REVERED
BY ALL

REVERED BY ALL

The Life and Works of
Rabbi Israel Meir Kagan — Hafets Hayyim
(1838-1933)

by

LESTER SAMUEL ECKMAN

SECOND REVISED EDITION

SHENGOLD PUBLISHERS, INC.

New York City

ISBN 0-88400-002-8

Library of Congress Catalog Card Number: 73-89418

Copyright © 1974 by Lester Samuel Eckman

Published by
Shengold Publishers, Inc.
45 West 45th Street, New York, N.Y. 10036
In cooperation with
Judaic Research Institute

Printed in the United States of America

INTRODUCTION

Lester Samuel Eckman

Rabbi Israel Meir Kagan, who lived from 1838 to 1933, was an outstanding rabbi, scholar, author, thinker, and spiritual leader of the East European Jewish community. His career represents a long, unbroken chain of study, piety, and devotion to his people. Rabbi Kagan commanded the respect of the non-Jewish world as well, and he was one of the very few religious leaders treated with deference by the early Bolsheviks, who admired his extremely simple mode of life and his kindness to others.

Among the problems that Rabbi Kagan was deeply involved in solving were these: the moral laxity within the Jewish community; the rise of the Enlightenment and Zionism among the Jews; the plight of Soviet Jewry; the Jewish soldier serving in a non-Jewish army; the problems created by emigration from a stable Jewish community to a predominantly non-Jewish environment; continuing traditional religious education for Jews, and the growing discrimination against Jews by the Polish government.

The general purpose of this study is to examine and illustrate the impact of the life and works of Rabbi Israel Meir Kagan on the moral, social, religious and political life of the Jews in Poland and Russia during his lifetime. More specifically: in examining Rabbi Kagan's views on moral laxity, we will discuss his unique works *Hafets Hayyim (He Who Desires Life)* and *Ahavath Chesed (Loving-Kindness),* as well as his books on family purity—*Geder Olam (Everlasting Fence), Toharath Yisroel (Purity of Israel),* and *Baith Misroel (House of Israel).* In examining his views on the secular enlightenment among the Jews, we will discuss his works *Chomas Hadas (Fortress of Faith)* and *Torath Habaith (Home and Family Study).* His views on the problems of the Jewish soldier will be illustrated through a discussion of his work, *Mahaneh Israel (Camp of Israel);* his advice to immigrants will be discussed by examining his book, *Nidhei Israel (Dispersed of Israel).* His concern for traditional religious education and for the political problems of his day will be seen in the work, *Michtevei Hafets Hayyim (Letters of Hafets Hayyim).*

Rabbi Kagan was a prolific writer and several other of his works are dicussed herein. He also played an important personal role in the affairs of his time. His letters and other writings were gathered together after his death and published in *Michtevei Hafets Hayyim,* which has proved invaluable in examining his views on all aspects of Jewish life and in determining the part he played in dealing with the problems of his time.

This study does not include extensive investigations of Rabbi Kagan's works dealing with *Midrashic (homiletic)* interpretations of the Hebrew Bible, or of his work, *Likutei Halakhoth (Collection of Laws),* or of his work, *Mishnah Berurah*—his *Halakhic* commentary on the *Orah Hayyim.* It does not attempt to evaluate Rabbi Kagan as a Talmudic scholar, nor does it include a consideration of articles which appeared in the daily press of his time concerning him or concerning the problems he dealt with.

The lessons to be gleaned from the works of Rabbi Israel Meir Kagan can serve as a shining beacon of inspiration to mankind in these perplexing times. By relating his enduring teachings to our contemporary lives and times, we can be better equipped, mentally, morally and spiritually, to confront the awesome challenges of the present and the future.

*   *   *   *   *

I wish to express my abiding gratitude to the distinguished scholars and educators Professors Zvi Ankori, Salo W. Baron and the late Henry Roberts of Columbia University; Dr. Leon Katz, Professor Abraham Katsh, President of Dropsie University, Professors Baruch Levine, Frank Manuel and Francis E. Peters of New York University; and Rabbis Joseph David Epstein and Pinchas M. Teitz, whose guidance and direction have been a constant source of inspiration in the eternal quest to expand the frontiers of knowledge.

CONTENTS

REVERED
BY ALL

CHAPTER ONE

THE BIOGRAPHY OF ISRAEL MEIR KAGAN

Rabbi Israel Meir Kagan was born in Zhetel, Poland on February 6, 1838. His father, Ariah Zev, was an observant Jew and Talmudical scholar. His mother, Dobrosah, taught him to read the Prayer Book; but as was the custom, his father began to instruct him in the Bible and Talmud at a tender age. When Israel Meir was ten, he and his father left for Vilna, where the young boy studied in the *yeshiva*[1] (then headed by Rabbi Haim Nachman Parnes[2]) under the special guidance of Rabbi Jacob ben Yehuda Teitz.[3] Ariah Zev remained in Vilna to care for Israel Meir, earning his livelihood by tutoring sons of the rich in the *yeshiva*. In 1849 he passed away in a cholera plague.[4]

Israel Meir continued with his studies in Vilna, where he lived with Rabbi Israel Gordon, who looked after the fatherless boy and played an active role in his education. Israel

---

[1]*Yeshiva* is a Talmudical school. The term can refer to both higher schools of learning (*yeshivoth godolot*) and the elementary institutions (*yeshivoth ketanot*) in Russia.

[2]Dov Katz *Tenuath Ha-Musar* (Tel-Aviv: Abraham Zioni, 1963), IV, 21.

[3]*Ibid.*

[4]Kagan, *Michtevei Hafets Hayyim*, p. 2. Dobrosah was later remarried to Rabbi Simon of Radun.

Meir's older brother, Aaron, also instructed him for three years (1852-1855) in Vilna[5] and wielded a strong influence on his moral and intellectual growth.

In 1847 the Russian government opened two rabbinical seminaries teaching both secular and Judaic studies. One was established in Vilna, the other in Zhitomir. The Vilna *Maskilim*,[6] hoping to gain recognition for the school as a training center for rabbis, sought both a distinguished scholar for its director and brilliant students. The *Maskilim*, who had the power to recommend persons for the directorship to the Minister of Education Uvarov, chose Rabbi Israel Salanter (1810-1883) [7] as *Rosh Yeshiva*[8] of the school and made attempts to persuade Israel Meir to enroll as a student.[9] Rabbi Salanter, however, shared the view of most rabbis that the seminary at Vilna would be a liability rather than an asset to traditional Judaism, and he turned down the offer. The Vilna *Maskilim* tried to persuade him to accept the position by having Uvarov speak to him. When Salanter realized that Uvarov could compel him to accept the position, he

---

[5]*Ibid.*

[6]The term *Maskilim* refers to adherents of the *Haskalah*, or Jewish Enlightenment Movement, which began in the eighteenth century in Germany and spread in the nineteenth century to Eastern Europe. The *Haskalah* was one aspect of the general Western European Enlightenment. One of its main purposes was to bring secular education—especially the language of the land—to the Jewish masses. The *Maskilim* endeavored to accommodate the Jews of the ghetto to the social, economic, and cultural ways of contemporary society. See Salo W. Baron, *A Social and Religious History of the Jews* (New York: Columbia University Press, 1937), II, 213-224. See also, Simon M. Dubnow, *History of the Jews in Russia and Poland* (Philadelphia: The Jewish Publication Society of America, 1918), II, 59ff; and Salo W. Baron, *The Russian Jews: Under Tsars and Soviets* (New York: Macmillan Co., 1964), p. 125.

[7]Rabbi Israel Salanter was the founder of the *Musar* (moralist) movement. His carefully selected student body devoted most of its time to traditional Talmudic studies; but the spiritual leader of the *yeshiva* also introduced periodic *Musar* talks. These talks molded the character and the lives of the students. They were not conventional lectures, but intense addresses meant to affect the listeners deeply and to create in them a longing for a life of self-improvement. See Katz, *Tenuath Ha-Musar*, Volume I; and Menahem G. Glenn, *Israel Salanter: Religious Ethical Thinker* (New York: Bloch Publishing Co., 1953).

[8]A *Rosh Yeshiva* is a Talmudist who lectures in a *yeshiva*.

[9]A. D. Lebensohn, one of the founders of the *haskalah* movement, made an effort to persuade Israel Meir to join the circle of Vilna *Maskilim*. See Katz, *Tenuath Ha-Musar*, IV, p. 163.

left Vilna.[10] Israel Meir, who had been influenced by Israel Salanter's moralistic teaching, rejected the flattering attention paid to him and determined to proceed with what was considered the "pure course" of the Torah.[11] Kagan saw in the *haskalah* movement a design to destroy the authority of the rabbis and to undermine traditional Judaism.[12] He was convinced that Tsar Nicholas I was using the *haskalah* as an instrument to bring about Jewish assimilation.[13]

During his student years in Vilna Israel Meir devoted so much time to his studies that he neglected his health and became seriously ill. Suffering from physical and nervous exhaustion, he was forced to interrupt his Talmudical studies. He consulted many doctors and ultimately recovered to live a very long and productive life.[14] His sickness, however, made him especially sensitive to the plight of his students, and he became scrupulous in watching over their health and well-being. He encouraged them to get at least eight hours of sleep each night and always impressed upon them the importance of having a healthy body as a repository for a healthy soul.[15]

Because of his prominence as a Talmudic scholar, many rich Jews wanted to have Kagan as a son-in-law; and Kagan's mother and older brother favored a marriage offering financial security; but in 1855, at the age of seventeen, Israel Meir married Frieda, the daughter of his step-father, Rabbi Simon.[16] In marrying Frieda, he was apparently rebelling against two customs of the time: one, that he should follow the advice of his parent or his brother concerning his mate, and two, that a Talmudical scholar should expect and receive a substantial dowry from his wife's family. He settled down with his wife in Radun, a small town which later be-

---

[10]*Ibid.*

[11]*Ibid.*, IV, 21ff.

[12]Interview by the author with Rabbi Mendel Zaks, son-in-law of Rabbi Kagan, June 28, 1967.

[13]*Ibid*; see also Dubnow, *History of the Jews in Russia and Poland*, II, 51.

[14]Kagan, *Michtevei Hafets Hayyim*, I, 5.

[15]Letter from Rabbi Mendel Zaks, June 28, 1967. See also, Kagan, *Michtevei Hafets Hayyim*, I, 5.

[16]*Ibid.*, p. 3.

came one of the most famous Jewish communities in Europe, largely due to his presence there. In later years, Kagan remarked more than once to his son, Ariah, "I am grateful to your mother for enabling me to acquire Torah knowledge by her willingness to sacrifice clothes and a comfortable dwelling."[17]

Kagan agreed to accept from the townspeople the position of Rabbi of Radun; but he insisted on serving without remuneration. However, the venture lasted only a few months. When someone refused to accept his decision in a case of religious law, he "resigned his position and indeed never again accepted public office. He preferred to remain a layman."[18]

Frieda Kagan then opened a small grocery shop, in order to make a living; "but as a result of his endeavors to offer the finest merchandise at the smallest profit, and his over-scrupulousness in not expanding his clientele, he could not long flourish in the competitive realm of business."[19] One can conclude that Kagan did not desire to cultivate the necessary skills and temperament to function either as the Rabbi of a Jewish community or as a businessman—both endeavors necessitating skills in politics and craftiness. He turned to professional teaching and taught Talmud from 1864 to 1869 in yeshivoth in Minsk and Washilishok.

In 1869, at the age of thirty-one, a dream of his life was realized when he became Rosh Yeshiva in Radun. The "Yeshivath Hafets Hayyim," as it was later known, gradually became a leading center of Talmudic learning. Rabbi Kagan was successful in enlisting the support of the Jews in Radun and its surroundings for the construction and upkeep of the yeshiva. In the early years of the yeshiva, the Jews of Radun allowed out-of-town students to eat in their homes. Later, a kitchen was established to provide regular sustenance for the students. Rabbi Kagan's wife and daughters were responsible for collecting the necessary food from the Jews in the community and for preparing the meals.

---

[17]Ibid., p. 5.
[18]Yosher, "Israel Meir Ha-Kohen—Hafets Hayyim," p. 462.
[19]Ibid.

Before the Second World War, students were given money for food, clothing, mail, and other necessities. A married student received an additional stipend for his wife and family. In the beginning, only students from Radun and surrounding towns came to study at the *yeshiva*, but as it grew students from distant places were attracted as well. Kagan guided each student with fatherly-love and understanding. Even though he had failed in the world of business and as a town rabbi, he displayed the necessary skills, initiative, and even fund-raising ability to win support from the very same townspeople for building and maintaining a *yeshiva*.

Rabbi Kagan earned his living, however, not from his post as head of the *yeshiva*, but from the sale of his numerous books. He permitted himself only a small profit and refused to receive anything above the price he had originally set.[20]

Rabbi Kagan's preoccupation with his writings did not deter him from observing the rise of the Palestine *Hoveve Zion*[21] and its offspring, the Bilu,[22] which preceded Herzlian

---

[20]When a Rothschild paid him three hundred francs for copies of his books, Rabbi Kagan took only thirty francs. He dispatched the remainder to Rothschild with a note suggesting he send the money to the seminary, if he were willing. To Rothschild such an experience was inspiring and he made an increased contribution to the rabbinical seminary of Radun. See Yosher, "Israel Meir Ha-Kohen—Hafets Hayyim," p. 462.

[21]The *Hoveve Zion* (Lovers of Zion) movement was a group of scattered societies that had begun to emerge in the 1860's. They met at a conference in Kattowitz, Silesia, in November 1884, organized a federation, and elected Leo Pinsker (1821-1891) as their President. Their aim was to restore Jewish national life by colonizing Palestine. Of the vast literature on the *Hoveve Zion* the following may be mentioned: Nahum Sokolow, *A History of Zionism 1600-1918*, with an introduction by A. J. Balfour (London, 1919), II, 281ff; S. L. Citron, *Toldot Hibbat Zion* (Odessa, 1914), Vol. I; and B. Dinaburg, *Hibbat Zion* (Tel-Aviv: Dvir, 1932), Vol. I.

[22]Bilu is an abbreviation for the Hebrew words *Beth Ya'cob Lechu ve-Nelcha* ("House of Jacob, come, let us go," Isaiah 2:5). The members of this group were the first to settle in Palestine after the pogroms of 1881 in Europe. They were largely university students who were moved by the tragic events in Russia to search for meaning in life as workers of the soil in Palestine. Their aim was to encourage and strengthen immigration and colonization through the establishment of agricultural colonies, built on cooperative-social foundations. One of the first colonies founded by Bilu was Rishon Le-Zion. See the Manifesto of the Bilu in Sokolow, *History of Zionism*, II, 332ff. See also, Ismar Elbogen, *A Century of Jewish Life*, translated by Moses Hadas (Philadelphia: Jewish Publication Society of America, 1944), pp. 255ff. and 263.

Zionism[23] and Simon Dubnow's Diaspora Nationalism which was espoused by the Bund.[24]

At first Rabbi Kagan reacted to the settlement of the pioneers in Israel with enthusiasm and a conviction that the Messianic age was approaching. In anticipation of the restoration of the Holy Temple and the reinstatement of sacrificial offerings, he added *Seder Kodashim* (Talmudic order dealing with Temple and sacrificial ritual) to the curriculum of study at the *yeshiva* at Radun. As the Zionist movement grew and

---

[23]Theodor Herzl (1860-1904), in Paris as a correspondent for the famous newspaper *Neue Freie Presse*, was aroused by the Dreyfus case. He struggled with the Jewish problem and arrived at a solution: the Jewish people must have a Jewish state. A charter for such a state in Palestine must be obtained from Turkey. A Jewish society must be launched to organize the mass emigration of Jewish people to Palestine. A source of immense value on Theodore Herzl and his work are his *Tagebucher*, edited by Leon Kellner (Berlin: Judisicher Verlag, 1922-23), 3 vols., and his *Gesemmelte Zionistische Werke* (Berlin, 1934), 5 vols. See also his work, *A Jewish State*, translated by S. d'Avigdor, 2nd rev. with a forward by Israel Cohen (London, 1934).

[24]Simon M. Dubnow, a Russian Jewish historian, developed his own interpretation of Jewish history, claiming that the spiritual powers of the Jewish people and their unity were preserved by the organized Jewish community during the two thousand years of exile. He believed that the unity of the Jews did not depend upon a national territory, or upon an independent state. Their unity was kept alive by communal organizations, within whose framework Jewish culture and religion had continued growing for two thousands years after their dispersion. See Dubnow, *History of the Jews in Russia and Poland*, II, 55-58; 132-42; and Dubnow, *Nationalism and History: Essays on Old and New Judaism*, edited with an introduction by Koppel S. Pinson (Philadelphia: Jewish Publication Society of America, 1918).

Bund is the name adopted by the Jewish Socialist Party, organized in Russia in 1897. Its influence was particularly strong among the Jewish workers in densely Jewish population centers such as those of Warsaw, Minsk, Vitebsk, and Bialystok. The Bund, a militant group, participated in the overthrow of the Russian Tsarist Government by organizing demonstrations and strikes. After the Russian Revolution of 1917, a part of the Bund joined the Jewish section of the Communist Party, while those who did not were persecuted by the Soviets. In Poland, the Bund established schools, conducted cultural work in the Yiddish language, formed youth groups and workers' cooperatives. It opposed Zionism and was antagonistic to Hebrew as the Jewish national tongue. The aim of the Bund was to develop the political and socialist consciousness of the Jewish masses and to emphasize equality. See Koppel S. Pinson, "Arkady Kremer, Vladimir Medem and the Ideology of the Jewish Bund," in *Jewish Social Studies*, VII (1945), 233-64; and Jacob Sholem Hertz, *Doires Bundisten*, 2 vols. (New York: Verlag Unzer Zeit, 1956). See also Baron, *The Russian Jews*, pp. 168-172, 205, 244.

spread, other rabbis began to complain about Rabbi Kagan's silence and his failure to denounce the leaders of the Zionist movement in general and their mocking of religion in particular. "By nature Rabbi Kagan avoided quarrels; and in the Zionist movement's dispute he tried to remain publicly neutral in order to prevent further altercation.[25] Nevertheless, his private writings indicate his disappointment and grief at hearing that the leaders of Zionism were encouraging a break from the traditional practices of the Torah— both in Russia and in the Palestinian colonies. His distress included secular as well as religious Jews. Although he seemed to recognize the demands that emigration had placed upon the pioneers and did not feel, as did some Orthodox Jews, that the pioneers should engross themselves in prayer and the study of Torah, he did feel that the precepts of the Torah should remain the basis for their lives and actions.[26]

The first decades of the twentieth century brought to Russian Jewry a series of bestial pogroms. There were massacres at Kishinev in 1903, at Bialystok in 1905, and in other Russian cities and towns.[27]

The massacres led to increased emigration from Russia, and to the Jewish self-defense body.[28] The misery of European Jews continued, and was in fact intensified, during the

---

[25]Kagan, *Michtevei Hafets Hayyim*, I, 73. See pp. 109-125 for a more detailed discussion of Kagan's views on Zionism.

[26]*Ibid.*

[27]The Kishinev Pogrom was instigated by P. A. Krushevan, editor of the conservative newspaper, *Bessarbets*, which was heavily subsidized by the Tsarist government. In two days (April 6-7) of killing and plundering, forty-five Jews were killed, eighty-six were seriously hurt, and five hundred were less seriously wounded. The pogrom caused 1,500 houses and shops to be looted or destroyed. See Baron, *The Russian Jews*, p. 69; and "The Kishinev Pogrom," in the *American Jewish Year Book* (1903-1904), V, 19-22, 39, 109, 111-112, 129-130, 133-141.

Bialystok was one of the 660 other Jewish communities that suffered from the wave of plundering and killing. In a span of one week (October 19-25), the pogrom of 1905 cost the Jews of Russia about one thousand dead and seventy-eight thousand wounded, and property losses of 131 million. See "The Bialystok Pogrom," in the *American Jewish Year Book* (1906-1907), VIII, 36-37, 79-89.

[28]See Baron, *The Russian Jews*, p. 60; and Dubnow, *History of Jews in Russia and Poland*, III, 80, 87ff, 96, 116ff, 120, 129, 150; see also Louis Greenberg, *The Jews in Russia* (New Haven: Yale University Press, 1944), pp. 52, 54, 81, 155, 158.

First World War.[29] That war, with the chaos created in Poland, sent Rabbi Kagan and many of his students out of Radun and set them wandering as refugees in Russia for several years. There they were eyewitnesses to the violence of Tsarist Russia being torn by the Bolshevik revolution within and the German army without. They also fell victim to the arrests and pogroms of the Tsarist military and, later, suffered through renewed pogroms under the "whites" as they fought with the revolutionary "reds."[30]

Many Bolsheviks—non-Jewish as well as Jewish—held Rabbi Kagan in high esteem because of his simplicity in dress, his humility, and his concern for the common man.[31] But, although he was personally well-treated by the Communists, he was concerned for the future of Jews in Soviet Russia, and indeed for the future of religion in general. He watched the closing of religious schools and the conversion of study houses to clubs for social and political purposes. He saw teachers and *Roshei Yeshivoth* exiled to Siberia. And he stood by helpless as Jews were forced by the Communists to desecrate the Sabbath.[32]

With the help of General Wladyslaw Sikorski, Rabbi Kagan returned to Radun in 1921 and lived in independent Poland from 1921 to 1933. He established a good rapport with the Polish government, enabling him to help defend the rights and causes of the Jews in that country.[33] He par-

---

[29]See Baron, *The Russian Jews*, pp. 187-200.

[30]During his time in Russia, Rabbi Kagan remained involved and concerned with the plight of his fellow Jews. One of his students, a young boy from Memel, Germany, was arrested on the basis of false information, tried by a Tsarist military court and sentenced to ten years of imprisonment. Upon hearing the verdict, Rabbi Kagan remarked: "Fools, they sentenced him to imprisonment for ten years; it never occurred to them that their corrupt system may not last ten months, or perhaps ten weeks." Yosher, "Israel Meir Ha-Kohen—Hafets Hayyim," p. 469. March, 1917, the date of the fall of Tsarist rule in Russia, was in fact then less than ten weeks away.

Rabbi Kagan also made public appeals for the Relief Fund for Passover and wrote articles requesting economic help for the hunger-stricken Jews and their children. *Ibid.*, pp. 460ff.

[31]*Ibid.*, p. 470.

[32]Letter from Rabbis Kagan and Hayyim Ozer Grodzenski, Adar, 1931, in Kagan, *Michtevei Hafets Hayyim*, p. 56.

[33]*Ibid.*, II, 215-221; 224-225; 238-243.

ticipated in many Polish conferences dealing with religious, educational, and communal matters,[34] and he continued to write.

He found time in his busy life to participate in religious, educational, and communal gatherings. He believed in personal contact with people and made every effort to keep appointments with scholars as well as with laymen. His presence in conferences and his direct contact with people were evidence of his warmth and humility, and of his concern for the political, religious, economic, and social welfare of his people.

At this time the community of religious Jews included the Hasidim. Rabbi Kagan was well respected by the Hasidic rabbis—especially the Gerer Rebbe, Rabbi Abraham Mordecai Alter—and by their followers. In communal elections, Hasidic Jews often united with Orthodox Jews to oppose secular candidates in the election. Whenever this happened, the religious candidates were elected, since the Hasidic rabbis had a large following. Since Rabbi Kagan was often instrumental in uniting Hasidic and Orthodox Jewry, he was a very powerful person with whom the secular Zionists, Bundists, and others had to reckon—at times with fear.

While in Poland, Rabbi Kagan continued to display concern for his brethren in the Soviet Union. He wrote a letter to the Pope asking him to use his influence in alleviating religious and cultural persecution in Russia although, for political reasons, he was unable to send the text to the Pope.[35] He also spoke to his close colleagues about taking physical action against Jewish Communists in the Soviet Union who were active in the persecution of their brethren.[36] But this plan never materialized either.

During these years Rabbi Kagan also participated actively in providing religious education not only to poor boys, but also to girls. He was active in helping Sara Schenierer, the founder of the *Beth Yaacov* movement, spread religious edu-

---

[34]Ibid., II, 86-87; 125-129; 134-139; 143-151.
[35]For details, see pp. 141-142.
[36]*Ibid.*

cation among the girls. In his busy schedule he tried to find
time to address audiences of women on diverse religious subjects. For example, in 1931, at the age of ninety-three, he
spoke to thousands of men and women in the large synagogue
in Vilna on the significance of keeping the family purity laws.
Women in the big cities in particular had been influenced by
secular education and had become lax in observing the family purity laws.[37]

He also was active in the Agudat Israel organization, the
world organization of Orthodox Judaism. The purpose of
the Agudat Israel was to search for solutions to the contemporary problems of Judaism in the spirit of the Torah. From
its inception, Rabbi Kagan had been an outstanding guide
in the organization.[38]

In the last years of his life, Rabbi Kagan prayed and
prepared himself for the days of the Messiah which he believed were about to come. He prayed for Israel's rehabilitation as a Jewish state, re-established on Torah foundations,
with the Holy Temple restored and sacrificial offerings reinstated.[39]

Before his death, Rabbi Kagan also seems to have fore-
seen the Nazi destruction of European Jewry. Speaking to
his foremost disciple, Rabbi Elhanan Wasserman, he said, "I
don't exaggerate because the time is coming that all of us
will be exposed to real danger. Not economic starvation, but
slaughter of us, our women, and our children." And in 1930
he told his students: "A terrible storm is blowing, a dreadful
holocaust is approaching. The First World War would appear to be a child's play in comparison to the future destruction. You don't know, but I foresee what will happen in the
next ten years."[40] In later chapters we will examine to what
extent Rabbi Kagan acted wisely upon this prediction—a
prediction which turned out to be disastrously accurate, and

---

[37]Kagan, *Michtevei Hafets Hayyim*, II, 195-197.
[38]*Ibid.*, II, 134-137. See details pp. 169-171.
[39]Kagan, *Michtevei Hafets Hayyim*, I, 77. Interview by the author with
Rabbi Zaks, 1967.
[40]Moses M. Yosher, *Ha-Hafets Hayyim* (Tel-Aviv: Nezach, 1959), II,
621.

the force of which might have been lessened by early emigration of Jews to Israel or America.

Kagan's Standing Among His Contemporaries

Rabbi Israel Meir Kagan was an outstanding rabbi, a codifier of Jewish law, a scholar, and a thinker. His career represents a long, unbroken chain of study, piety, and devotion to his people. He occupied a prominent position as religious guide of the Jews of Eastern Europe and commanded the respect of the non-Jewish world as well. He was one of the very few religious leaders treated with deference by the early Bolsheviks.

One contemporary of Rabbi Kagan, Rabbi Abraham Mordecai Alter (known as the Gerer Rebbe), urged Jewish scholars and laymen alike to study the works of Rabbi Kagan, particularly the *Hafets Hayyim*, for his strong and important statements against slander.[41]

Rabbi Hayyim Grodzenski (1863-1940), a rabbi and scholar of Vilna, found it fitting to eulogize Rabbi Kagan in the following terms:

> Behold, at the end of the year, the Holy Ark was taken; "the angels overpowered the mortals"[42] . . .
> the saint of the priesthood and the elder of the generation, who has illuminated the whole Jewish dispersion with his righteousness and his learning, and his precious writings, is no longer with us, and he has left no one like him. . . .[43]

Rabbi Aaron Lewin, a member of the Polish *Sejm*, and chief rabbi of Reisa, Galacia, referred to Rabbi Kagan as "the *Tsaddik* (righteous person) and prominent elder of our generation, to whom all Jews look up for spiritual guid-

[41]Letter from Rebbe Abraham Alter, Jerusalem, 1936, quoted in *Osef Michtavim* (Jerusalem, 1936), letter 12.

[42]*Tractate Ktuvoth*, p. 104. When Rabbi Judah I, codifier of the *Mishnah* (175) died, Rabbi Kapara eulogized him using the metaphor of the Holy Ark and the angels.

[43]Letter from Rabbi Hayyim Ozer Grodzenski to Rabbis, 1933, in Kagan, *Michtevei Hafets Hayyim*, II, 260ff.

ance."[44] Rabbi Joseph Epstein, a younger contemporary of Rabbi Kagan and presently a *Rosh Yeshiva* at Yeshiva University in New York City, also wrote about Kagan in glowing terms.[45]

Notwithstanding the eminent position he achieved among his contemporaries, Rabbi Kagan walked humbly before God and man—"his greatness consisted of his simplicity in behavior and in speech, even though he was a spiritual giant." Rabbi Epstein adds: "Humility was his greatest attribute and all those who knew him were moved and inspired by this quality of his."[46]

Rabbi Israel Meir Kagan's Writings

Rabbi Kagan was one of the most prolific writers of rabbinic literature. Four of his works are unique: *Hafets Hayyim (He Who Desires Life)*,[47] *Mahaneh Israel (Camp of Israel)*,[48] *Ahavath Chesed (Loving Kindness)*,[49] and *Nidhei Israel (Dispersed of Israel)*.[50] They represent the first attempt to gather Biblical, Talmudic, Midrashic and rabbinic sources and compile them as codes of rabbinic law. The books deal with such diverse topics as gossip and tale-bearing, religious and ethical aspects of military life, religious and social problems of immigration, and various other aspects of human relations.

His pen enriched almost every aspect of rabbinic literature. He wrote books and manuals attempting to stem the tide of the Bund—in particular *Chomas Hadas (Fortress of*

---

[44]Letter from Rabbi Aaron Lewin, in *ibid.*, pp. 242ff.

[45]Letter from Rabbi Joseph Epstein to the author, Brooklyn, June 28, 1967.

[46]*Ibid.*

[47]Israel Meir Kagan, *Hafets Hayyim* (Warsaw, 1873). The title comes from Psalms 34:13-14: "Who is the man that desires life and loves to enjoy happiness for many days? Keep your tongue from evil, and your lips from speaking guile." Rabbi Kagan became known throughout the world by the title of the book.

[48]Israel Meir Kagan, *Mahaneh Israel* (New York: Saphrograph Co., 1943. First appeared in 1881.

[49]Israel Meir Kagan, *Ahavath Chesed* (Warsaw, 1888).

[50]Israel Meir Kagan, *Nidhei Israel* (Warsaw, 1893).

Faith);[51] and he dealt with home and religious study in
Torath Habaith (Home and Religious Study).[52] He wrote a
commentary, *Mishnah Berurah (Lucid Learning),*[53] on the
first part of the *Shulhan Arukh;*[54] and a commentary, *Likutei
Halakhoth (Collections of Laws),*[55] on the tractates *Zebahim*
and *Menahoth* which deal with temple and sacrificial ritual.
He also composed works on family purity: *Geder Olam
(Everlasting Fence),*[56] *Toharath Yisroel (Purity of Israel),*[57]
and *Baith Yisroel (House of Israel).*[58] After his death, his son,
Ariah Leib Kagan, edited the *Michtevei Hafets Hayyim (Letters, Articles and Speeches of Hafets Hayyim)* which contains
articles, letters and speeches dealing with the religious, political, social, military, economic, and educational life of the
Jews during the first three decades of the current century.

Hafets Hayyim

Rabbi Kagan's vital contribution to rabbinic literature
was *Hafets Hayyim (He Who Desires Life),* which deals with
gossip and tale-bearing. It is not easy to ascertain what
prompts a creative man to write a certain work; but the moral
climate of Rabbi Kagan's time seems to have given urgency
to this particular work. His lifetime was marked by a breakdown of morality affecting every segment of Jewish life.[59]

One example of this breakdown is the controversy between

---

[51]Israel Meir Kagan, *Chomas Hadas* (Petersburg, 1905).

[52]Israel Meir Kagan, *Torath Habaith* (Petersburg, 1907).

[53]Israel Meir Kagan, *Mishnah Berurah* (Warsaw, 1884).

[54]*Shulhan Arukh* is the authoritative Jewish religious code, prepared
by Rabbi Joseph Karo. It is divided, as the *Arbaah Turim (Four Rows),*
into four parts: one summarizing the laws pertaining to prayers, Sabbath
and holidays; a second on dietary laws, laws of mourning and other ritual
matters; a third on civil laws; and a fourth on the laws relating to marriage,
divorce and similar matters.

[55]Israel Meir Kagan, *Likutei Halakhoth* (Petersburg, 1900-1925).

[56]Israel Meier Kagan, *Geder Olam* (Warsaw, 1890).

[57]Israel Meir Kagan, *Toharath Yisroel* (Jerusalem, 1967). First appeared
in 1890.

[58]Israel Meir Kagan, *Baith Yisroel* (Petersburg, 1928).

[59]Rabbi Salanter's disciple, Rabbi Isaac Blazer (1837-1907), wrote:
"Slanderers have become powerful; and men committed to resisting evil are
looked upon with disdain . . . falsehood is clothed by the garment of
righteousness . . . and justice is in a position of silence." Isaac Blazer, *Or
Israel* (Vilna, 1900), p. 4.

the rabbis and the *Maskilim*—both parties indulging in gossip and tale-bearing. The *Maskilim* ridiculed and mocked the rabbis and Jewish traditions and did not hesitate to denounce the rabbis before the Russian authorities and to blame them for the failure of Jews to be assimilated into the Russian culture.[60] The rabbis also resorted to slander and tale-bearing in order to counter the *Maskilim*.[61]

The *Hafets Hayyim* was the first rabbinic code to summarize all the laws prohibiting gossip and tale-bearing, and to point out the enormity of evil that may result from it.

Mahanel Israel

A major event of Rabbi Kagan's lifetime was the conscription of Jews into the Tsarist army. It prompted Rabbi Kagan to write his unique code, *Mahaneh Israel (Camp of Israel)*, dealing with matters pertaining to military life, including: the proper ritual for Jewish soldiers, sex laws, gossip, compassion, the study of Torah, and other matters. *Mahaneh Israel* was to guide the Jewish soldier away from home who was thrown into a strange environment often hostile to Judaism.[62]

One of Rabbi Kagan's recommendations was early marriage prior to conscription. He felt that the possibilities of intermarriage and assimilation—strong possibilities since the

---

[60]Abraham Mapu (1808-1867), for example, was a *maskil* who portrayed Rabbi Gadial in the darkest colors in his work, *Avit Zavua* (Warsaw: Alexander Ganz, 1873-74), p. 225. The poet, Judah Leib Gordon (1830-1892) also depicts Rabbi Vosfi's soul as Tartaric and greedy for Jewish money. See "Kotzo Shel Yod," in *Kol Shirei Gordon* (Tel Aviv: Dvir, 1931), IV, 28; see also Greenberg, *The Jews in Russia*, I, 120.

[61]Rabbi Kagan himself lived through such a distressing experience in Radun. The community rabbi was threatened with the loss of his post because of a rumor that his two sons were followers of the *Haskalah*. A distinguished rabbi was asked for his judgment. Rabbi Kagan argued that discharging the rabbi because of a rumor, even if the facts were true, was wrong. The distinguished rabbi rebuked young Kagan for meddling in the affair and recommended dismissal of the community rabbi. The latter was forced to move to another city and shortly thereafter died, apparently from grief and frustration. Ultimately, his two sons became outstanding rabbis, in spite of the rumor that almost ruined their reputation and destroyed their father's life. (Kagan, *Michtevei Hafets Hayyim*, I, 14-15.)

[62]*Ibid.*, pp. 8-22.

men were conscripted at a very early age and placed into a hostile, Christian environment—would be lessened if the men committed themselves before entering the service. There was, of course, a great deal of controversy surrounding this recommendation, and Rabbi Kagan became involved in a major disagreement with the famous Rabbi Meir Malbin (1809-1879).[63]

Ahavath Chesed

The political and economic discriminations against the Jews of Tsarist Russia heightened Rabbi Kagan's interest in the ordinary Jew. In 1888 he set forth the legal and moral principles dealing with various aspects of human relations in *Ahavath Chesed (Loving-Kindness)*. It covers topics such as the laws concerning loans, pledges, wages, the importance of showing hospitality to guests, the *mitzvah* of visiting the sick, mourning the dead and comforting the mourners.[64]

Nidhei Israel and Shem Olam

In the 1880's a wave of savage Jew-baiting swept through Russia, resulting in a mass emigration of Jews to America and Palestine. Rabbi Kagan's concern with the lot of these wandering Jews motivated him to write two immigrant guides, *Nidhei Israel (Dispersed of Israel)* and *Shem Olam (Everlasting Memorial)*.[65] They contain laws of prayer, Sabbath and holidays, and deal with dietary laws, the use of scissors in rounding the corners of the head and beard, study of Torah and education of children, family purity, gossip, and loving-kindness.[66] Since Rabbi Kagan held that it is permissible to use a pair of scissors in rounding the corners of the head and beard, a controversy arose between him and the Hasidic rabbis.[67]

---

[63]*Ibid.*, p. 19.
[64]*Ibid.*, pp. 36-38.
[65]Israel Meir Kagan, *Shem Olam* (Warsaw, 1893).
[66]Kagan, *Michtevei Hafets Hayyim*, I, pp. 54-58.
[67]See p. 103 for details.

Chomas Hadas

In 1905 the Rabbi published his *Chomas Hadas (Fortress of Faith),* dealing with the following subjects: out of respect for the Almighty; our mutual responsibility, a reason for duty; fear not the opponents—strengthen Torah; the man with the ability must found a *yeshiva;* the great sin of depriving one's child of a Torah education; the extent to which man must strive for Torah while he is alive; the tremendous importance of supporting Torah, and the great need for Torah. Rabbi Kagan wrote the work to counteract the influence of the Bundists and the secular Zionists who competed for mass support among the Jews.[68]

Torath Habaith

In 1907 Rabbi Kagan published *Torath Habaith (Home and Religious Study).* He stressed the importance of Torah study and of the practice of its precepts in the home. He believed that only by seeing an example set in the home can children apply their Torah study to their own lives. He admonished Jews who find it difficult to study Torah because they are used to idleness or newspaper reading to cease wasting their leisure time and begin studying Torah. He reminded them that only study will lead to practice and proper observance of the precepts of Torah.[69]

Mishnah Berurah

The Rabbi rejected the method of *pilpul* in his *Mishnah Berurah (Lucid Learning).*[70] He maintained that learning to apply the teachings of Torah to practical situations was most important, and that time was too short and precious to

---

[68]Interview by the author with Rabbi Zaks.

[69]Kagan, *Torath Habaith,* pp. 12, 14.

[70]*Pilpul* is a casuistic method used in Talmud study, which explores all possible sides of an argument. It was first used in *yeshivoth* in Germany, and was introduced to Poland in the sixteenth century by the famous Talmudic scholar, Rabbi Jacob Pollack. *Pilpul* is often associated with hairsplitting argumentation and not with practical decisions. See Dubnow, *History of the Jews in Russia and Poland,* I, 119ff, 122, 236, 256.

waste on speculation and dialectics.[71] In this opinion he followed the anti-pilpulistic approach of the Gaon of Vilna (1729-1797), who opposed the use of *pilpul* in the study of rabbinics and who emphasized the search for accurate and authentic sources.[72]

Rabbi Kagan's son, Ariah Leib Kagan, confirmed his father's use of this method. "The *Mishnah Berurah* is patterned along this method. He cited Biblical and Talmudical sources, followed by codifiers such as Rif, Rambam, Tosafoth, Rosh and Ramban, . . . and his thorough research was intended to clarify the *Halakhah* in the *Tur* and the *Shulhan Arukh*."[73]

---

[71]Kagan, *Michtevei Hafets Hayyim*, I, 9.

[72]*Ibid.*

[73]Kagan, *Michtevei Hafets Hayyim*, I, 8ff. Rif refers to Isaac Al-Fasi (1013-1103), who made a compendium of the Talmudic laws eliminating all irrelevant discussions and formulating clear-cut decisions.

Rambam refers to Rabbi Moses ben Maimon (1134-1204), (Maimonides), who wrote the *Mishnah Torah*, a code divided into fourteen books embracing the entire field of Jewish law. The *Mishnah Torah* is written in clear, precise Hebrew.

Tosafoth refers to Rabbi Jacob ben Meir, known as Rabbenu Tam (our perfect Rabbi), (1100-1171), a grandson of Rashi, who was the head of the school of Talmudists whose works are called *Tosafoth* (additions). These scholars analyzed the opinions of the Talmud. Their comments and discussions are characterized by keen critical examination of Talmudic law.

Rosh refers to Asher ben Jehiel (1250-1328), who wrote commentaries on the first and sixth orders of the *Mishnah* and short supplementary notes on certain tractates of the Talmud. His main work was a *Halakhic* compendium.

Ramban refers to Moses ben Nahman (1194-1270), who is also known as Nahmanides. His fame as a champion of the Jewish faith arose after a forced dispute between Christians and Jews. His commentary on the Bible continues to be highly regarded for its profound interpretations based on reason and *Halakhah*.

Tur refers to Jacob, the son of Asher (1250-1340), who prepared a code of his own in which the whole religious jurisprudence was methodically arranged into four parts: (1) *Orah Hayyim (The Path of Life)* embracing all laws of religious conduct of a Jew from the time he rises in the morning until he retires in the evening, namely all laws of prayer, benedictions, synagogue ritual, law of phylacteries and similar subjects, laws of the Sabbath, and laws of all festivals. (2) *Yoreh Deah (Teacher of Knowledge)* dealing with the dietary laws, and the prescriptions referring to avoidance of idolatry, interest, superstition, non-Jewish customs, the rules about ritual cleanliness, vows, reverence for elders and teachers, study, charity, circumcision, servants, proselytes, Torah, the mezuzah, plants, animals, clothing, rights of the first born, priestly dues, excommunication, sickness, death and mourning. (3) *Eben-ha-Ezer (The Stone of Help)*, whose name is taken from I Samuel, 3:13 and is an allusion to both the stone of judg-

Rabbi Kagan published the first volume of the *Mishnah Berurah* in 1884 and the concluding sixth one in 1907. The work deals with the first section of the *Shulhan Arukh* known as the *Orah Hayyim (Way of Life).* The *Orah Hayyim* contains laws relating to the religious conduct of the Jew upon rising in the morning, fringes, phylacteries, prayers, dietary observance, the Sabbath and holidays, benedictions, the new moon, and synagogue ritual. The Rabbi maintained that the *Orah Hayyim* was important to every Jew and should be an open book to the layman. He felt that every Jew should possess a copy.[74] Yet he also recognized that few Jews engross themselves in the study of the book even among the pious. The reason is twofold:

> The study of the *Shulhan Arukh* without the *Tur* is obscure, and in our time it has become difficult to resolve the doubts that appear in the *Shulhan Arukh,* because people confront severe hardships. Also people are confused in following the *Shulhan Arukh* because of the diversity of opinion among the later commentators of the Code of Karo.[75]

According to Rabbi Kagan, when Rabbi Joseph Karo wrote the *Shulhan Arukh* he hoped that Jews would study the *Tur* along with it. The *Shulhan Arukh* does not provide sources and explanations of the laws, so doubts arise about whether a law is derived from the Torah or from an enactment of the rabbis.[76] The *Tur* does provide these explanations and sources. But, because of the economic and political situation, the Jews in Eastern Europe did not have the time or patience to search for clarification and explanation in the

---

ment of the **High** Priest's breastplate, and to the fact that in Gen. 2:20 woman is called *Ezer,* helpmate. This part deals with laws concerning marriage, divorce, and other family relations. (4) *Hoshen ha-Mishpat (The Breastplate of Judgement)* borrowed from Exodus 28:15 deals with civil and criminal law, which bears on civil life and the dispensation of justice in all its phases.

[74]Kagan, *Michtevei Hafets Hayyim,* I, 8ff.
[75]Kagan *Mishnah Berurah,* I, 3b.
[76]*Ibid.*

Tur.[77] In addition to the laws and customs which are commanded by the Torah and those decreed by the Sages, the *Shulhan Arukh* contains laws which one should not do in the "beginning" but as a *fait accompli* are legitimate. The diversified opinions of the *Shulhan Arukh's* later commentators concerning the laws and customs challenged the Jew to make difficult decisions.[78]

To help the layman study the *Shulhan Arukh*—in particular the *Orah Hayyim*—Rabbi Kagan prepared three commentaries on it: (1) *Mishnah Berurah* (Lucid Learning), which explains every law in the *Orah Hayyim* in light of Talmudic and rabbinic sources so that the reason and motive for the law would be clear; (2) *Sha'ar Hazion (Gate of Zion)*, which cites the Talmudic and rabbinic sources used by Rabbi Kagan in preparing the *Mishnah Berurah*; and (3) *Biur Halakhah (Explanation of Laws)*, which is another aid to the *Mishnah Berurah* and explains some laws further while clarifying more complicated matters.[79]

In general, it may be said that in the *Mishnah Berurah* Rabbi Kagan follows the path of leniency rather than rigidity in interpreting the law. For example, Jews in Poland and Lithuania used wine made of raisins for *Kiddush* (a ceremony and prayer by which the holiness of the Sabbath is proclaimed by the Jew in his home) and for *Havdolah* (a religious ceremony that marks the outgoing of the Sabbath. The word "Havdolah" means "separation," and Jewish law

---

[77]*Ibid.*
[78]*Ibid.*
[79]An illustration from the text will clarify Rabbi Kagan's method. The *Orah Hayyim* states that Jewish residents of a city may compel each other to build a synagogue and to buy a Torah Scroll as well as sacred books for study (see *Shulhan Arukh, Orah Hayyim*: Laws relating to the building of a synagogue, cap. 150). The questions and doubts that arise from this law are: "What does the word 'compel' mean?" "How many Jews are needed to have a synagogue in a community?" "Can a minority insist that a synagogue should be constructed against the will of a majority?" "If the community lacks sufficient money for building a synagogue, are its constituents obligated to contribute separately to the temporary rental of a synagogue as well as to the fund for the building of one?" "May members of other faiths participate in the construction of a synagogue?" "Suppose Jews do not have enough money to build a *Beth Midrash* (adjoining study room) within the synagogue, of what value will the sacred books

prohibits the resumption of ordinary work after the Sabbath before a formal declaration of "separation" has been proclaimed). Raisin wine was used because of the high price of grapes. Rabbi Kagan permitted the Jews to recite the blessing over the wine even though it was made of raisin, and even though it was made of water and little more than one-sixth pure grape wine.[80]

Likutei Halakhoth

Rabbi Kagan believed that his were the "days of the coming of the Messiah . . . and if we had the means we would buy land and settle in Palestine."[81] Since he and his sons were of the priestly caste,[82] he thought that they would need to know the laws of sacrifices and Temple ritual because they were convinced that they might be called to Temple service. Although it may be difficult for modern readers to understand the strength of Rabbi Kagan's belief in the rebuilding of the Temple and in the reinstituting of sacrifices, as late as

be?" These questions led Rabbi Kagan to discuss the subject in the *Mishnah Berurah*. There he referred to the law of Rambam that as long as there are ten Jewish men a house of worship must be established. He also cited the ruling of Moses Isserles that even a minority can compel a majority to construct a synagogue (see Moses Isserles, *Haggahoth*, paragraph 163). Rabbi Kagan held that if ten Jews cannot afford to build a structure for worship, they are still obligated to rent a building to serve as a synagogue. He also ruled that one must contribute to the rental of a synagogue as well as to the fund for the construction of a new one (Kagan, *Mishnah Berurah*, II, 60ff).

Rabbi Kagan's commentary on this subject in the *Sha'ar Hazion* states that it is self-evident that a building must be rented for worship as long as there are insufficient funds to erect one. Since he gives no source which helped him to arrive at this particular conclusion, he himself is the author of the ruling (see *ibid.*, p. 60).

In *Biur Halakhah* the Rabbi gives details concerning the extent of a non-Jew's participation in the construction work of a synagogue. He held that only the roof may be constructed by a non-Jew while the other parts must be done by Jews. He also ruled that a house of study must be constructed along with a house of prayer since the study of Torah takes precedence over prayer (see tractate *Sabbath*, p. 10 and Kagan, *Mishnah Berurah*, II, 60ff).

[80]Kagan, *Mishnah Berurah*, III, 100.

[81]Kagan, *Michtevei Hafets Hayyim*, I, 44.

[82]The descendants of Aaron and his sons were known as the "priestly caste" and were responsible for carrying out the sacrificial and Temple ritual. Rabbi Kagan wrote that, if the Temple were reconstructed, the priestly caste would again assume its sacrificial and Temple duties.

1946 the author was taught by rabbis to believe with all his heart and all his might in the coming of the Messiah and the reconstruction of the Temple. For two thousand years in exile, Jews had longed and hoped for the coming of the Annointed One to hasten the redemption and the rebuilding of the Temple. Orthodox Jews throughout the world and in Israel still retain prayers referring to the rebuilding of the Temple and reinstitution of the sacrifices in their daily, Sabbath, and High Holiday liturgy. Even the conservative movement retains such prayers in its prayer-book. Rabbi Kagan prepared a *halakhic* condensation of the *Seder Kodashim (Order of Holiness)* to meet this need. The first volume of *Likutei Halakhoth* appeared in 1900 and the concluding one in 1925.[83] A controversy arose over his writing of *Likutei Halakhoth,* opponents arguing that it might replace the direct study of the sources.[84]

Geder Olam, Toharath Yisroel, Baith Yisroel

Rabbi Kagan's writings also include his concern for the observance of family purity—the obligation for which lies with the married Jewish woman.[85] He felt that Jewish women had become lax in carrying out the regulations concerning family purity. These rules had been observed faithfully for centuries and played an important role in the religious role of the Jewish woman as well as in the promotion of good health. As Dr. Jacob Smithline, a pioneer in the medical explanation of the need for *Mikvah,* wrote:

Abstinence . . . has a threefold advantage; firstly,

---

[83]Kagan, *Michtevei Hafets Hayyim.*
[84]For details, see pp. 115-116.
[85]God has commanded the Jews (Leviticus 18:19); "To a woman in the state of her separation (*Nidah*) thou shalt not approach . . ." The Hebrew term *Nidah* means "isolation," and applies to a woman during her menstrual period, because then she is to be separated from her husband. A woman becomes a *Nidah* whenever she perceives vaginal bleeding, however slight. From the moment she becoms a *Nidah* until she immerses in a *Mikvah* (ritual font), sexual intercourse is strictly forbidden. See Rabbi David Miller, *The Secret of the Jewish Law* (New York: Hebrew Publishing Company, 1927), IV, 21-43.

that of the promotion of physical repair in the woman; secondly, that of giving the female time to regain her vitality; thirdly, it may enhance tenderness and love in the male for his mate. . . . There is a resulting spiritual upwelling that brings forth the finest and noblest qualities of the human soul.[86]

Rabbi Kagan corresponded with Dr. Smithline and praised his work and medical knowledge on behalf of family purity laws.[87] In 1921 the late professor L. Duncan Bulkey, senior physician of the New York Skin and Cancer Hospital, noted "The consensus of opinion seems to be that Orthodox Jews, observing their ritual life, are much less subject to cancer than the rest of the population."[88]

Geder Olam appeared in 1890. It includes laws dealing with the observance of the purity laws and with the covering of a woman's hair.[89] In 1910 Rabbi Kagan felt it was necessary to write another work on family purity laws, which he called *Toharath Yisroel*; and in 1928 he wrote *Baith Yisroel.* In the last, he devotes his third chapter to the importance of observing the family purity laws. He states:

And now because of our multiple sins, we hear the alarming reports that in the big cities women began to be lax in observing the family purity laws by avoiding going to the ritual bath because they have baths in their homes which they think can take the place of the ritual bath. However, they are violating the law of the Torah which requires specific measures for the bath.[90]

---

[86]Dr. Joseph Smithline, "Scientific Aspects of Sexual Hygiene," in *Torah Laws for the Modern Woman* (New York: G. M. T. Typographic Corp., 1965), pp. 29ff.

Letter of Rabbi Israel Meir Kagan to Dr. Smithline, the ninth day of Cheevan, in *ibid.,* p. 1.

[88]Smithline, "Scientific Aspects of Sexual Hygiene," p. 32.

[89]According to the *Shulhan Arukh,* a Jewish woman is obligated to observe the laws relating to the covering of the hair by wearing a hat, wig, or kerchief in the presence of other men. Today, very Orthodox women still observe the laws governing the covering of the hair.

[90]Rabbi Israel Meir Kagan, *Baith Yisroel,* p. 17.

In 1928 Rabbis Kagan and Grodzenski urged rabbis throughout the world to strengthen the observance of the family purity laws. They exhorted Jews to do what they could to restore the ritual bath in America, in Soviet Russia, and in other lands where Jews settled.[91] Their call was somewhat successful. As of 1965, there were over one-hundred and seventy ritual baths in major American cities; seventeen in Brooklyn alone, others in such remote places as Des Moines, Iowa, Fargo, North Dakota, and Sheboygan, Wisconsin. It is also interesting to note that East Germany, Hungary, Wales, and Turkey each have one ritual bath.[92] Rabbis Kagan and Grodzenski were influential in the establishment of the United Jewish Women for Taharas Hamishpocho, Inc., whose purpose is to disseminate literature concerning the observance of family purity laws as well as to build ritual baths in areas where none exist.[93]

The preceding survey of Rabbi Kagan's writings is intended to demonstrate the prolific nature of his work and to indicate the scope of his interests and concerns. A few of his books and articles have been discussed here in greater detail as they will not be analyzed further. *Hafets Hayyim, Ahavath Chesed, Nidhei Israel* and *Mahaneh Israel* merit detailed treatment in later chapters because of their uniqueness and their impact on his as well as our own time.

> . . . who is able to assess and to evaluate his accomplishments for the dissemination of Torah in behalf of the education of Jewish children . . . the Jewish family . . . but the matter of safeguarding one's tongue consumed his whole being; this was the soul of all his accomplishments and in behalf of this cause his holy and pure life served as a symbol and example.[94]

As we have seen, Rabbi Kagan began his adult life by

---

[91]Rabbis Israel Meir Kagan and Hayyim Ozer Grodzenski, "Taharas Hamispocha," in Kagan *Michtevei Hafets Hayyim*, II, 41ff.

[92]Smithline, "Scientific Aspects of Sexual Hygiene," pp. 52-58.

[93]*Ibid.*, p. 6. Headquarters are in New York City.

[94]Letter from Rabbi Joseph Epstein to the author, June 28, 1967.

marrying more for spiritual than material reasons. He evidenced that humility in all his actions that would later win the esteem of the Bolsheviks, and also the guilessness and distaste for dissembling that made a profession both as community Rabbi and as storekeeper impossible. His devotion to the Torah and his spirituality pervaded his actions throughout his life as well as all his writings. He saw the Torah as the central rationale for Jewish existence and felt that what he interpreted as the spirit of Torah should be infused into every aspect of daily life. His belief in the spiritual joy of understanding and practicing the tenets of the Torah and his simple and serene faith in God and His creation caused him to grieve deeply for those who were led astray, but his fundamentalist attitude was never punitive or exclusionary. He remained concerned for the lives of all Jews and his writings stand as testimony to his efforts to reach those who had gone or been led astray as well as the faithful.

This chapter has offered a brief summary of his life and writings and has established points of reference and background for subsequent chapters, which will deal in more detail with the historical problems dealt with by Rabbi Kagan and with his abiding concern—the avoidance of gossip and tale-bearing.

Chapter Two

POSITIONS AND RESPONSES

As has been seen, Rabbi Israel Meir Kagan turned his attention to several important historical problems. The six problems discussed in this chapter are: (1) military conscription in Eastern Europe, (2) poverty and social welfare in Jewish communities, (3) emigration as a response to the conditions of Eastern European Jewry, (4) the Zionist question, (5) Jews under Communism, and (6) Poland between the wars. In each case the general problem will be delineated, Rabbi Kagan's response will be discussed and a conclusion will follow. For organizational purposes, the problems have been arranged in roughly chronological order.

MILITARY CONSCRIPTION IN·EASTERN EUROPE

The Russian conscription law of 1874 and the problems within the Jewish community occasioned by it gave rise to one of Rabbi Kagan's major publications—*Mahaneh Israel*. This section contains a general discussion of the difficulties faced by European Jews in this regard. *Mahaneh Israel* will be examined in detail to illustrate specific recommendations made to the young men—including discussions on the importance of prayer, fringes and phylacteries and Torah study, on the observance of the Sabbath and Kashruth (dietary laws) , on hope and on ethical conduct. The section concludes with an evaluation of the book and of Kagan's response to this problem.

The Conscription Law of 1874

The Jewish community of Russia was victimized in two ways by the canton system of Nicholas I.[1] First, the Jews were compelled to do military service while being deprived of basic civil rights; and, secondly, Tsar Nicholas used the military service to force the assimilation of Jews into Russian life. Not satisfied with merely imposing a military obligation upon the Jews, Nicholas used the military service as an educational and disciplinary agency for the Jews. The barracks were "to serve as a school, or rather as a factory . . . for producing de-Judaized Jews, who were Russified, and if possible, Christianized."[2] Indeed, Nicholas wanted to demoralize the Jewish community by touching one of the chief strengths of Jewish life, the young. "Records of the number of conversions are incomplete, but from those available we can ascertain that the percentage of converts was very high,

---

[1]The term "canton system" was applied to Jewish children in Tsarist Russia who were recruited for military service. In 1827 Tsar Nicholas I (1825-1855) conscripted Jews for the first time for military duty. The recruits served for twenty-five years beginning at the age of eighteen, normally. Jewish children were taken, however, at the age of twelve and placed in preparatory establishments for military training. The cantonists were sent to remote areas and every effort was made to baptize them as Christians. Many did not survive the rigorous discipline in the preparatory establishments. Many saved themselves by accepting Russian Orthodox Christianity. Naturally, Jews did everything within their power to keep their children from being conscripted into Nicholas' army. To frustrate their attempts at evasion, Nicholas ordered the leaders of each community to fulfill a quota of children. The rich often tried to buy substitutes for their children, while informers and professional kidnappers added to the demoralization and terror within the Jewish community. (See Dubnow, *History of the Jews in Russia and Poland*, pp. 13-29; and Baron, *The Russian Jews*, pp. 35-38; and A. A. Kizevetter, *Storicheski Ocherki*, (Moscow, 1912), pp. 402-502. Kizevetter, a contemporary of Nicholas I, provides valuable primary source material on the life and reign of Nicholas I, but he fails even to mention Nicholas' discriminatory policies, especially the canton system towards the Jews. The reason for such subjective historical writing was probably Kizvetter's fear of exile to Siberia or death for reporting the shortcomings of a Russian Tsar.

[2]Dubnow, *History of the Jews in Russia and Poland*, II, 15.

in many instance reaching one hundred per cent."[3] "In the battalions of Saratov in the year 1845, for example, all the Jewish cantonists were baptized, including 130 who came in May and were forced to convert within two weeks. In the same year the Perm battalion reported similar successes to the Holy Synod."[4] "These results were due to the special pressures brought to bear upon the military and religious officials through the intensified program instituted by Nicholas in 1843" and in previous years the achievements had not been quite so gratifying. For example, in the half battalion of Verkhne-Uralsk, "only one third of the Jewish children were won over to baptism between the years 1836 to 1842, and the battalion of Saratov—which reported such perfect results in 1845—converted only 687 out of its 1,304 Jewish recruits during the years 1828 to 1842."[5]

According to Salo Baron, the total number of conversions may not have exceeded 60,000 in the entire thirty-year period, and the Jewish population, which at the time of the conscription of the minors may have averaged 3,000,000, could have sustained such losses without serious interruption in its numerical expansion.[6] However, the agony and sense of tragedy felt by those parents whose sons were taken from them to serve in the army must have been severe.

This tragedy made a strong impression upon Rabbi Kagan and throughout his life he showed great understanding and compassion for the soldiers of Tsar Nicholas I. Once he saw a husky Jew in a hotel in Vilna asking the waitress for chicken and whiskey. He started to eat the meal without washing his hands and without reciting a blessing. Rabbi Kagan was about to approach the man to tell him that a Jew has to wash his hands before eating and recite a blessing; but the owner of the hotel warned him away from the illiterate and pugnacious man. He told the Rabbi that the soldier has been captured at the age of seven along with other chil-

---

[3]Greenberg, *The Jews in Russia*, I, 51.
[4]*Ibid.*
[5]*Ibid.*; see also Saul M. Ginsburg, *Historische Werk* (New York, 1937), II, 63, 102.
[6]Baron, *The Russian Jews*, p. 37.

dren and conscripted. He was sent to Siberia and lived there until the age of eighteen with Russians. Then he was conscripted for army duty for twenty-five years. He had not even learned the Hebrew alphabet. From such a man one should not expect much. But Rabbi Kagan began speaking with him and asked him whether the hotel owner's story was true. When the soldier answered affirmatively, Rabbi Kagan said: "Your suffering in this world will bring you repose in the world to come, along with the righteous and learned. Very few Jews have been exposed to such suffering on behalf of Judaism and God as your experience indicates that you were."[7] The soldier began to cry at the warm words of the Rabbi; and, upon learning that he was Kagan, he kissed him. With the understanding and compassion of Rabbi Kagan, he became a religious Jew.[8]

This story is illustrative of warmth, understanding and compassion that Rabbi Kagan had for the common man in general and for the soldier in particular. His humility seemed to break through every social, economic and cultural barrier of his day which usually protected the rich and learned leaders of the Jewish community from those who suffered more.

The plight of the Jewish soldier under Alexander II (1855-1881), who began his reign after the Crimean War, did not improve. In that war the Russian army of Nicholas I was badly beaten by the Turks. Their defeat had proved to the world that sheer weight of manpower and perfection in drilling, so impressive in parade grounds, were no substitute for training, organization, and modernized equipment. Of some 2,200,000 men called into the army by 1856, a mere fraction took active part in fighting. The ruinous cost of maintaining this huge army and its failure to prevent the disastrous outcome of the war pointed to the necessity for fundamental army reform.[9]

---

[7]Yosher, *Ha-Hafets Hayyim*, I, 174ff.

[8]*Ibid.*

[9]Michael T. Florinsky, *Russia: A History and An Interpretation* (New York: Macmillan Co., 1964), II, 906ff; see also Alexander Kornilov, *Kurs Istorii Rossii v XIX Veke (Lectures in the History of Russia in the Nineteenth Century)* (Moscow, 1912-1914), II, 63-71.

Alexander II, known in Russia as liberator of the peasants, appointed General Dimitry Miliutin, Minister of War from 1861 to 1881, to reorganize the army. General Miliutin did so by introducing important technical innovations such as the general staff, the medical service, army engineers, military courts, the liberal arts program at military schools, and up-to-date arms and equipment. The most significant contributions, however, were the "humanization of discipline, the bettering of conditions of service, and the introduction of conscription borne equally by all social classes."[10]

The conscription law of January 1, 1874 stated that every able-bodied man, irrespective of social status, was to enter the service at the age of twenty. The normal term of active service was six years, with an additional nine years required in the reserve followed by five years in the militia. The reserve and the militia were called up only in an emergency. The law did not draft all males of twenty—breadwinners and only sons could be drafted solely by the order of the Tsar. Furthermore, the term of military service for young men graduated from elementary schools was cut from the normal six years to four years; for graduates of secondary schools to three years or to eighteen months, according to the grade completed; and for graduates from colleges to six months. All this was to ensure more time for the military service. Graduates from colleges, however, were able to enter as volunteers—which shortened their term of service to three months.[11]

Rabbi Kagan's Position and Response

Although Miliutin's reforms removed some of the worst aspects of Russian military service, Rabbi Kagan was greatly disturbed by the new general recruiting law of 1874. It

---

[10]Florinsky, *Russia: A History and An Interpretation*, II, 906ff.

[11]See Kornilov, *Kurs Istorii Rossii v XIX Veke*, II, 63-71. Even though Kornilov deals with the law, he does not specify its impact on the Jews. See also Sergei Fedorovich Platanov, *History of Russia*, translated by E. Arnsberg and edited by F. A. Golder (New York: Macmillan Co., 1905), pp. 377-378. Platanov does not mention the impact of the law of 1874 on the Jews. See also Kagan, *Michtevei Hafets Hayyim*, p. 18.

threatened the very existence of the *yeshivoth* since their students were now to be drafted for the first time. The religious recruits who did not also have a secular education were required to serve six years rather than six months to three years. They were sent to remote locations in Russia proper or to Siberia. Rabbi Kagan feared that tens of thousands of Jewish soldiers would be exposed to forbidden foods and laxity in observance of the laws of the Torah.[12] And he dreaded the possibility of conversion and intermarriage of a young Jewish soldier in a Christian environment. He urged Jews to continue to marry before entering the army, as they had before the law of 1874. He hoped that a married soldier would avoid violating laws relating to sexual matters and intermarriage. In spite of the famous public disagreement with Rabbi Malbim (1809-1879)[13] on this issue, Rabbi Kagan remained convinced that early marriage would be beneficial.[14]

In 1881, Rabbi Kagan published *Mahaneh Israel*, designed to provide a religious and ethical code for the Jewish soldier. Since no similar code was available, Rabbi Kagan searched Talmudic and Rabbinic sources to form the basis for the code.

The Talmud offered no precedents for him, as it contains little more than a definition of three types of war: optional war, preventive war, and duty-bound warfare.[15] The war of conquest under Joshua, for example, is held by the Talmud to be a war of duty, while the wars of the house of David for extending the dominion were political,[16] and therefore fell into the category of optional war.

Maimonides went into more detail, stating that a king

---

[12]Kagan, *Michtevei Hafets Hayyim*, p. 18.

[13]He wrote a commentary on the Scriptures, characterized by a fine perception of the niceties of the Hebrew language.

[14]Kagan, *Michtevei Hafets Hayyim*, p. 19. Rabbi Kagan wrote an article about early marriage which the Russian government censored because it held that it was more useful for government to enlist single than married men. The article was finally published in Prussia. ("A Message for the Time," reproduced in *Mahaneh Israel*, pp. 175-197).

[15]Tractate *Sotah*, p. 44; *Megillah*, p. 15.

[16]*Mishnah Torah: Sefer Sofhtim*, p. 324. These wars required the consent of the high court.

does not need the permission of the high court to wage a war for what he defined as religious causes, such as the wars of Joshua and the war of Amalek.[17] On the other hand, the king had to have the consent of the high court of seventy-one members to declare a political or secular war in order to extend the dominion.[18] According to Maimonides, it is necessary to attempt to make a peace treaty with an enemy, but if the enemy refuses, a declaration of war can be made. An offer of peace must be extended whether it is a war for obligatory causes or for political causes to extend the dominion.[19] If a nation accepts peace and wishes to practice the seven civilized precepts of the children of Noah, not even one human being may be killed but those who submit must work for the king in such tasks as the building of fortifications, the king's palace, and similar projects.[20] Here again, Rabbi Kagan could find no precedent for his particular concern— the everyday religious and ethical life of the Jewish soldier serving in a foreign (Tsarist Russian) army. Since Jews were not drafted into foreign armies until the nineteenth century, rabbis had never been involved in the problems of the Jewish draftee. Thus Rabbi Kagan had to be original and creative in compiling such a code for the Jewish soldier.

He did find some aid in the *Mishnah Torah* of Maimonides, the *Turim* of Rabbi Yaacov ben Asher, and especially in Karo's *Shulhan Arukh*. He drew heavily on the *Shulhan Arukh's* laws dealing with prayer, dietary laws, observance of the Sabbath, and similar matters. However, his creativity lay in selecting the important laws in the *Shulhan Arukh*, and systematizing and classifying them to be meaningful to a Jewish soldier. His originality is also evident in his lenient interpretation of laws in some circumstances and strict interpretation in others. He shows leniency in such matters as prayer, study of Torah, and dietary laws under emergency conditions, but he is uncompromising in such

[17]The wars of Joshua and the war of Amalek were fought, according to Maimonides, for the preservation of Judaism and of the Israel people.
[18]*Mishnah Tora: Sefer Sofhtim*, p. 324.
[19]*Ibid.*
[20]*Ibid.*

matters as sex laws, gossip and tale-bearing, the observance
of the Sabbath, and ethical laws.

Rabbi Kagan wrote:
Behold, if we were to look attentively at Torah observance at the present time, we would find it to be
very lax for settled Jews in general, and for the Jewish soldiers in particular. There are those Jews who
transgress the laws of the Torah with contempt
while others violate the Torah laws dealing with
martyrdom.[21]

He stated that the laxity in observance of Torah commands was due to ignorance. He pointed out that the Code
of Karo did not provide specific laws dealing with the religious life of a Jewish soldier. Many of the soldiers were stationed in places which did not have a rabbinical authority
to answer simple questions concerning observance. He wrote:

Therefore, I found it necessary to prepare a code for
soldiers based on sources and I searched in detail
to discover a decree . . . which will make it easier for
soldiers to keep the law; and I also investigated the
morals for every man in general and for the soldiers in particular, whose morals, if corrupted, can
bring disgrace to God. May God merit us to keep
the commands of the Torah between God and man
and those precepts between man and man.[22]

According to Kagan, there were other reasons for laxity
in the observance of the Torah laws. Some soldiers felt that
the new environment forced them to violate certain commands. Some felt that God had allowed them to be forsaken
by the rest of the Jewish people and thereby released them
from an obligation to obey the commands of the Torah.[23]
Other soldiers were lax in observing the Torah because of
the influense of irreligious friends in the army.[24]

[21]Kagan, *Mahaneh Israel*, p. 7.
[22]*Ibid.*
[23]*Ibid.*, pp. 15ff.
[24]*Ibid.*

Rabbi Kagan held that God does not forsake a man who is removed from the rest of the Jews. Even the irreligious soldier who is transported to a remote hostile environment still remains God's concern. The soldier who keeps the laws of the Torah in the trying days of army life is greatly to be admired. He will be inspired to be strong in his practice of Judaism by constantly recalling the trials and tribulations of Abraham and Joseph on behalf of God.

Prayer, Fringes, Phylacteries, and Torah-Study

In *Mahaneh Israel* Rabbi Kagan stressed the importance of prayer, fringes, phylacteries, and Torah-study, stating that prayer is greater than good deeds and sacrifices. In the *Mishnah Berurah*, he states that the purpose of a Jew in the world is to serve God through prayer since he was created by the Almighty for this specific task.[25] On the day before the soldier wages battle he should devote some time to prayer, solemn meditation, and repentance. He should examine his deeds, recite the confession which is said on Yom Kippur eve before Kol Nidre service,[26] and firmly resolve never again to commit the evils he has been wont to do. He should concentrate his energy in prayer and supplication before God that He, in His compassion, may remove all accusations on earth and heaven from him. He must recite the prayer "I Give Thanks Unto Thee," composed by Rabbi Kagan specifically for the Jewish soldier.

> I give thanks unto Thee, O my Lord, the God of my fathers, the God of Abraham, Isaac and Jacob; in the heavens above and on earth below there is no other God besides Thee. Thou wast, and art, and wilt be. In Thy hand lie my security as well as the power to destroy me; May it be Thy will to deliver me, that I should not die in battle, for Thou are all-Merciful. I pray to Thee, O gracious God; the

[25] Kagan, *Mishnah Berurah*, I, 7.
[26] The confession was composed by Rabbi Danzig (1748-1821), the author of the Code Chaye Adam which deals with the laws of Karo's *Shulhan Arukh's Orah Hayyim*.

soul is Thine and the body is of Thy making, have pity on Thy work. Make me worthy to continue serving Thee. Have mercy on Thy servants, the children of Thy proven ones who, though suffering poverty, degradation and oppression for so many centuries, are still calling on Thy name and believe in Thee and Thy Torah. Many thousands and tens of thousands readily offered themselves to be slaughtered and burned for the holiness of Thy name. Be merciful to our brothers in arms who are facing danger. Help us. O Lord, to promote, protect and safeguard the cherished institutions of our country for the sake of Thy divine glory. Deliver me, I beseech Thee, of the sin of killing my own brothers. May there come before Thee our great pain and that of our fathers, mothers, wives and children. They are all praying daily before Thee for our safety. May our merits and our righteous deeds be seen before Thee, and all our sins be thrown into the depths of the sea, and may Thy compassion overcome Thy anger against us. Aid us to triumph over our enemies and deliver us from all ills, from famine and from captivity, from grief and sorrow, from being plundered and tormented. Grant a perfect healing to all the sick and wounded people of our country.

O God, I pray Thee, heal them and realize in everyone of them the blessing "The Lord will sustain him upon the bed of painful disease." Those of our people who are well, permit them to continue in their state of health; protect them from the affliction of sickness. Guard us from all injury, deliver us from oppressors and adversaries, save us from all accusations and from every evil spirit and from all sorts of trouble that move about in the world. If it be Thy will that I die, may my death bring me forgiveness for all my sins, iniquities and transgressions that I have sinned or perverted or

dealt iniquitously before Thee and Thou shalt make
me worthy that my bones be placed at rest in accordance with the rites of the faith of Israel, and
prevent my body from being thrown about care-
lessly as prey for animals of the field and the fowl of
the skies. O Lord, grant me a portion in paradise
and a share in the future life, reserved for the righteous. I thank Thee and I believe that Thou art God
the Creator, who hast created all the worlds; that
Thou hast originated, made, formed, and established all that is found therein. Thou alone over-
seest all the worlds and there is no existence for
any of them without Thy providence. I believe that
because of Thy love for our ancestors, Thou hast
chose our nation Israel and given us Thy Torah
which is eternal, through Thy prophet and trusted
servant, Moses our teacher. Through him Thou
didst hand down the written law which is the very
Torah we possess and, orally, Thou also handed to
him the interpretation thereof, which is the Holy
Talmud. I believe that God gave the Torah to
Moses, and I believe that He spoke to His holy
prophets whose prophecies constitute the books of
the Prophets and the Scriptures. I further believe
that God will bring to his people Israel, their righteous Messiah at the time when, in His opinion,
they will deserve to be redeemed, and that there
will be a resurrection of the dead at the will of
the Creator, may He be blessed for Thy help I hope,
O Lord, I hope, O Lord, for Thy help. O Lord, for
Thy help I hope.[27]

Several questions can be asked: Was Rabbi Kagan not
naive to expect the Jewish soldier to pray and to be convinced
that prayer would save his life? Furthermore, why did Kagan
have to compose a special prayer for the Jewish soldier? If
Rabbi Kagan were naive, so were the Jewish soldiers, especially those who came from the *yeshivoth*. Religious life

and prayer were the way of life for the observant young men in the Jewish pale of settlement. Certainly, *yeshiva* students believed that prayer and faith in God would save their lives in time of battle. Rabbi Kagan was a keen student of the realities of his time and he tried to strengthen the faith of the Jewish soldier through the tools of his day, namely prayer and trust in God.

It would seem that there were many prayers in the Prayer Book and appropriate psalms for the Jewish soldier to recite before going into battle without the need to compose a new prayer. But if the prayer of Rabbi Kagan is analyzed carefully one can see that such a prayer was essential because of its unique nature. It manifested his great concern and love for the Jewish youth in the military service and it was also a message to the Jewish community at large to be concerned with the trials and tribulations of the Jewish soldier in remote places. Above all, his prayer contained the thirteen fundamental principles of the Jewish faith as enumerated by Maimonides. Even in battle the soldier was not exempt from these principles. Thus, in the matter of the principles, the Rabbi had the same standards for the soldier as for the average Jew. Certainly, such standards were hard to keep under the harsh conditions of military life, but the soldiers were aware that the standards had been set up by a man who cared deeply for their welfare.

Rabbi Kagan related that every Jewish soldier should take phylacteries along with him to his army post. If one of his phylacteries was lost, and he could not borrow from a friend, he could put on only one.[28] In the *Mishnah Berurah* he also stated that a poor Jew who must beg in order to buy phylacteries is exempt from putting them on, even though it is a prerequisite from the Torah. It would seem that Rabbi Kagan felt that the dignity of the man was more important than humiliating oneself by securing phylacteries through

---

[27]Kagan, *Mahaneh Israel*, pp. 74-75. See also Kagan's prayer for the Jewish soldier, translated into English in Moses M. Yosher, *Israel in the Ranks* (New York: Shulsinger Bros., 1943), pp. 138-140.

[28]Kagan, *Mahaneh Israel*, p. 30; see also *Mishnah Berurah*, I, 70.

begging.[29] Since Karo's *Shulhan Arukh: Orah Hayyim* completely neglects the religious life of the Jewish soldier,[30] Rabbi Kagan felt it permissible to be lenient in the case of using phylacteries. He also stated that a Jewish soldier must be particularly careful to wear fringes while in the army because they represent the numerical value of the 613 commands of the Torah. The putting on of fringes add holiness to a Jew and prevents him from committing transgressions.[31] Again, in the *Mishnah Berurah*, Kagan held that poor persons who must beg to obtain fringes are exempt from wearing them since self-respect is more important. [32] He held that one can insert the fringes inside his garment if he deals with non-Jews.[33]

It may seem difficult, from our standpoint, to comprehend the importance of a soldier wearing fringes and putting on phylacteries. But these were tangible and visible symbols of the soldier's devotion to the high standards set for him as a religious man. The challenges facing a Jewish soldier were difficult ones and Rabbi Kagan seems to have understood that only strong, tangible evidence of faith would sustain a young man in his attempt to remain faithful.

A soldier should devote some time to the study of Torah, Rabbi Kagan wrote, for Torah study is always required. Such study will tell the soldier how to carry out the commands of the Torah and will keep him away from gossip, quarrels and fraud. Studying Torah will also set an example for the other soldiers to follow.[34] The Rabbi warned that in the beginning the study of Torah may engender mockery by non-Jewish soldiers and even some fellow Jews. Despite the derision, the soldier must strengthen himself and continue to study and observe. Rabbi Moses Isserles of the sixteenth century wrote: "A person must disregard mockery in the case of

---

[29]Kagan, *Mishnah Berurah*, I, 63.

[30]Karo, *Shulhan Arukh, Orah Hayyim*, pp. 39-79, makes no mention of the religious problems of a soldier.

[31]Kagan, *Mahaneh Israel*, pp. 39ff; see also Kagan, *Mishnah Berurah*, p. 62.

[32]Kagan, *Mishnah Berurah*, p. 67.

[33]*Ibid.*, p. 28.

[34]Kagan, *Mahaneh Israel*, pp. 39ff.

serving God.''[35] According to Rabbi Kagan, the reward of a soldier who accepts ridicule in his determination to serve God and to keep the practices of the Torah is great. If derision overpowers a soldier, laxity in the study of Torah will lead to other trespasses. Sensitivity to derison will lead to the removing of the yoke of the Torah; and the soldier will become a flagrant sinner.

Rabbi Kagan wrote that a soldier studying Torah would be highly respected by his commander because the commander will know that the soldier is not a thief, a drunkard, or a troublemaker. In the end the mockery will stop and he will be able to continue the study of Torah and the practice of the Jewish commandments without ridicule.[36] The following incident was related by Rabbi Kagan:

> A religious soldier asked his commander for a leave on an army holiday. The commander permitted the pious soldier furlough for a day. He went to a certain house on the base to study Torah. By chance, the commander walked into the same house and saw the soldier studying with great enthusiasm. The commander was bewildered and told him, "I thought that when you asked me to excuse you for the day it was to go with other soldiers to celebrate in the taverns." The soldier then replied, "Believe me, my commander, the day that I am engrossed in the study of Torah . . . is a day of great joy in my life and a day of purpose in my life." The soldier related to his commander the morals of the Torah and the commander was very impressed by the answer of his religious soldier. The commander informed other commanders of the righteousness and morality of the Jewish soldier.[37]

In the *Mishnah Berurah*, Rabbi Kagan maintains the traditional requirement for daily morning and evening Torah

---

[35]*Ibid.*
[36]*Ibid.*, p. 40.
[37]*Ibid.*, pp. 41ff.

study, but remains flexible about the amount of time to be spent at it.[38]

Observance of the Sabbath

The observance of the Sabbath and all laws pertaining to it are discussed in detail in *Mahaneh Israel*. The soldier must remember that the Sabbath is the sign and the covenent between God and the Jews. The Torah warns the Jew twelve times to keep the Sabbath holy. According to the Sages, observance of the Sabbath is as if observing the whole Torah; and transgressing the Sabbath is as if denying the whole Torah.

Although Rabbi Kagan expected a Jewish soldier to observe the Sabbath as rigidly as any other Jew, he was aware of the difficulties and had high praise for the soldier who attempted to keep the Sabbath. For example, he did not consider a soldier who was forced by his commander to work on the Sabbath a violator of the Sabbath.[39] But he was aware that military commanders gave soldiers in military camps a choice of jobs. Some jobs did not require work on the Sabbath, and Kagan urged the Jewish soldier to select these. In dealing with the problem of two Jewish soldiers—both commanded to dig a ditch on the Sabbath—Rabbi Kagan held that one soldier could not require the other to dig alone in order to avoid violating the Sabbath himself.[40]

Observance of Kashruth

The Jewish soldier was prohibited—as are all Jews—from eating certain foods. Rabbi Kagan reminded the soldiers that observance of Kashruth is a positive Torah command and that a Jew's sense of holiness remains strong through such observance.[41] When kosher meat was unavailable, the soldier could subsist on a vegetarian diet.[42]

---

[38]Kagan, *Mishnah Berurah*, I, 88ff.
[39]Kagan, *Mahaneh Israel*, p. 49.
[40]*Ibid.*, p. 52.
[41]Kagan, *Mahaneh Israel*, pp. 55-59.
[42]*Ibid.*, pp. 251ff. During the Second World War, Rabbi Moses M. Yosher, a former student of Rabbi Kagan, wrote *Israel in the Ranks*, a

Rabbi Kagan pointed out that there are different degrees in the prohibition of forbidden foods. Some articles of food are under a more stringent ban than others. For example, drinking non-kosher soup is less a transgression than eating *trefa*.[43] He also advised the soldier to minimize the transgressions he must commit to survive when subsistence on a restricted diet proves impossible.[44]

The National Jewish Welfare Board's manual, "Kashruth Observance in the Military Establishment of the United States," is also based on *Mahaneh Israel*. This contemporary *kashruth* guide states:

> No serviceman should lightly discard the standards of observance to which he is accustomed. On the contrary, he should make a tremendous effort to maintain them. It is, however, gross ignorance to argue, for example, that since one may be forced by circumstances to use non-kosher dishes, one may as well disregard the laws of kashruth completely. One's guiding principle should be that, under all circumstances, he will observe as many cherished religious practices as possible. A stubborn determination to abide by all of the regulations of *kashruth* may lead some men to total abandonment of Jewish dietary practice. On the other hand, steadfast resolu-

---

religious guide of faith and practice for the Jewish soldier, based to a large extent on Kagan's *Mahaneh Israel*. Distributed to Jewish soldiers during the war, it guided them in particular in the observance of diety laws and other religious observances: 'When kosher meat is unavailable, it is well to remember that one can frequently subsist on a purely vegetarian diet . . . even a soldier may at times select a variety of vegetables and other healthful foods on which he can subsist." (Yosher, *Israel in the Ranks*, p. 70.)

[43]Kagan, *Mahaneh Israel*, pp. 254ff. Forbidden foods are called *trefa*.

[44]*Ibid.*, pp. 55-59. Yosher agrees on both points: "However, there are different degrees in the prohibition of non-kosher foods . . . the drinking of *trefa* soup is less a violation than the eating of *trefa* meat." (Yosher, *Israel in the Ranks*, p. 70); "Hence, when the soldier is in a condition that he cannot subsist on a restricted diet, he should try to minimize as much as possible the violation that he feels compelled to commit." (Yosher, *Israel in the Ranks*, p. 71).

tion to maintain a maximum practice will in all likelihood be successful.[45]

This manual for U.S. Jewish soldiers presents exactly the same views as Rabbi Kagan's on *kashruth*.[46]

Not content with merely writing about this problem, Rabbi Kagan traveled from city to city collecting money to provide kosher food for the soldiers stationed nearby. After difficult negotiations with the commanders of the Jewish soldiers, the Rabbi and his committee obtained permission to establish three centers for dispensing kosher food. These centers were in the vicinities of Vilna, Grodna, and Oran where there were many Jewish soldiers.[47]

In 1923, Rabbi Kagan published an article in the newspaper *Der Jud* on the matter of kosher food for Jewish soldiers. He wrote:

> Everyone has to know that a soldier of the Jewish faith did not become as lax in keeping the Torah as other Jews . . . since the government does not

---

[45]"Kashruth Observance in the Military Establishment of the United States," published by the Commission on Jewish Chaplaincy of National Jewish Welfare Board, p. 2.

[46]*Ibid.*, pp. 2ff. The author wrote also to Rabbi Shlomo Goren concerning the influence of *Mahaneh Israel* in the armed forces of Israel. He answered:

> I want to stress the point that the important writing *Mahaneh Israel* of the Gaon and Zaddik Chefetz Chaim . . . was not found relevant for Israel's Defence Forces since his main aim was to indoctrinate Jewish soldiers among non-Jews but he did not lay down any principles how to maintain a sovereign Jewish army, navy, and airforce according to *Hallacha*. This is the reason why we did not make any use of his book in our military forces. On the other hand we made great use of his tremendous collection and research of the *Mishnah Berurah* and *Biur Hallacha* on *Shulhan Arukh*, to form the *Hallachic* criteria of everyday's life in Israel Defense Forces.

(Letter from General Rabbi Shlomo Goren, Chief Rabbi, Israel Defence Forces to the author, January 15, 1971. A similar letter stating the same reason as Goren's as to why *Mahaneh Israel* was not influential in the armed forces of Israel was received on November 23, 1970 by the author from Rabbi Mordecai Piron, head of Israel's Defence Forces' wing dealing with the religious life of the Israeli soldier.)

[47]Kagan, *Michtevei Hafets Hayyim*, p. 21.

force the Jewish soldier to eat forbidden foods, Jews
are responsible for helping the soldier.[48]

Importance of Hope

In *Mahaneh Israel*, Rabbi Kagan held that hope is crucial
to a soldier, especially in battle. He must trust in God to
help him and must share hope and confidence with his fellow soldiers by emulating the example of Jonathan's inspiration to David in time of trouble.[49] If a soldier returns safely
from battle, he shall be even more grateful to God, and shall
recite a prayer to God for saving his life. If he is taken cap-
tive by the enemy, he must maintain his trust in God that
he will be set free.[50]

Ethical Conduct

A Jewish soldier must act with humility, understanding,
and loving-kindness to his fellow soldiers. Give and take
should be their relationship. In three things loving-kindness
is greater than charity; the rabbis said, "Charity is with
money, loving-kindness is with the body; charity is given to
the poor, loving-kindness is given to the poor and the rich;
and loving-kindness enables a person to enjoy the fruits of
this world as well as the world to come."[51]

Gossip and informing are prohibited by the Torah; thus
Jewish soldiers must be careful to avoid gossip and slander,
which can cause mockery by non-Jewish soldiers. Soldiers
should not quarrel because this can also cause slander and
ridicule by non-Jewish soldiers. Strife among Jews and mockery by non-Jews lead to the desecration of God's name. A
person who does not answer his friend in the time of a dispute and thereby brings harmony is meritorious for, as the
Sages said, "because of harmony the world exists."[52] Drunken-

---

[48]Rabbi Israel Meir Kagan, "Kosher Essen Far Yuddishe Zelner,"
("Kosher Food for Jewish Soldiers"), *Michtevei Hafets Hayyim*, pp.
199ff.

[49]Kagan, *Mahaneh Israel*, p. 65.

[50]*Ibid.*, p. 66.

[51]*Ibid.*, p. 103; see also *Sukkah*, p. 491.

[52]*Hulin*, p. 89.

ness, gambling, and trespassing of sex laws are prohibited to the soldier. A Jewish soldier must observe all the laws of the Torah and must comport himself ethically at all times.

The book, *Mahaneh Israel*, was distributed among Jewish soldiers. Some began to gather a quorum for prayer and to practice loving-kindness to each other; some began to write books dealing with Torah. They kept the Sabbath as much as possible and they abstained from violating prohibitions of the Torah. Some wrote to Rabbi Kagan about the utility of the book and claimed that it helped them to be God-fearing and pious Jews.[53]

During the Russo-Japanese War, Rabbi Kagan sent important chapters of the book to soldiers. One of them related the following incident:

> During the Russo-Japanese War, the book saved me many times from death. Once the commander saw me and some friends studying the pamphlets of the book. He began to scream: "Don't you know that in a few hours we shall attack the enemy, and in such a danger you waste time with books of vanity? Pray to God for your lives." One of us answered the commander: "My master, we are not wasting time, for the pages contain prayers and requests from God, without them we are weak."[54]

Conclusion

Neither Rabbi Kagan nor his contemporaries such as Rabbi Israel Salanter and Moses Lilienblum organized the Jewish community to disobey the conscription law of 1874. But each reacted in his own particular fashion to the problems posed by the law. Rabbi Israel Salanter, in an 1879 article in *Ha-Meliz*, expressed his concern over a government complaint that Jewish youth of military age were failing to report for duty and over government charges of chaotic conditions within the Jewish community created by faulty birth

---

[53]Kagan, *Michtevei Hafets Hayyim*, p. 20. Leib Eckman, father of the author, has also expressed these thoughts about the book.
[54]*Ibid.*

certificates and ignorance of the details of the conscription law of 1874.[55] He urged the leaders of the Jewish community to explain to the Jews the details of the law and to encourage them to obtain birth certificates indicating their correct age. He was also disturbed that there were incidents of some recruits having to serve in the army twice because of registration in more than one place and that more Jewish recruits were conscripted than the law really required. Rabbi Salanter held that the primary reason for some youths dodging the draft was the fear that they would be drafted twice, reasoning that if they were to be drafted twice it would be better to avoid the draft completely. But he pointed out that dual conscription could be avoided by proper registration in one place.[56]

Rabbi Salanter, living in Memel, Germany, was primarily concerned to educate Russian Jews in the intricacies of their conscription law and to encourage them to obey the law by understanding it. He did not object to the law itself, since he felt it applied to all Russians equally. And he did not address himself to the religious and moral problems of the Jewish soldier.

The *Haskalah* movement looked upon the conscription law of 1874 as a socially just law, since no particular class or ethnic group was exempt from it. Naturally, the *Maskilim* were not concerned with the religious problems of the Jewish soldier in the army. Moses Lilienblum, one of the most important spokesmen for the *Haskalah,* shared the general *Haskalah* opinion of the law. He condemned richer Jews for bribing physicians to declare their sons physically unfit, thus causing an increase in recruitment of poorer youth to meet the quotas.[57] Lilienblum felt that the conscription law of 1874 could provide an opportunity for the sons of the rich and the poor to live together, to fight together, and to overcome social prejudices.

Although Rabbi Kagan seems to have agreed that the

---

[55]Israel Salanter, "Ma'orer Ha-Nirdamin," *Ha-Meliz* (8) (1879), 149-154.
[56]*Ibid.*
[57]Moses Lilienblum, "Nefesh Tahath Nefesh," *Ha-Meliz,* (4), (1878), 75-80,

law was not to be disobeyed, he analyzed the results of the law as containing the roots of intermarriage and conversion and, therefore, a threat of destruction to the *yeshivoth* and to future spiritual and communal leadership in the Orthodox Jewish community. His response was a direct attempt to counter these anticipated results.

Mahaneh Israel was written with a dual purpose. On the one hand Rabbi Kagan wanted to help all Jewish soldiers cope with their strange and often hostile environment; on the other, he hoped specifically to aid *yeshiva* students who became soldiers. If those young men were helped to observe the Torah as carefully as possible while in the army, they might return to the Jewish community to continue their studies and to assume positions of leadership. His deepest concerns were not the mere observance of laws involving sexual matters, *kashruth*, phylacteries and fringes, but rather the very survival of Orthodox Judaism in Eastern Europe and leadership within the Jewish community—both of which he felt were threatened by the conscription law of 1874. Rabbi Kagan feared that the Jewish community would be faced with a shortage of rabbis, teachers, and communal leaders, since these leaders usually came from the ranks of the *yeshivoth*—the very young men who were now being drafted for the first time. The shortage would come about as more and more young men were conscripted at an early age and were either converted to Christianity or intermarried. Such a shortage, the Rabbi feared, would lead to a degeneration of Judaism itself in Eastern Europe. Indeed, Rabbi Kagan was a man of foresight and analytical reasoning in pointing out the inherent dangers of the conscription law.

It was for the future existence of traditional Jewish values and practices in Eastern Europe, and *Mahaneh Israel* was his direct and powerful attempt to avoid the twin evils of emigration and conscription. Rather than emigrate— and thereby be lost to the European community—the *yeshivah* students could submit to conscription but use his book as a religious and moral guide to help prevent intermarriage and conversion while serving in the army.

The question arises whether Rabbi Kagan's response was based on thorough investigation and familiarity with the problems of a soldier. In general one can conclude that *Mahaneh Israel* is unique in that it deals with the specific concerns of the soldier rather than Jewry as a whole; and Rabbi Kagan shows a remarkable understanding of the soldier's religious, moral, social, and economic problems. Throughout his life, in Russia and Poland, he was an eyewitness to the trials and tribulations of the soldiers. In identifying closely with them, he won their respect and confidence. *Mahaneh Israel* was his attempt to provide a program for the soldier in dealing with his problems. For example, Rabbi Kagan recommended early marriage to provide a deterrent to sexual temptation; he recommended gathering a quorum for prayer, studying Torah in a group, practicing loving-kindness to each other and abstinence from violating the prohibitions of the Torah. He took the concept of emergency which is part of *Halakhah* and applied it to the program for the soldier. He also organized kosher food centers in the vicinities of Vilna, Grodno, and Oran. As late as 1923 he continued to write articles on the matter of kosher food for Jewish soldiers. We have evidence that Kagan's *Mahaneh Israel* was constructive and practical: the soldier who wrote to him from the Russo-Japanese War said, "My master, we are not wasting time, for the pages contain prayers and requests from God, without them we are weak."[58] Indeed, the plural number indicates that at least more than one soldier was pre-occupied with the study of *Mahaneh Israel*. Rabbi Shlomo Goren wrote to the author that *Mahaneh Israel* was a practical guide for the Jewish soldier fighting alongside non-Jews but it might not be used within the Israeli Defense Forces.[59]

None of the three—Kagan, Salanter, or Lilienblum—took the perhaps untenable position of opposing the war and the conscription on general moral grounds, although Rabbi

---

[58]Kagan, *Michtevei Hafets Hayyim*, p. 20.
[59]Letter from General Rabbi Shlomo Goren, Chief Rabbi, Israel Defense Forces to the author, January 15, 1971.

Kagan's guide was certainly an attempt to help the soldier maintain in his conduct as much of his morality as was possible.

POVERTY AND SOCIAL WELFARE
IN JEWISH COMMUNITIES

This section explores the conditions from 1800 to 1903 that prompted the writing of *Ahavath Chesed* and deals with Kagan's views on loans and on employer-employee relations. It discusses the Rabbi's explanation of *chesed;* the rationale for loving kindness, and reasons for the neglect of *chesed.* It also includes his views on daily performance of *chesed,* the *gemiluth chesed* fund, the importance of charity, showing hospitality, visiting the sick, *chesed* to the dead and comfort for the mourners, gladdening the groom and bride, verbal *chesed,* and a conclusion.

Historical Background

Rabbi Kagan believed that one of the major contributing factors to the development of the disease of gossip and talebearing was the poverty which most Jews suffered. "Poverty," he said, "breeds enmity and jealousy." It destroys the bridges between people and creates a void which is difficult to fill. *Ahavath Chesed* was Rabbi Kagan's attempt to fill that void.

The book was written in 1888, during the reign of Tsar Alexander III. This was a time of special hardship and persecution for Jews in Russia. The May Laws of 1882[1] decreed

---

[1]The May Laws of 1882 prohibited Jews from settling anew outside of the towns and villages. They suspended the "completion of instruments of purchase of real property and merchandise in the name of the Jews" outside the towns and villages. They also restricted Jews from doing business on Sundays or on Christian holidays. As a result of the provisions of the May Laws, the Jews suffered economic hardships within the confines of the pale of settlement. See Dubnow, *History of the Jews in Russia and Poland*, II, 316; and Baron, *The Russian Jews*, pp. 56, 57, 96, 261; see also Kornilov, *Kurs Istorii Rossii v XIX Veke*, pp. 306-307. Kornilov mentions the effect of the May Laws on Jews since he and other historians

the expulsion of Jews from the villages and prohibited them from carrying on their business in a normal way. Corrupt officials looked for bribes to supplement their meager bureaucratic wages. The looting during the pogroms impoverished the Jews of their personal and business possessions. In the light of such economic misery and persecution, it was easy to understand why so much bitterness prevailed and why Rabbi Kagan felt it necessary to write his book to counteract the bitterness.

As a result of the pogroms and discriminations, emigration increased and unemployment among the Russian Jews grew by leaps and bounds as a result of the depression of 1882-1887. Even Jewish artisans found that their respective skills in tailoring, shoemaking, or the food industry were of little avail in mechanized factories producing textiles, shoes, or food products.[2] Jewish merchants and workers had to pay an inordinant price for the transition to an industrial society.[3]

All Russians suffered from the general dislocations of the early Industrial Revolution. In 1882, a law was passed forbidding the employment of children under twelve years of age and setting an eight-hour limit on the working day for those aged twelve to fifteen. The latter were not permitted to work at all on Saturday and Sunday. In 1855 night work was forbidden for all women and all persons under seventeen in textile mills. This prohibition was later extended to other industries. Strikes and refusal to work were prohibited but the shortage of factory inspectors led to laxity in enforc-

---

became more courageous in exposing the shortcomings of the Tsars when Alexander III, the last of the strong Tsars, died.

Under Alexander III the government not only continued to enforce the May Laws, but added other prohibitions, among them *numerus clausus* for secondary schools and universities. Under the pretext that students of the Jewish faith were "quick in joining the ranks of the revolutionary workers," a quota for Jewish students was established. In 1887, a quota of 10 percent was set for schools within the pale, 5 percent outside the pale, and 3 percent in St. Petersburg and Moscow. Subsequently, these percentages were reduced to 7, 3 and 2 respectively. See Baron, *The Russian Jews*, p. 57.

[2]Baron, *The Russian Jews*, p. 115.

[3]*Ibid.*, p. 116.

ing the labor laws.[4] Thus the rich became richer and the poor became poorer during this period in the early development of modern capitalism. The Jewish masses sank to the lowest depths of poverty, and some came to feel it was the moral duty of the Rothschilds, the Poliakovs, and other wealthy Jews, to help them.

Rabbi Kagan's Position and Response

Rabbi Simlai had explained: "The Torah begins with an act of kindness (gemiluth chesed) and ends with an act of kindness. It begins with chesed, as it is written: 'And God made for Adam and his wife garments of skins and clothed them.'[5] It ends with chesed as it is written: 'And he (Moses) was buried in the valley in the land of Moab.' "[6]

Rabbi Kagan acknowledged these and other contributions to rabbinic literature on the subject of chesed.[7] He pointed out numerous passages scattered throughout the Torah, Talmud, and rabbinic literature on the subject. But, in response to the ills of early industrialism, he attempted to gather these passages into a coherent code of law on the specific subject of human relations—an attempt not only to inspire the wealthy to share their riches with the poor but also to encourage the poor to help each other.

Rabbi Kagan's Views on Loans

Rabbi Kagan discussed the Torah's positive command to lend money, based on the imperative statement, "You shall surely lend to him."[8] Lending is superior to charity, Rabbi Kagan avers, because the poor man is spared the shame of accepting gifts. His dignity is thereby preserved while his financial condition is strengthened.[9] In lending, a man also

---

[4]Florinsky, *Russia: A History and an Interpretation*, I, 1105; see also Petr I. Liashchenko, *History of the National Economy of Russia to the Revolution*, translated by L. M. Herman (New York: Macmillan, 1949), for details on economic conditions.

[5]Genesis 2:21.

[6]*Sotah* 14a.

[7]Rabbi Israel Meir Kagan, *Ahavath Chesed*, p. 7.

[8]Deut. 15:8.

[9]Kagan, *Ahavath Chesed*, p. 14.

fulfills the Torah command: "And if your brother be waxed poor and his hand fail with you, you shall uphold him . . ."[10] This *mitzvah* is also fulfilled by lending to the rich for a certain period of time, when they are pressed for money, since kindness may be done both to the rich and to the poor. But the poor take priority, and for that reason the Torah explicitly mentions the poor in its reference to the *mitzvah*.[11]

The precept of lending also applies to utensils and other articles. All such acts emanate from the virtue of *chesed* which God desires us to embody, as it is said, "For He delights in *chesed*."[12] Money loans, however, constitute the greater *mitzvah*, because the Torah mentions a separate reference to them.[13] Since the Sages, according to Rabbi Kagan, made no mention of a fixed measure for loans, the logical approach would be for each person to act in accordance with his means, and should extend whatever favor he can to his friends.[14]

For what period must a loan be granted? Here too the logical answer is that this depends on what each person is able to afford. The lender is not obligated to extend the loan longer than for a day if he cannot. The converse holds true also. If the lender can afford to, he is obliged to grant the loan for thirty days, when the borrower requires the amount for a longer period of time.[15]

The Torah obligation to lend to one's fellow man includes in its prescription both the instance when a security pledge is given and the instance when no such pledge is given, the borrower himself being sufficiently reliable. Rabbi Kagan presents the different points of view concerning an instance when no pledge is given. The view of the *Mekiltha* is that lending money to the needy is a command of the Torah, therefore one must lend even without a pledge.[16] According

---

[10]Lev. 25:35.

[11]Kagan, *Ahavath Chesed*, p. 14.

[12]Micah 7:18.

[13]Kagan, *Ahavath Chesed*, p. 14.

[14]Tractate *Yerushalmi*, Chapter One, Peah, paragraph one.

[15]Kagan, *Ahavath Chesed*, p. 14; see also tractate *Makoth*, p. 3, which states that one who makes a loan to his neighbor without terms cannot claim payment before thirty days.

[16]*Mekiltha*, p. 7.

to the tractate *Makoth*, since lending money depends upon a pledge, one cannot assume that it is obligatory to lend without a pledge; however, in a time of emergency, one must lend without a pledge.[17] Rabbi Kagan held that one must lend even without a pledge, but if one does so, he should present the money in the presence of witnesses, take a note from the borrower, or at least obtain his signature.[18]

Loans should be extended to all: man or woman, rich or poor, adult or minor. Even if a person is known as a habitual transgressor of the precepts of the Torah, a loan should be extended to him in his time of need.[19] Necessity must be the determining factor in extending a loan rather than the individual's observance of Torah or his character.

Answers to Questions about Loans

In this section the author will present selective inquiries concerning loans and will give the answer of Rabbi Kagan.

1. Is a person obligated to lend money to one who is not trustworthy in paying the loan? If one knows that the borrower is not trustworthy in paying loans, it is better not to lend without taking a pledge than to lend and be compelled to keep asking the debtor for repayment, because the creditor will then transgress the prohibition, "He shall not exact it of his neighbor."[20]

2. Who is obligated to grant free loans? All Jews— whether they be male or female, rich or poor (lending to one in poorer circumstances than they) —are obliged, in accordance with their means, to grant free loans. A woman is obligated to loan even if she has no husband. If she has a husband, she is exempt from giving monetary loans but not from loaning household utensils.[21]

3. Is one who is making a living by lending money

---

[17]Tractate *Makoth*, p. 3; see also tractate *Gittin*, p. 37.
[18]Kagan, *Ahavath Chesed*, p .15.
[19]*Ibid.*, pp. 18ff.
[20]Deut. 15:2, quoted in Kagan, *Ahavath Chesed*, p. 15.
[21]Kagan, *Ahavath Chesed*, pp. 17ff.

obliged to grant free loans? A person whose occupation is to lend money is still obliged to grant free loans to the poor in accordance with one's means.[22]

4. If the request is addressed to one engrossed in full time Torah study and the *mitzvah* cannot be fulfilled by others, is he permitted to interrupt his studies to give the loan? Rabbi Kagan ruled that if the request is addressed to such a person and the *mitzvah* cannot be fulfilled by others, he must interrupt his studies and give the loan. It makes no difference in this case whether the others are unwilling or unable to do the favor.[23]

5. Is a storekeeper obliged to extend credit to his customers? The Rabbi held that there are many reasons why a storekeeper is not obliged to extend credit to his customers. Firstly, his principal source of income is the selling of his wares. He reinvests the proceeds to replenish his stocks. Moreover, customer credit does not belong in the category of loans, as is indicated in the Mishnah (*Shevi'ith,* Chapter 10). Therefore, to extend credit is not included in this *mitzvah.* Nevertheless it seems that if a poor customer requests the needed items, the storekeeper is not exempt from this obligation, providd he is able to comply with the request.[24]

6. Should a loan be extended to a foe? The law to extend *chesed,* as commanded by the Torah, makes no differentiation between friend and foe, even in giving one hundred times. The Scripture has stated this explicitly in the *mitzvah* of restoring lost property: "If you meet your enemy's ox or his ass going astray, you shall surely bring it back to him again."[25] The precept of "unloading" makes the same point: "If you see the ass of him that hates you lying under its burden, you shall not forbear to pass by him. You shall surely release it with him."[26] The Gemara (*Bava Metzia* 31a) adds that one is obliged to help even a hundred times.[27]

22*Ibid.,* p. 18.
23*Ibid.*
24*Ibid.*
25Exodus 23:4.
26*Ibid.*
27Kagan, *Ahavath Chesed,* p. 19.

Rabbi Kagan's Views on Employer-Employee Relations

Rabbi Kagan wrote: "I have further seen fit to append to these laws the regulations governing paying the employees, since this matter is of great importance."[28] It involves a number of explicit Torah prohibitions, such as "thou shalt not oppress they neighbor nor rob him; there shall not abide all night the wages of a hired servant with thee until the morning."[29] According to Rabbi Kagan, many employers treated these laws lightly because they found it easier to defer payment for some minor reason—such as being too lazy to go to withdraw their deposits or to change a large bill so as to pay the worker on time. Legally the employer is obliged to comply with all the regulations, even if the employee is well-to-do. How much more careful must one be to pay the worker on time when he is poor, so that he and his family will have the necessities to live. To withhold the wages of a poor man is comparable to taking his life and the life of his household.[30]

Rabbi Kagan wrote, ". . . now, because of our many sins, employers find it easy to reduce the worker's wages. Frequently, too . . . employees knock at the doors of their employers day and night, yet no one pays attention to them, especially where the transaction involves a small amount."[31] The employers do not take heed that Torah jurisprudence does not distinguish between a case involving one cent and that involving one hundred dollars, and many of the guilty are otherwise honest and virtuous individuals who fulfill all other precepts punctiliously.

The Rabbi held that all this occurs because of extreme ignorance of the law and if the employers were aware of its significance they would take the most meticulous care to pay on time.[32] For this reason, Rabbi Kagan searched for and

---

[28]*Ibid.*, p.33.
[29]Lev. 19:13.
[30]Kagan, *Ahavath Chesed*, p. 33.
[31]*Ibid.*
[32]*Ibid.*

collected all the details of this law in order to alert everyone to fulfill properly all its requirements.[33]

Rabbi Kagan was convinced that the ills of industrialism could be overcome by applying religious precepts to the employer-employee relations. Perhaps his approach to such problems was simplistic in an age of science and technology and increasing secularism, but he did provide moral and spiritual strength to those who tried to right the economic injustices that were intensified by the Industrial Revolution.

Replies to Questions about Employer-Employee Relations

1. If a working man dies, does the son inherit his father's rights with respect to the employer's violation of withholding the wages? According to Rabbi Kagan, if a working man dies the son does not inherit his father's rights with respect to the employer's violation of withholding the wages. The employer does not transgress the prohibition unless he has the money to pay the employee, since the Torah commands: "The wages of a hired worker shall not abide with you,"[34]—"with you" implying that you have it.

2. If an employer hires two workers and has sufficient money only to pay one, what is the law? It appeared to Rabbi Kagan that the employer should divide the money between the two. The employer does not commit any transgression, since this is all the money he has. Even if one of the workers demands his wages before the other, the employer should still hold back half for the second, because the latter will certainly demand his wages. The Talmud (*Shevouth* 45a) declares that it is a presumption in law that a hired working man does not leave his wages unclaimed. If the employer knows that the other will not mind, he may pay the first his complete wages at this time. The principle pertains to a case where the two employees are either both rich or both poor.[35]

3. In the case of an employer hiring two workers, one

[33]*Ibid.*
[34]Lev. 19:13.
[35]*Ibid.*, p. 36.

rich and the other poor, and he only has sufficient money available to pay one of them, what is the ruling? The poor man takes precedence, because the scripture has stated, "For he is poor,"[36] and the Sages interpreted the verse to mean that the poor man takes precedence over the rich.[37]

4. Should an employer hire a worker if he knows that in this instance he cannot pay him on time? An employee usually expects to be paid on time, as the Torah points out: "He sets his heart on it."[38] Therefore an employer should never hire a working man when he knows for sure that he will be unable to pay him, unless he has reached an understanding with the employee beforehand.[39]

Chesed in the Bible

It is important to trace the Biblical concepts of *chesed* so that differences between them can be ascertained and the ones which Rabbi Kagan used be placed in proper perspective. One concept of *chesed* is its secular meaning. This includes: a *chesed* relationship between relatives by blood or marriage, related clans and related tribes;[40] host and guest;[41] allies and their relatives;[42] friends;[43] ruler and subject;[44] those

---

[36]Deut. 24:75.

[37]Kagan, *Ahavath Chesed*, p. 41.

[38]Deut. 24:15.

[39]Kagan, *Ahavath Chesed*, p. 41.

[40]In Gen. 47:29 Jacob, about to die, requests from his son, Joseph, to swear to him that he will show him *chesed y'emeth*. In Ruth 2:20 Naomi blesses her kinsman, Boaz, for having shown *chesed* to Ruth.

[41]In Gen. 19:19 the men whom Lot welcomes as his guests show him *chesed*. In Jos. 2:12, 14 Rahab renders *chesed* to the spies who found refuge in her house.

[42]In I Sam. 20:8 David, reminding Jonathan of God's covenant between them entreats Jonathan to show him *chesed*. Jonathan implores David, I Sam. 20:14, 15, to practice forever toward him and his house the *chesed* which had been sworn to him in the name of God. In II Sam. 9:1, 3, 7, David manifests *chesed* to Jonathan's son.

[43]In II Sam. 16:17 Absalom asks Hushai whether in his relationship to David, Hushai had shown him *chesed*. David wishes to reciprocate to Hanun, the son of his friend Nahash, II Sam. 10:2, the same *chesed* that Nahash had displayed towards him.

[44]In II Sam. 3:8 Abner speaks of the *chesed* he had shown to King Saul and his son Eshbaal. Esther 2:9, 17 speaks of the *chesed* which Esther had obtained from King Ahasuerus.

who have gained merit by providing aid, and the parties
thereby put under obligation.[45]

The above indicates that *chesed* exists between people
who are in some close relationship to one another. Our next
concern is to explain what *chesed* is. It is necessary to deal
with the extent to which the meaning of the word is influenced
by the fact that *chesed* can be practiced only between persons who share an ethically binding relationship. The con-
ceptual content of the word will be analyzed on the basis of
further investigation of those passages in which the word
occurs in a purely secular sense. The analysis yields the following conclusions: *chesed* is conduct corresponding to a
mutual relationship of rights and duties.[46] *Chesed* is conduct
in accordance with a mutual relationship of rights and
duties.[47] *Chesed* can be confirmed by an oath.[48] It constitutes
the essence of a covenant.[49] The component parts of the general concept consist of reciprocity,[50] mutual assistance, sin-
cerity, friendliness, love, loyalty, brotherliness, and duty.[51]

A second concept of *chesed* is its religious meaning. In this
context *chesed* is the reciprocal conduct of men toward one
another and at the same time the proper relationship toward

[45]In Judges 1:24 we read that the spies scouting Bethel promise to
show *chesed* to an individual whom they saw leaving the city if he would
indicate to them a way of entering the city. King David commands
Solomon to display *chesed* forever to the members of the house of Barzillai.

[46]In ancient Israel, ancient and present-day Arabia, a mutual relationship of rights and duties prevailed among the members of a family or
among those who believed themselves to be of similar ancestry. The family
and tribal bonds were of paramount importance. See W. R. Smith, *The
Prophets of Israel* (Edinburgh, 1882), p. 161. See also Nelson Glueck,
Hesed in the Bible (Cincinnati, Hebrew Union College Press, 1967), p. 38.

[47]In I Sam. 20:8 *chesed* is meant as conduct in accordance with the
mutual relationship of rights and duties between allies.

[48]In II Sam. 21:7 the King spared Mephibosheth, the son of Saul's son
Jonathan because of the oath which took place between David and Jonathan.

[49]David and Jonathan made a sacred covenant. Through this covenant
their friendship was transformed into brotherhood and *chesed* was the
mode of conduct each had to assume toward the other. The covenant
obliged both of them to take care of the welfare and safety of the other.

[50]*Chesed* which calls for reciprocity can be illustrated in I Kings 2:7.
David ordered Solomon to consider the members of Barzillai's family as
members of his own house for they provided the troops of David with
food and clothing. This act obligated King David, even at the time of his
death, to accept them as members of his own family.

[51]See Glueck, *Hesed in the Bible*, p. 55.

God.[52] As reciprocal ethical and religious conduct, *chesed* fulfills the demands of justice, loyalty, righteousness, and honesty. These concepts are embraced in its meaning.[53] Knowledge of God and fear of God (which can be used synonymously) are also components of *chesed*.[54] The meaning of *chesed* can best be translated as religiosity, piety, kindness, and love of mankind.[55] It is very closely related to mercy, but is distinguished from it in that *chesed* is obligatory.[56]

Explanation of Chesed

How tenaciously should an individual cling to the virtue of *chesed*? The extent of the required attachment is defined in the verse: "It has been told to you, O man, what is good and what God requires of you: only to act justly and to love kindness . . ."[57] At first sight, it would seem that it should have been sufficient for Scripture to state: "to act with justice and kindness" or else "to love justice and kindness," but by using the expression "It has been told to you . . . ," Scripture must have intended to bring forth an idea which man would be unable to discover on his own.[58] It is common knowledge that it is very important to act justly and to do kindness, but the true meaning of the Scriptural intent becomes clear from the statement, "If a person's coat has been taken from him as a result of a court's verdict, he should sing for joy."[59] Rabbi Kagan illustrated this by the following story.

---

[52]In Hos. 2:25; 1:9 there is a reciprocal relationship between God and man. In Hos. 10:12 we see the conditions which Israel has to fulfill in order to come to terms with God. "Sow in justice and you will harvest in *chesed*. When men practice justice and charity among themselves they find the way to God and their salvation. Only through mutual reciprocity of charity and loving kindness does mankind, in everyday life, display the proper attitude and conduct toward God."
[53]See Glueck, *Hesed in the Bible*, p. 59.
[54]In Hos. 6:6; "I desire *chesed* and not sacrifice, the knowledge of God, not burnt offerings." This indicates that without *chesed* there is no knowledge of God, and a knowledge of God presupposes *chesed*. See Glueck, *Hesed in the Bible*, p. 58.
[55]*Ibid.*, p. 69.
[56]*Ibid.*
[57]Michah 6:1.
[58]Kagan, *Ahavath Chesed*, p. 43.
[59]Tractate *Sanhedrin*, 7a.

A band of rebels lived in a certain city and many joined them. To strenghen their bond with one another, they agreed to wear similar garments. Thus, they would be different from the rest of the population. One day they crowded into the local tavern and drank heavily. Some of them refused to pay for their drinks and the owner would not permit them to leave until they had left their clothes behind as security for their debts. They stalked out angrily. Shortly afterwards the conspiracy became known to the king; their actions were investigated and they were rounded up to be executed. Those who did not wear the uniform were saved. They said to one another:

> We thought that the tavern owner had done us harm by forcing us to leave our clothes behind. In truth he did us a great favor. He saved our lives. Let us go and applaud him for what happened now. For the future, let us make up our minds not to follow the evil ways of our friends, so that we avoid being caught like them.[60]

So one must realize that the appropriation of another's property may cause him to lose even that part of his possessions which he acquired honestly—especially when even his very clothes are tainted by dishonest or forceful acquisition. When the prophet stated: "It has been told to you, O man, what is good," he intended to convey that, contrary to the common belief that it is good for a man to amass wealth, what is ultimately to his monetary advantage is to act justly, to scrutinize all his transactions so as to ensure that his profits were acquired through means approved by Torah law. In this manner, a person will make sure that his possessions remain with him. This is what Scripture means by "only to do justice."

"To love *chesed*" means that no one should think that it is sufficient to ensure that his possessions are free from the taint of dishonesty, and believe that they will therefore remain with him, and that good will be bestowed on him on

---

[60]Kagan, *Ahavath Chesed*, p. 43.

this account. He is also obligated to do kindness and give charity proportionate to his means.

As for the choice of words, "to act justly and love *chesed*," rather than "to act with justice and *chesed*," the prophet intended to convey meaning to an area where almost everyone is at fault. Indeed, we all perform acts of kindness but we are often kind only under pressure. So the prophet urges us: "What does God require of you? Only to love kindness." A person must not believe that by occasional acts of kindness he has discharged his duty. Instead, one must possess a love for this *mitzvah*. There is a difference between what a person does because of pressure and what he does out of love. The Torah requires us to act lovingly and not begrudgingly or coldly.[61]

The Rationale for Loving Kindness

God created man in His image. The commentators take the statement to refer to God's attributes. God gave man the power to emulate His attributes, to do good and to act with kindness toward his fellowmen. As Scripture states: "God is good to all . . ."[62] "He gives food to all flesh for his *chesed* endures forever."[63] The existence of the whole world, then, depends on this trait. Whoever follows in this path will bear the stamp of God, while whoever refrains from exercising this characteristic and questions himself, "Why should I do good to others?" removes himself completely from God.[64] Therefore, it is self-evident that the existence of all mankind depends upon the traits of charity and kindness, for each and every man is confronted by changing circumstances during his lifetime. On each occasion he needs cooperation and help to cope with the particular situation.[65]

Charity and kindness are important reasons for God's forgiveness of a sinner. Throughout the Torah, God urged man

---

61*Ibid.*, pp. 43ff.
62Psalms 145:9.
63Psalms 136:25.
64Kagan, *Ahavath Chesed*, p. 44.
65*Ibid.*, pp. 45ff.

to embody *chesed* for it is through the practice of charity and kindness that the sinner transforms his personality.[66]

Reasons for the Neglect of Chesed

According to Rabbi Kagan, there are five things which prevent the performance of *chesed*: fear, ignorance, illusions of being exempt, parsimony, and indolence. Some people fear that the debtor will not repay the loan and they themselves may need the money at short notice. Fear also plays an important role in preventing the performance of *chesed* when a person is apprehensive that the public will become aware of his wealth.[67]

Some people are lax in carrying out the precept of *chesed* because of sheer ignorance. They are unaware of the important and obligatory nature of the *mitzvah,* and they do not know the reward it carries. They fail to realize that it is as much a positive command of the Torah as *Sukkah*; every Jew exerts much effort in building a *Sukkah*. However, even a small inconvenience is sufficient for many to avoid the performance of *chesed*. When we do act, it is with reluctance and sadness, without a trace of pleasure.[68]

Rabbi Kagan described the following case and asked every intelligent person to apply it to all similar situations. If one person meets another in the street and asks him: "Brother, would you lend me a dollar for a short time?", the latter will find a thousand reasons for turning down the request even if he considers the person asking for the loan reliable. Sometimes he will respond that it is too much effort for him to go home to get the money, the borrower should have come at another time, or he should have come to him at home. If the poor man pleads with him and he at last goes home or changes the bill and lends the money to the borrower, he does so unwillingly and sadly because of the trouble to which he was put.[69]

On the other hand, suppose a man whom you held to be

---

[66]*Ibid.*
[67]*Ibid.,* pp. 53ff.
[68]*Ibid.,* p. 54.
[69]*Ibid.,* p. 55.

reliable met you in the street and said, "Quickly, brother, go to your home. I have a good business proposition to tell you about. The down payment is small. After the transaction is completed, you will give me a modest sum for my recommendation." Would you tell the person, "I am too tired to go back home or to obtain a certified check." No, you would hurry home and find ways and means of carrying through the deal for yourself. If the venture proved to be a success, you would praise the person for giving you the good advice.[70]

So indeed is our case. When one person approaches another for a free loan, the transaction is a minor one as far as the borrower himself is concerned—he will merely gain a few pieces of silver. The lender, however, the bestower of kindness, has been approached to engage in a major undertaking involving a positive precept of the Torah, the reward for which is eternal. The lender should be happy and should rush to perform the *mitzvah* of *chesed*.[71]

The illusion that one is exempt is used by many because they argue with their conscience: "Am I the only one in the whole city? Let him go to those others. They are richer than I." This argument is fallacious because it is uncertain whether others will be willing to help. Furthermore, since the person originally approached has the means, he is not absolved from the positive command just because there happen to be richer men in the city than he.[72]

Some people avoid the *mitzvah* of *chesed* out of parsimony. The Sages have already stated: "When the niggardly and plunderers of the poor multiplied, those who hardened their hearts and closed their hands against lending to the poor also increased, and they transgressed what is written in the Torah: 'Beware that there be not a base thought in your heart . . .' "[73]

Parsimony is a very ugly trait which leads an individual to refrain from giving charity and performing acts of kind-

---

[70]*Ibid.*
[71]*Ibid.*
[72]*Ibid.*, p. 56.
[73]Deut. 15:9 quoted in Tractate *Sotah*, 47b.

ness. It causes a person to repress all feelings of compassion
and pity for the poor. Sometimes his niggardly nature gains
such control over a man that he even begrudges himself the
benefit of possessions. Furthermore, the miser influences his
friends to withhold help from the less fortunate, because he
does not want to appear alone in his wickedness.[74] Great
insight into human behavior such as this was one of Rabbi
Kagan's major contributions in this work. The Rabbi urged
that a man keep away from miserliness and train himself to
be kind to others. Then others will display compassion and
pity toward him, too. He should always remember that money
was given to him by God not for his own use alone, but that
he might be ready to extend his hand to the poor and needy.[75]
In the *Mishnah Berurah*, Rabbi Kagan advocates a middle
of the road standard of living. A person must manage his
budget intelligently so that he can enjoy his Sabbaths and
holidays and at the same time help others.[76]

Some people are too lazy to occupy themselves with lending and the subsequent responsibility to collect the loan.
Rabbi Kagan held that indolence is indeed the most frequent
factor preventing a person from serving God. Through lazi-
ness one remains devoid of Torah, of *mitzvoth*, of *teshuvah*
(repentance), because it is the nature of the indolent always
to postpone all things until tomorrow and the day after.[77]

A person must conduct himself in the affairs of the Torah
and *mitzvoth* as he does in his own business. If a person owns
a store, he will not hesitate to stand behind the counter in
the cold weather. He will weigh out a quantity for one customer, then for a second, and so on, even though his profit
on each sale is rather small. He will wait for customers to
come, and when they do he will be so overjoyed that he will
not feel the cold. Surely, how much more should a person
exert himself to carry out the *mitzvoth* of the Torah dealing
with charity and kindness.[78]

---

[74]Kagan, *Ahavath Chesed*, pp. 56ff.
[75]*Ibid.*, p. 57.
[76]Kagan, *Mishnah Berurah*, V, 304ff.
[77]Kagan, *Ahavath Chesed*, p. 58.
[78]*Ibid.*, p. 59.

Daily Performance of Chesed

Rabbi Kagan held that a person should be especially careful not to be remiss in performing *chesed* even for a single day of his life, in the same manner that one takes care to set fixed times for daily Torah study.[79] Some people think that after they have once discharged *chesed* towards a fellow man they have fulfilled their obligation for several weeks to come, even though they are still capable of helping others. On the contrary, a man must perform *chesed* every day of his life, whenever a need presents itself to him, even if he is called upon several times in a single day.

If a person were to examine carefully the days of his life that have already passed, he would find most of them devoid of this holy trait, and some of them even empty of Torah and the fear of God. Therefore, a person must see to it that the remaining days of his life do not pass without daily Torah study and acts of *chesed*.[80]

Gemiluth Chesed Fund

Rabbi Kagan recommended setting aside a sum of money in one's home—each person according to what he can afford—for a permanent *Gemiluth Chesed* fund.[81] Firstly, one can invent all kinds of excuses and rationalizations for not being charitable. Even when one is amenable to giving, the members of one's household might not be and will try to discredit anyone who approaches one. Such an unpleasant experience could be avoided if the money were already set aside, and one would find no difficulty in fulfilling the precept of *chesed*.[82]

Rabbi Kagan urged Jews to establish, in addition to the sum of money set aside for small loans, Free Loan Societies in each city for larger loans.[83] He wrote: "I know that the reader will think to himself: 'Why should I set a sum aside such as the Free Loan Societies in each city, and then hand

[79] *Ibid.*, pp. 59ff.
[80] *Ibid.*, p. 60.
[81] *Ibid.*, p. 61.
[82] *Ibid.*, p. 61.
[83] *Ibid.*, pp. 61, 63ff.

out small loans? It is better for me to lend a large single sum . . . as a single loan to a respectable person, for after all *gemiluth chesed* is a *mitzvah* whether the loan is made to the poor or rich.' " This is a fallacy, because it is a greater *mitzvah* to lend to the poor. Also, in business, if a person engages in a number of small transactions involving a small amount, the total profit will be larger than if the total amount was used in a single transaction. So, too, in a case in which an individual gives a number of loans, each for a small amount as is customary, he can perform hundreds of small *mitzvoth* in the course of one year. This would not be so if he lent a single large sum to one individual, since in the same period he might only perform a few *mitzvoth*.[84]

Even if, through his constant preoccupation with this *mitzvah*, a person occasionally incurs the loss of money, he should not suffer grief, since obviously no business in the world, whether it be a store or other enterprise, large or small, can entirely avoid bad debts and other such losses. Very few undertakings are fully guaranteed against any loss whatever. Nevertheless, a large part of the world engages in business, day and night, because it is not necessary to consider one transaction, but rather the overall operation of the business to determine whether it is profitable or not.[85]

The Importance of Charity

According to the Talmud (*Sukkah* 49b) , *gemiluth chesed* is greater in three things than charity: charity is given in the form of money, *gemiluth chesed* is given in the form of money and personal participation. Charity is primarily for the poor, while *gemiluth chesed* is for the poor as well as for the rich. Charity involves the living only, while *gemiluth chesed* involves the living and the dead. Nevertheless, Rabbi Kagan points out areas in which charity is greater than *gemiluth chesed*. Charity is an outright gift, while a *gemiluth chesed* loan is advanced for a limited period after which the lender recovers his money. Moreover, the giving of charity

---

84 *Ibid.,* p. 61.
85 *Ibid.,* pp. 62-64.

involves the person in an inner struggle with himself. When a person gives charity and thereby reduces his assets, the struggle is more difficult. Lending money, on the other hand, involves a lesser struggle since the lender will ultimately recover the loan.[86]

According to Rabbi Kagan, the charitable acts of the patriarchs were instrumental in the history of the Jewish people. They are praised by God for their acts of charity.[87] Abraham is selected by God because he practiced charity: "For I have known him, to the end that he may command his children and his household after him, that they keep the way of the Lord, to do righteousness and justice . . ."[88] Isaac is praised in the Torah because of acts of charity: "And Isaac sowed in that land, and found in the same year a hundredfold; and the Lord blessed him."[89]

Rabbi Kagan held that Biblical and Talmudic laws governing charity were relevant to modern times. He objected to the practice in many communities of concerning themselves only with their own poor and closing their door to the poor of other communities. This is a mistake, he asserted, because no one has the right to forbid the entrance of needy individuals from any community.[90] He pointed out that the rich (who can afford to support the poor of other cities as well as their own) are the first to object.[91] In the *Mishnah Berurah* the Rabbi held that during Jewish holidays the leaders of Jewish communities must collect the necessary funds so that the poor will also celebrate the festivals with dignity.[92]

Rabbi Kagan also praised the establishment of homes for the aged. He said that it was equivalent to adding life to the old and weak and that one who saves a life is like one who saves the world. This is an area which has an important

---

[86]*Ibid.*, pp. 70-74.
[87]*Ibid.*
[88]Gen. 18:19.
[89]Gen. 26:12.
[90]Kagan, *Ahavath Chesed*, p. 71.
[91]*Ibid.*
[92]Kagan, *Mishnah Berurah*, V, 306.

message for our own day. An elderly person without proper contacts has to wait a long time before a place is found for him in an old age home. Some commercial old age homes charge such exhorbitant prices that the poorer elderly are denied entrance.

Recognizing that the care of the aged and the poor required funds, Rabbi Kagan undertook to raise money for institutions for the needy. He developed a program for allocating charity in a permanent manner. One is to set aside a tenth of his income from his assets and another tenth from his profits. The fund that will be established from the assets is to be used for charity and on occasions when emergencies prevail he himself may borrow from this fund on condition that he will return the money. Thus, he is allowed to make a loan to himself. From the second fund to be established from profits after taking inventory every half year or at least once a year, two-thirds is to be used for the poor and one-third for reserve.[93]

Showing Hospitality

Showing hospitality to guests is a form of kindness. Since a whole section of the Torah is alloted to the *mitzvah* of showing hospitality, this fact indicates that we are to observe it all our lives.[94] After the episode of the visiting angels, Scripture praised Abraham since he would train his children also to follow in his righteous path.

Since the Torah describes Abraham's hospitality in detail, its purpose is to teach us by example how to treat guests.[95] The holy books have admonished that, when guests come, one should receive them cordially. Food should be placed before them, since the visitor might be poor and hungry and ashamed to ask. The host should be gracious, even though he might be beset with worries. Rabbi Kagan held that food, drink, and sleeping quarters must be provided for a guest. However, if individual members of the community cannot

---

[93]Kagan, *Ahavath Chesed*, pp. 74-76.
[94]*Ibid.*, p. 90.
[95]*Ibid.*, p. 92.

accommodate a guest with all the three requirements, then the community as a whole must establish a hostel for wayfarers. He was influential in the establishment of *Hachnasath Orchim* (Hostels for Wayfarers) Societies in many of the Jewish communities of Eastern Europe.[96] He wrote, "it has now become the standard practice in Jewry to found a *Hachnasath Orchim* Society which devotes itself to the fulfillment of this *mitzvah*.[97]

Visiting the Sick

The *mitzvah* of *bikkur cholim* (visiting the sick) is another aspect of *gemiluth chesed*. The *mitzvah* of visiting the sick has no fixed measure or limitation. The distinguished is required to visit the plain person. The precept can be performed several times a day, unless this becomes burdensome to the patient.[98] Relatives and close friends come as soon as a man takes ill; casual acquaintances wait until the third day, so as not to hamper his chances of recovery. If the patient is seriously ill, all come to him without delay.[99]

One may pray for the sick in any language he wishes because he is addressing his words directly to God. When not in the patient's presence, however, he should use Hebrew. His petition should include the patient among the rest of the sick ones of Israel. He should say, "May the Allpresent have mercy upon you among the sick ones of Israel." For Sabbath, the formula is, "It is Sabbath, and it is forbidden to cry out. But the cure will come speedily, and His mercies are many. Have a peaceful Sabbath."[100]

Rabbi Kagan related that in his time people were lax in observing this *mitzvah*, especially when the sick person was poor. Yet, he wrote, they could not consider themselves exempt because the obligation existed whether the patient was rich or—even more so—poor. If the poor man was not

---

[96]*Ibid.*, p. 94.
[97]*Ibid.*
[98]*Yoreh Deah*, Chap. 335.
[99]Kagan, *Ahavath Chesed*, pp. 94ff.; see also Karo, *Shulhan Arukh, Yoreh Deah*, Chap. 335.
[100]Kagan, *Ahavath Chesed*, pp. 94ff.

visited, his very life might be endangered because he usually could not afford the food he needed in illness and sometimes he could not afford to call a doctor or to buy medicine. His sufferings were aggravated in the winter when the severe cold crushed his depressed spirit. His worries would increase after lying in bed for several days with no one to care for him or to revive him. All these factors weaken his resistance and reinforce his illness, and may cause his death.[101] How should we appraise this dreadful state of affairs? People have to confess and say, "Our hand has not shed this blood." The Sages have interpreted this verse to mean, "We did not let him go without food." This would have been considered shedding blood, since it might possibly have contributed to his death. How much more direct is the case here since the person is already ill; no attention is paid to him, and so his death has been hastened. Certainly this would be too great a sin to bear.[102]

Rabbi Kagan was instrumental in forming *Bikkur Cholim* Societies. He wrote:

> Indeed in many communities the practice has now been adopted of forming a *Bikkur Cholim* Society for the purpose of caring for these unfortunate souls when they are ill, to see that they receive the proper medical care, proper food and all other necessities. How commendable would it be were this the universal practice, especially since human life is often involved.[103]

Chesed to the Dead and Comfort to the Mourners

Burying the dead, beside being a commandment of the Torah, (as it says; "You shall surely bury him,"[104]) is also part of *gemiluth chesed*. It is an even higher form, *chesed shel emath* (true kindness), because no reciprocity can be expected.[105] Since the Torah speaks at great length about the

---

[101]*Ibid.*, p. 96.
[102]*Ibid.*
[103]*Ibid.*
[104]Deut. 21:22.
[105]Kagan, *Ahavath Chesed*, p. 100.

death of Sarah and Jacob, it shows the importance of *gemiluth chesed* in the case of burying the dead. If the deceased has relatives, the main duty of attending to his burial will lie with them; however, the whole community is duty-bound to participate in the funeral.

Comforting the mourners also belongs in the category of *chesed*. Many treat the *mitzvah* of comforting the mourners lightly—especially when the mourners are poor. But in truth the grief and loss of the poor are all the harder to bear, because these unfortunates derive pleasure from nothing else except their loved ones. Great is the reward of those who come to comfort the poor.[106]

Gladdening the Groom and Bride

To gladden the groom and bride is also considered an important obligation and is a form of *gemiluth chesed*. The duty of gladdening groom and bride reaches its highest form where not many guests are present, when the couples are poor, or when children of parents who have become bereft of their wealth, marry. It is a great *mitzvah* to attend such weddings and bring joy to the couples.[107]

One must contribute to families who cannot afford the wedding costs or other such matters. Rabbi Kagan was active in organizing *Hachnasath Kallah* (Dowering the Bride) Societies for helping orphans, or even those who had parents but were poor, to marry. In addition to making it possible for such girls to marry, and thereby guarding them from evil, a great *chesed* is done to the poor parents, who worry day and night once their daughters reach marriageable age and they are unable to help them.[108]

Verbal Chesed

The Sages have pointed out that *chesed* can involved one's self and one's money. The *chesed* involving one's self can be divided into three types: deeds, words, and thoughts.

---

[106]*Ibid.*, pp. 100-102.
[107]*Ibid.*, pp. 102ff.
[108]*Ibid.*, p. 103.

Chesed involving deeds and thoughts have been discussed previously. Here we will consider verbal *chesed.*

When one studies the Torah in order to teach others one is performing verbal *chesed.* If a person is angry at a friend and another person intercedes and so stills the first man's anger, he is performing an act of *chesed.* If one is in a position to prevent harm from befalling another by word of mouth, this is considered *chesed* also. Good advice in the conduct of business offered to a friend is considered an act of *chesed.* If a person can have someone do a favor for a friend, this too falls in the category of *chesed.*[109]

During the First World War, Rabbi Israel Meir Kagan witnessed the hunger, sickness, and tragedy of war when he and his students emigrated to Russia. In 1916, he wrote that people were starving and that there were many formerly rich people who were ashamed to reveal their starvation. He suggested:

> . . . every city must appoint leaders to provide food so that people will not die of hunger . . . since there is an increase of hunger everywhere, and thousands and tens of thousands of people lack even bread, every person shall be very cautious in carrying out the precepts of charity according to law; and a person much take at least the middle of the road in giving charity.[110]

In the same article, he described the misery of captives and pointed out that the lack of food and shelter led to disease in adults as well as children and that people were faced with living in the streets with no separate quarters for men and women. The Rabbi reminded his readers that it was the duty of every Jew to help such victims.

Conclusion

In modern times, a book reviewer can use statistical devices to convince the reader of wide readership—and supposed

---

[109]*Ibid.*, pp. 106ff.

[110]Rabbi Israel Meir Kagan, "Rodeph Tzedekah v'Chesed," *Michtevei Hafets Hayyim,* II, 2.

impact—of a book. No such figures are available for a work such as *Ahavath Chesed*. One is forced to rely on less objective means. One may look, for example, at the hundreds of *Gemiluth Hasadim* institutions, the many institutions for visiting the sick, for providing lodging to the needy and to the visitor, and for hospitality in general that were established during Rabbi Kagan's lifetime. One may enumerate, through Rabbi Kagan's papers and letters, the number of people who wrote to him asking for advice on establishing *gemiluth chesed* institutions.[111]

To one familiar with Jewish literature it is evident that *Ahavath Chesed* represents a unique and difficult synthesis of a tremendous body of material from many and diverse sources; to a sympathetic reader it offers convincing and powerful arguments for the necessity and importance of practicing *chesed* in one's daily life, and to the seeker of solutions, it offers specific programs for organizing charity and kindness. One could go further and suggest that—were they tried, even now—some of his obviously just prescriptions might go far in alleviating the ills stemming from poverty and corruption in our own society.

Another factor which must strike a reader who cares to go further than merely reading the work is the evidence that Rabbi Kagan wrote from a very deep conviction and that the work is in many ways a reflection of his own standards of conduct. The work's uniqueness lies in three main areas. Firstly, Rabbi Kagan protested against the modern notion of the insularity of a town or village and the concept that one's moral responsibility ceases at the geographical boundaries of a town or village. He urged a more universal recognition of the needs of all Jews and argued against the notion of ignoring the suffering of those who may be out of sight.[112]

Secondly, *Ahavath Chesed* offers a program of regular charity. It recommends setting aside one tenth of one's income from assets and one tenth from one's profits.[113]

---

[111]Kagan, *Michtevei Hafets Hayyim*, p. 37.
[112]Kagan, *Ahavath Chesed*, p. 71.
[113]*Ibid.*, pp. 74-76.

Thirdly, one must note Rabbi Kagan's remarkable psychological insights into the reasons for neglect of *chesed*.[114]

Rabbi Kagan was also the first clergyman in modern Europe to deal with such problems as loans, *gemiluth chesed,* and employer-employee relations.

In general, Rabbi Kagan's response to the problems of poverty and social welfare in Jewish communities was a constructive one that offered specific programs for alleviating the symptoms.

EMIGRATION AS A RESPONSE TO THE CONDITIONS OF EASTERN EUROPEAN JEWRY

Rabbi Kagan's book, *Nidhei Israel (The Dispersed of Israel),* appeared in 1893 in response to events during the reign of Tsar Aleander III.[1] In this section, we will examine Alexander's government policy with respect to the Jews, Pobedonostsov's[2] attitude toward the Jews, the spread of pogroms, and the May Laws and other restrictive measures. The resulting mass emigration and other responses to discrimination will be described. *Nidhei Israel* was Rabbi Kagan's response to emigration, and in discussing that work we will deal with his analysis of the causes for laxity in observance of the Torah, his outlook on the presence of God and His testing of men, his recommendations as to determining Jewishness, and his recommendation concerning methods of education for the dispersed, for prayer, for Torah study, for the role of the Rabbi, for shaving of beards, for dietary laws, and for the Sabbath. A conclusion will be offered at the close of the section.

Governmental Policy of Alexander III

After the assassination of Alexander II in 1882, his son,

---

[114]*Ibid.,* pp. 53ff; pp. 70-74.

[1]Kagan, *Michtevei Hafets Hayyim,* I, 54ff; see also Rabbi Reuben Katz, *Shaar Reuben* (Jerusalem: Mossad Harav Kook, 1952), p. 30.

[2]Constantine Pobedonostsev (1827-1907), an advisor to Tsar Alexander III, was a vehement anti-Semite.

Alexander III, became Tsar. By education and disposition, he was a despot in the fullest sense of the word. In his early life his character was molded by instruction from the eminent historian, S. M. Solovev, who set him on the path to a philosophy of nationalism.[3]

Autocracy—with no popular representation in central government and with impotent local governments—was the method by which Alexander III hoped to elevate Russia to the status of a supreme power. To achieve this end, he nurtured the philosophy of Panslavism. On April 25, 1881 he wrote:

> I understand only one policy, to exact from every situation all that is needed by and is useful to Russia, and to disregard all other considerations, and to act in a straightforward and resolute manner. We can have no policy except one that is purely Russian and national; this is the only policy we can and must follow.[4]

Alexander's policies of autocracy, orthodox Christianity, and nationalism brought with them administrative centralization and discrimination against religious and ethnic minorities.[5]

Pobedonostsev's Attitude Toward the Jews

Constantine Pobedonostsev (1827-1907), a jurist, was a teacher to Alexander III and quite influential. He hated Jews and he conscientiously spread anti-Semitism throughout the country. He reinforced Alexander's belief that the Jews were responsible for the crucifixion of Jesus.[6] And he encouraged the Russian press to keep up their campaign against the Jews —a campaign which grew in its dimensions. Not only the conservative press, like *Novoe Vremia (New Times)*, and

---

[3]Florinsky, *Russia: A History and an Interpretation*, II, 1086; see also Kornilov, *Istorii Rossii v XIX Veke*, III pp. 265-319 for details on the life and reign of Tsar Alexander III.

[4]Florinsky, *Russia: A History and an Interpretation*, II, 1088.

[5]*Ibid.*

[6]*Ibid.*, p. 1119; see also Constantine Pobedonostsev, *Reflection of a Russian Statesman* (London: Grant Richards, 1848), for details on his views on Jews.

Grazhdanin (The Citizen), but also the liberal press began to use anti-Semitic slogans, and to single out the Jews for attacks. The anti-Semitic forces took full advantage of the fact that a Jewish woman, Jessie Helfman, was involved in the murder of Alexander II.

Pogroms

In 1881 an anti-Semitic outburst took place in Elizabethgrad, New Russia, a large city with a population of fifteen thousand Jews. On the eve of Greek Orthodox Easter, the local Christians, gathering on the streets, spoke of the fact that the *Zhyds*[7] were about to be beaten. The Jews became frightened. The police, prepared to keep public order during the first day of Easter, called out a small brigade of soldiers. The first days of the holiday passed serenely. On the fourth day,[8] April 15th, the troops departed from the streets and the pogrom began. The organizers of the pogrom encouraged a drunken Russian to cause trouble in the tavern of a Jew. When the tavernkeeper pushed the troublemaker into the street, the waiting crowd began to shout, "The Jews are beating our people," and they began to attack passing Jews.[9]

All this was the prearranged signal for a riot. Jewish stores in the market place were invaded and destroyed and the merchandise looted. At first the police and the military scattered the rioters, but on the second day the pogrom was renewed with greater zeal and better leadership and the military and police authorities assumed a passive role. The pogrom movement spread to Kiev.

> At twelve o'clock at noon, the air suddenly resounded with wild shouts, whistling, jeering, hooting, and laughing. An immense crowd of young boys, artisans, laborers, was on the march. The destruction of Jewish houses began. Window panes

---

[7]An abusive term for Jews.
[8]The Greek Orthodox Easter lasts officially three days, but an additional day is celebrated by the population.
[9]Dubnow, *History of the Jews in Russia and Poland*, II, 249.

and doors began to fly about . . . the mob, having gained access to the houses and stores, began to throw upon the streets absolutely everything that fell into their hands.[10]

Soon after, pogroms swept into Volhynia, Podolia, Odessa, and adjacent villages and townlets. When these anti-Semitic outbreaks began to attract unfavorable comments both at home and abroad, the government decided to initiate reforms. In February, 1883 the Tsar appointed a committee, headed by Count Pahlen, a former Minister of Justice, to investigate the issue and make recommendations for new legislation. The committee's report of 1888 claimed that discrimination brought nothing but disaster.

> The very history of Russian legislation . . . teaches us that there is one way and one solution—the emancipation of the Jews and their assimilation with the rest of the population under the protection of the same laws.[11]

However, Alexander III rejected these recommendations. He dissolved Pahlen's committee and placed all its findings in the archives.[12] Thus the policy of discrimination and hatred for the Jews prevailed, and the Temporary Rules, which were adopted May 3, 1883, remained in force.

May Laws

The Temporary Rules contain the following provisions:

> First, to forbid the Jews henceforth to settle anew outside of the towns and townlets. Second, to suspend the completion of instruments of purchase of real property and merchandise in the name of Jews outside towns and townlets. Third, to forbid the Jews to carry on business on Sundays, and Christian holidays.[13]

---

[10]*Ibid.*, pp. 252ff.

[11]Quoted in Florinsky, *Russia: A History and an Interpretation*, p. 1120.

[12]"Pahlen Commission," *Evreiskaia Enciclopedia*, Vol. 6, 862-863.

[13]Dubnow, *History of the Jews in Russia and Poland*, p. 312; see also Kornilov, *Istorii Rossii V XIX Veke*, III, 306-307.

The word "Temporary" in the title made it unnecessary for the orders to obtain the approval of the State Council where the Minister of Interior, Nicholas Pavlovich Ignatyev, feared opposition. Temporary orders required only the acquiescence of the cabinet and the signature of the Emperor. But the Temporary Rules were never regarded by their author as temporary, and indeed, they remained in effect until the abdication of Nicholas II in 1917.

The May Laws, as the Temporary Rules were subsequently known, constituted an economic pogrom against the Jews. They prohibited the Jews from engaging in any business activity on Sundays and Christian holidays, which caused an economic burden for the Jews. The rule not only forced a day of idleness upon the poor Jews who had already observed their own Sabbath the day before, but it also excluded them from engaging in business with the many peasants visiting the towns on Sundays. The other two measures made it impossible for Jews to have anything to do with land or to reside in the arable districts. Jews were criticized for not participating in agriculture, but here the legislative machinery itself was used to deter any Jewish connection with farming.

Additional Restrictive Measures

Then came further restrictive measures: quotas for Jewish students in secondary and higher schools (1887), the exclusion of the Jews from the legal profession (1889), the *zemstvos* (1890), and the municipalities (1892). The purpose of the restrictions in education and in the legal profession was to reduce the number of those "privileged" Jews who, under the law passed in the reign of Alexander II, "had been awarded for their completion of a course of studies in an institution of higher learning by the right of unrestricted residence throughout the Empire."[14] The "highly placed obscurantists" contended that the Jewish students exerted an injurious influence upon their Christian comrades from a religious as well as a moral point of view.[15] The political po-

---

[14]Dubnow, *History of the Jews in Russia and Poland*, p. 348.
[15]*Ibid.*

lice[16] reported that Jewish students in colleges "are quick in joining the ranks of the revolutionary workers."[17] Pobedonostsev looked upon popular education in general as a harmful force, fraught with danger to monarchical absolutism and the church.

> There can be but little doubt that the previously-mentioned imperial resolutions indicating the necessity of curtailing the number of Jews in the Russian educational establishments were inspired by the Grand Inquisitor.[18]

A mere enumeration of legal restriction does not depict the full measure of their harmful implications. Discrimination breeds the possibility of bribery—to which petty Russian officials were easily susceptible. But reprieve from the execution of unjust laws bought by bribes was risky, creating a vicious circle involving the unfortunate victims and their greedy protectors.

Mass Emigration

One response to the pogroms and discriminatory legislation was mass emigration. It was to be expected that migrants should seek refuge in those lands which had long-standing reputations of giving asylum to the oppressed. Russian and Galician refugees settled in England, especially in London. They lived closely together in miserable quarters and worked for low wages. Jews also found shelter in South Africa, Canada, Australia, and Argentina.

By far the greatest number emigrated to the United States. Jewish emigration to America during the first three years of the eighteen eighties grew rapidly. In 1881 there were 8,193 immigrants; in 1882, 17,497; in 1883, 6,907 From 1884 to 1886 the number of Jews emigrating from Russia remained constant, averaging 15,000 to 17,000 annually. During the last three years of the decade, emigration

---

[16]The secret police charged with keeping track of the followers of liberal and revolutionary tendencies.

[17]Dubnow, *History of the Jews in Russia and Poland*, p. 348.

[18]*Ibid.*, p. 349.

increased in 1887 to 28,944, in 1888 to 31,256, and in 1889 to 31,889.[19] The exodus from Russia gained momentum after a decree which fined a person for evading the draft and the initiation of the educational quota.

Contemporary Reaction to Discrimination and Emigration

While the desire for emigration from Russia grew, revolutionary forces were developing within Russia proper to do away with the discriminatory laws. In Geneva in 1883, Russian revolutionary migrants formed a new socialist organization, *Grupa Osvosbozhdeniia Truda* (Group for the Emancipation of Labor). In Russia George Plekhanov (1857-1918) founded the Liberation of Labor, which was the first social democratic organization in Russia. The Jewish socialists, Paul B. Alexrod and Lev Deich, were members of the group. Plekhanov and his supporters maintained that

> it was only through economic struggle that people could gradually learn the meaning and the need for political struggle.[20]

Axelrod's goal in life was to "emancipate all the poor and oppressed in Russia," and he considered Marxism "a liberating force for living and suffering men."[21]

In the Jewish pale of settlement there were also socialist circles. The aim of the socialist was to teach the workers reading, mathematics, the natural sciences, and the elementary concepts of socialism. Russian, rather than Yiddish, was the language of propaganda. Basically, the content of propaganda was the same for Jewish as for non-Jewish revolutionary groups. The leaders of these circles were often intellectuals banished by the government to the Jewish pale of settlement. The importance of the cells to the workers can be seen from the following words of a worker who spoke in Vilna on May 1, 1882.

---

[19]*Ibid.*, p. 373.

[20]Leonard Schapiro, *The Communist Party of the Soviet Union* (New York: Vintage Books, 1964), p. 8.

[21]*Ibid.*, p. 9.

We dare not sit with folded hands and wait for assistance from above. We shall be saved and emancipated only through our own efforts. As far as possible each should seek to educate himself and others and thus contribute toward the formation of at least small socialist groups, for the time being. Through these circles we shall be able to become members of the great universal struggling workers' party which, acting in unison, will achieve its human rights. Then shall be inaugurated genuine freedom, fraternity, and equality for all mankind, Jews not excluded.[22]

Another worker at the same gathering stressed the significance of acquiring political freedom:

The entire enlightened world marches forward and is approaching the new order of the future. Only our beloved Russia is still far from the goal . . . so it is up to us to pave the way with our young forces. We must first explain to our sisters and brothers that the emancipation of each individual worker will be achieved only upon the emancipation of the entire working class. But in our country we are greatly handicapped by the lack of freedom of the press, assembly, and organization. Our first step, therefore, has to be the achievement of a constitution.[23]

From these modest socialist circles in the Jewish pale emerged the Bund. The Bund, which considered itself part of the Russian Democratic Party, hoped to develop the political and socialist consciousness of the Jewish masses and to stress civil equality for the Jews. The Bund's reaction to the discriminatory laws of Alexander III was to teach socialism and revolution and thereby encourage Jews to remain in Russia rather than to emigrate.

During the time of discriminatory legislation and emigration, an assembly of forty Jewish leaders, among them representatives of the Musar movement, was called together

---

[22]Greenberg, *The Jews in Russia*, II, 143.
[23]*Ibid.*

under the chairmanship of Baron Horace Gunzburg in St. Petersburg in April, 1882. They passed a resolution completely rejecting organized emigration as incompatible with the "historic rights of the Jews in their present fatherland.[24]

Rabbi Israel Salanter approved Jewish emigration to America in preference to Palestine because he felt that Jews in America would have a better opportunity to earn a living.[25] He was disturbed about the questionable morality and laxity of religious observance in the immigrant communities, but he hoped that with economic betterment there would be a spiritual and moral regeneration. On the other hand, Rabbi Kagan opposed emigration altogether because he feared the ensuing neglect of Jewish ritual and custom among the immigrants in a new and strange environment, even if it should prove temporary.[26]

Jews already in the West also reacted to the discriminatory laws. The following is part of the text of the Me-

> To His Memorial Majesty, Alexander III, Emperor of all the Russians. We, the citizens of London, respectfully approach your Majesty, and humbly beg your gracious leave to plead the cause of the afflicted. Cries of distress have reached us from thousands of suffering in your vast Empire, and we Englishmen, with pity in our souls for all who suffer, turn to your Majesty to implore for them your Sovereign aid and clemency.
>
> Five million of your Majesty's subjects groan beneath the yoke of exceptional and restrictive laws. Remnants of a race whence all religion sprang ours and yours, and every creed on earth that owns one God—men who cling with all devotion to their ancient faith and forms of worship, these Hebrews are in your Empire subject to such laws that under them they cannot live and thrive. Those laws built up in

---

[24]Baron, *The Russian Jews*, p. 87.

[25]See letter of Rabbi Ariah Leib Frumkin, a contemporary of Rabbi Salanter in Katz, *Tenuath Ha-Musar*, I, 212ff.

[26]Kagan, *Michtevei Hafets Hayyim*, p. 54.

morial to the Tsar voted by Jews at the Guildhall meeting:

> bygone times when intolerance was the rule in al-
> most every state, have been intensified by later or-
> dinances and weigh as grievous burdens on the He-
> brew subjects of your Majesty, raising a barrier be-
> tween them and their Christian fellow-subjects,
> making them a pariah caste, degraded and despised
> as if an accursed race . . .
>
> For they have virtues. These Israelites declared
> aliens by the laws are patriots still. They serve in the
> Imperial Army beyond their due proportion, they
> fight with zeal and valor in Russia's battles, and shed
> their life-blood for their country's cause. Ever loyal
> to your Majesty, they strive to obey the law, though
> its yoke be heavy, and true to the dictates of their
> Ancient Book, they pray in their Synagogues for the
> welfare of your Throne and Home. . . .
>
> And, mighty Sire, permit the sunshine of your
> Imperial Grace to brighten their dark homes, and
> let them feel the warmth of your paternal favor.
> As every passing year your Majesty's vast Empire
> widens and grows, so enter a new sphere of conquest,
> proclaimed by thy emancipation Emperor of five
> million hearts swelling with gratitude. . . .
>
> Signed on behalf of the
> citizens of London
> (Signed) Joseph Savory[27]

In a letter to Constantine Pobedonostsev, the Russian Jews who emigrated to England wrote the following:

> We, the signers of the letter, Russian Jews, who
> went to England not because of a crime committed
> against Russia, or because of unwillingness to as-
> sume military obligation, or other responsibilities,
> but because of lack of economic opportunities for a

---

[27]"The Memorial to the Czar, by the Jews of England," reproduced in Jacobo Lipschitz, *Sichron Jakob (Memoirs of Rabbi Jacob Lipschitz)* (Kaunas, 1930), III, 44-48.

livelihood in the Jewish pale of settlement; and the grave poverty forced us to leave the birthplace and to search for a refuge and a livelihood through independent work in a foreign country. Therefore, even now we consider ourselves attached to our birthplace from a moral point of view; the welfare of the birthplace and the will-power to serve the economic, spiritual, and religious life of our brethren in Russia compel us to turn to your honor concerning the Jewish problem, confronting now Russia.[28]

In May, 1882 a second assembly gathered in Saint Petersburg to discuss emigration. Rabbis Isaac Elhanan, Elijahu Levinsohn, Zev Cohen, Benush Katznelson and others of the Musar movement participated in the meeting. The majority of the delegates expressed the view that there was merit in emigration, but that it could not solve the problem of all six million Jews living in Russia. They also felt that if communal leaders continued to occupy themselves with emigration, anti-Semites would spread malicious reports that the Jews did not love their mother country and were exploiters of the country, ready to leave at the first distress they experienced.[29] The assembly adopted a resolution calling for lobbying in the higher eschelons of the government to remove discrimination against the Jews.

Some lobbyists tried to find favor in the eyes of the minister of finance and the minister of justice, and others tried to befriend Pobedonostsev, whose influence on Alexander III was great. The accomplishments of the lobbyists were numerous. In 1882 Pobedonostsev wrote:

Behold, I honor and hold in high esteem the ancient people, the Jews, from whom Christianity inherited the fundamentals of her faith, but the young generation of the Jews furthered away from the tra-

---

[28]Letter from Russian Jews in England to Pobedonostsev (London, 1882), reproduced in *ibid.*, III, 70-76.
[29]*Ibid.*, p. 91.

ditional Judaism of their fathers and followed dangerous paths, which harm even us.[30]

In addition to this, the lobbying brought about the abolishment of several laws and decrees injurious to the Jews.

The *Hoveve Zion* movement responded to the discriminatory laws of Alexander III by advocating return to Israel. It actively encouraged emigration to Palestine and colonization there.[31]

Rabbi Kagan seems to have been alone among Jewish leaders in concerning himself not only with whether or not to emigrate but also how to live with the decision. Although he did not approve of emigration as a response to discrimination, he was ready to help the immigrant in his religious, social, and economic re-adjustment to a new and strange environment.

Rabbi Kagan's Position and Response

Rabbi Kagan experienced the pogroms, the economically discriminatory May Laws, the expulsion of Jews from Moscow, the educational and legal restrictions, the development of closed social circles, and the emergence of the Bund. He saw with his own eyes the results and the implications of these discriminations—bribery, lawbreaking, emigration, economic hardships, and participation in revolutionary movements. He was also eager to hear news of the immigrants and was deeply concerned about the loss of religious life that was often a part of adjustment to life in foreign lands. For a time, the immigrant Jew observed the Sabbath and dietary laws; but as social pressures grew he was carried into a new life and these practices often changed. As an immigrant, the Jew experienced many hardships. He was looked down upon and mocked and his life was one of poverty and drudgery. To rise out of his degraded circumstances, he felt that he should compete in work or trade on an equal footing with his Christian neighbors. Sabbath observance was brushed aside, and

---

[30]Constantine Pobedonostsev, "The Jews," *Ha-Meliz*, 18 (1882).
[31]See below, pp. 158-180.

other traditional practices also fell by the wayside. As he acquired economic stature, the immigrant Jew strove to achieve
a social position on a par with his native-born co-religionists.
Soon this desire found its satisfaction through secular education, the reform of Jewish worship, or intermarriage. The
traditional observance of the Sabbath was replaced by a type
of relaxation based upon lounging at home or engaging in
picnics and outings—practices which were foreign to the keeping of the Sabbath.[32]

According to Rabbi Ariah Leib Kagan, his father was very
disturbed by the pogroms, the expulsion of Jews from the
villages and from Moscow, the economic, political, and social
discriminations of Alexander III, but he was just as disturbed
by the letters he received from Jews in every area of the dispersion, each telling of great hardship. Ariah writes that his
father was saddened by the laxity in religious observance reported in America and other countries.[33] Rabbi Kagan knew
that the immigrant in the New World would experience difficulty in getting adjusted to a different economic, political,
cultural, and social environment, and he reasoned thus: if
older Jewish settlers in the United States and other parts of
the world work on the Sabbath and on holidays, surely the
new immigrant will work on the Sabbath and on holidays
because of economic and social pressures. The Rabbi

> was reluctant to bless the people departing to Amer-
> ica and other places, and he urged them to change
> their minds about settling in places where Torah is
> neglected.[34]

Rabbi Ariah Leib Kagan relates that in 1892, in Warsaw,
his father confided to him his grave concern over the plight

---

[32]Hyman Grinstein, *The Rise of the Jewish Community of New York*
(Philadelphia: Jewish Publication Society, 1945), p. 15.

[33]Rabbi Mendel Zaks informed the author that letters and travelers spread
the news about the laxity in observance of Judaism in the new places of
settlement. Simon Eckman, grandfather of the author, visited America
on several occasions. Upon returning, he too informed Rabbi Kagan of
the desecration of the Sabbath and the neglect of Torah study. See also,
Kagan, *Michtevei Hafets Hayyim*, p. 54.

[34]*Ibid.*

of the Jews in Russia and their resultant emigration to America, Africa and other parts of the world. Rabbi Israel Meir Kagan told his son that mass emigration was "a breakdown of the Jewish faith and assimilation with the non-Jewish population of their new places of settlement.[35] The son answered his father that it was impossible for Rabbi Israel Meir Kagan to control the mass emigration because "the majority of the emigrants have no place to settle because of the expulsion from the villages and Moscow by Alexander III."[36] He continued:

> If you are zealous of God's honor and His Torah, you must follow the emigrants and settle also in America. In America, travel from city to city and motivate them in the morning and in the evening to follow the teachings of the Torah, also to establish large gatherings to strengthen Torah and observance; and I brought proof from the Prophet Jeremiah who rebuked the Jews for departing to Egypt, but we read afterwards that he followed the Jews to Egypt and the Prophet preached the words of God to the Jews in Egypt.[37]

Rabbi Israel Meir Kagan was astounded by the advice of his son and did not answer him. After a half year had passed the son found a manuscript dealing with codes for the dispersed Jews in America and other countries. This was published in 1893 and was called *Nidhei Israel (The Dispersed of Israel)*. It was Rabbi Kagan's answer to his son's advice, and it was an excellent substitute for the Rabbi himself emigrating to America. People of the Jewish faith in America, England, Africa, and other countries began to study his laws dealing with the dispersed. On the recommendation of the most prominent rabbis, Rabbi Kagan translated the book into Yiddish so that women and laymen would also be able to learn from it. Rabbi Kagan's son relates that he used to send

---

[35]*Ibid.*, p. 55.
[36]*Ibid.*
[37]*Ibid.*

books to America, Africa and England, and that he even received an order for eighteen books from a rabbi in Ottawa, Canada.

Another reason for writing the book, according to Rabbi Mendel Zaks, was to discourage troubled Jewish youth from participating in the revolutionary movements and in the Bund by showing that Judaism can adjust to strange conditions in distant lands and can solve the religious problems of modern life.[38]

The title of the book comes from the verse, "If any of thine that are dispersed be in the uttermost parts of heaven from thence will the Lord thy God gather thee."[39] In the book, Rabbi Kagan discussed important principles of Judaism for Jews emigrating to foreign countries, and for those Jews lax in observance of the Torah at home. He wrote:

> And behold, when we discern now the keeping of precepts of the Torah, and its statutes in this world, indeed, it is very lax, even for those people living unpersecuted at home, and especially for people wandering in the distant lands, like America, Africa, and England. There are many who take lightly the keeping of the precepts of the Torah. There are some, who transgress contemptuously the commands and there are among them who disregard even those commandments for which one is commanded to endure martyrdom and not to infract them.[40]

*Four Causes for Laxity in Observance
of the Torah Commands*

According to Rabbi Kagan, there were four causes for laxity in observing the precepts of the Torah: first, there are those who attribute the transgression of the precepts to the intricate problems of adjustment in a new country. These immigrants do not take seriously the teachings of the Torah and reason that since God has punished them with wander-

---

[38]Interview by the author with Rabbi Mendel Zaks, June, 1967.
[39]Deut. 30:4.
[40]Kagan, *Nidhei Israel*, pp. 11ff.

ing to distant lands it is logical to assume that He has forsaken them. The effect of this is despair of keeping the law
of God and, at times, violation of the most significant laws,
such as those relating to the Sabbath, sex rules, and similar
matters.[41]

A second cause is a lack of knowledge concerning how to
conduct oneself according to the laws of the Torah. An absence of Jews who could teach the simplest laws and a lack
of persons dedicated to strengthening faith in God and Torah
led people to pursue the path of irreligion. Shame, which
prevents a person from departing from the ways of the Torah
in the old country, is absent in the new lands of refuge, and
it is easier for people to go astray.[42]

A third cause of laxity is the immigrant's discovery that
his acquaintances from the old world look with disdain upon
religious practice in America and other lands of new settlement. He is, therefore, enticed to feel, "I am not alone in
this matter. As will be with the rest of the people of the town,
so will it be with me."[43]

And, according to the Rabbi, the fourth cause is the
neglect of Torah study, which leads to the destruction of
Judaism.[44]

Rabbi Kagan pointed out that the first cause of laxity—
a belief often held by immigrant Jews that they had been
forsaken by God and were therefore exempt from obeying
the Torah—was an ancient problem. The Sages (*Sanhedrin*
105) said that when Israel was dispersed throughout the exile,
some men wanted to remove themselves from the yoke of
God. Ezekiel, the prophet, advised them to repent, and they
told him: "a servant who was sold by his master and a woman who was divorced by her husband have nothing to do
with the one who has rejected them; therefore, God has given
up the Jews as his select nation because he delivered them
to the nations." And God said to the prophet, "Ask them:

---

[41]*Ibid.*
[42]*Ibid.*
[43]*Ibid.*, p. 24.
[44]*Ibid.*, p. 28.

'Where is the book of the divorcement of your mother? Or
which of my creditors is it to whom I have sold' "[45] Rabbi
Kagan interpreted the passage to mean that living in the
diaspora did not imply being forsaken by God. The entire
world is the Lord's and it may be that the Jews have been
sent to live among heathens in order to cleanse their spirit.[46]

A Jew remains obligated to observe the commandments
of God in exile. When he worships the Lord and studies the
Torah, redemption will be given to him by God.[47] Rabbi
Kagan concludes with the following:

> It is clearly explained to us that even a wandering
> Jew to a distant land who is subjugated there to a
> certain idolatrous nation, even thus, he has not
> been forsaken by the Holy One and God is his ever-
> lasting portion and inheritance.[48]

Rabbi Kagan's Outlook on God's Presence and His Testing of Men

Rabbi Kagan believed that God measures the worth of
a human being not by how many precepts he follows, but
by the devotion and sacrifice he endures to fulfill even one
of God's commands. He quotes a rabbinic source claming that
one precept followed under suffering is equivalent to a hundred precepts without pain.[49] Many times God hides himself—which explains the emergence of evil and suffering—thus
giving each person an opportunity to rise above evil circumstances. God tested a generation of Jews in the desert to
purify them and develop in them a character strong enough
to surmount all difficulties and to maintain faithfulness to
the Torah under all circumstances. Man uplifts himself
through the performance of commandments under difficult
circumstances. The dispersion of the Jewish people throughout the world and their persecution and suffering can be ex-

---

[45]Tractate *Sanhedrin*, p. 105.
[46]Kagan, *Nidhei Israel*, pp. 12ff.
[47]*Ibid.*, p. 13.
[48]*Ibid.*
[49]*Ibid.*, pp. 16ff.

plained as a time for testing of the Jewish people's faith in God and His precepts. If the oppressed and needy faithfully resist evil under all circumstances God will eventually respond to their needs. Rabbi Kagan urged immigrant Jews to heed his views and see their troubles as a chance to prove their faith in God.[50]

Now that the world had witnessed the ultimate horrors of the suffering at places like Auschwitz, it may be more difficult than ever for some to take Rabbi Kagan's views seriously. But to some the faith offered by the Rabbi remains as comforting and strengthening even after Auschwitz as it was to many faithful immigrants before that holocaust.[51]

---

[50]*Ibid.*

[51]After the author lived through the horrors of the Second World War, he asked the question, "Where was God?"; and when his father was taken away from him by the Communists and millions of innocent people and children experienced the greatest tragedy and immeasurable barbaric sufferings that were recorded in the annals of history, the question recurred. Many people asked the same question about the exterminations at Auschwitz, Bergen Belsen, Dachau, and other death camps. Many of the survivors whom the author knows personally, including two of his brothers-in-law, are still asking the question.

It is indeed a very difficult question to answer in the light of what happened not only in Auschwitz, but what continues to happen in places such as Biafra, My Lai, East Pakistan, and the Middle East. It is easy to accept the philosophy of a man such as Rabbi Richard Rubenstein—whose views have been the subject of discussions between him and the author on numerous occasions, when he was Hillel director of Harvard University and while he was serving as Regional Director of Hillel in Pittsburgh, Pa. and the surrounding area—that God died in Auschwitz and thereby close the chapter on this question. The author feels, however, that he and others have found meaning in life and a belief in God and His goodness after Auschwitz through study of the Torah and of the works of great men such as Maimonides, Halevi, and Rabbi Israel Meir Kagan. The author's father, for example, spent five years in a Russian prison, but he never lost his faith in God that someday a miracle would happen and he would once more be re-united with his wife and four children. It was the philosophy of Rabbi Kagan that kept this man's faith in God and His commands strong under such difficult circumstances.

Whether God is dead after Auschwitz is irrelevant to the person who went through the "living hell" of Auschwitz or the suffering of a prison camp during wartime, and still believes in God. He too must answer the question, "Where was God?" And to many who do not presume to understand all the mysterious ways in which God may work and who accept that mystery Rabbi Kagan's views offer comfort and strength and add meaning to their lives—meaning, comfort and strength which would not be there were they to believe that God is simply dead.

Who Is a Jew?

Another important issue which has confronted the Jewish people in recent years is "Who is a Jew?" Rabbi Kagan dealt with this problem in *Nidhei Israel* and his views are as relevant now as they were then.

The issue has been raised in recent years because of marriages between Jews and non-Jews (especially among Russian immigrants) and between Israelis and women who did not convert to Judaism in accordance with Jewish law. The issue of who is a Jew was a problem which brought about a schism between Samaritans and Judaeans. Intermarriage then had even penetrated the high priesthood. Manasseh, grandson of the High Priest, Eliashib, had married the daughter of Sanballat the Hornite, governor of Samaria.[52] Nehemiah expelled Manasseh from the Temple and thus extinguished Sanballat's hopes of ever seeing Manasseh as a High Priest in the Temple in Jerusalem. Sanballat decided to construct a Temple in Samaria on Mt. Gerizim and install Manasseh as high priest. Such a temple would not only vie with the Temple in Jerusalem but might even overshadow it, since Manasseh of the Zadokite family would be its high priest. The leaders of the Judaeans, in order to nullify the high priesthood of Manasseh and remove the danger of a temple on Mt. Gerizim, enacted a law stating that if a Judaean married a woman of a foreign nation, the offspring of the marriage would not be considered Judaean.[53] The male offspring of Manasseh could not be priests—not even Judaeans. This it came about, through the political ambitions of Sanballat, that a child's status in Jewish law follows that of its mother.[54] The expulsion of Manasseh from the Temple and the enactment of this law was what brought about the schism between Samaritans and Judaeans.

Before we examine Rabbi Kagan's views on Jewishness

---

[52]Josephus, *Antiquities* 11:8, 2 (306-312).

[53]Solomon Zeitlin, "Offspring of Intermarriage," *Jewish Quarterly Review*, LI (October, 1960).

[54]*Ibid.*, p. 138. This law corresponded to the Jewish *halakhic* law stating that the mother determines the Jewishness of a child.

it might be well to trace Talmudic, rabbinic, and contemporary opinions in order to provide some historical perspective to our discussion.

Who Is a Jew? The Talmudic and Rabbinic Views

Rabbi Johanan replied in the name of Rabbi Simeon ben Yohai: "the Bible states, 'For he will turn away thy son from following Me . . .'[55] 'Thy son' born from an Israelitish woman is called 'thy son'[56] but 'thy son' who was born from a heathen is not called 'thy son'[57] but her son." Rabbi Rabina said: "From this it follows that the 'son of your daughter' who derives from a heathen is called 'thy son.'[58] One may ask whether Rabbi Rabina was of the opinion that if a heathen or a slave had intercourse with a daughter of Israel the child was considered fit?[59] The Gemara concludes 'though he is admittedly no bastard neither is he considered fit; he is rather regarded[60] as a tainted Israelite.[61]

Maimonides provided the following general guideline as to who is a Jew: a son born of a slave or of a heathen or of a non-Jewish maiden or of a heathen's daughter is not Jewish. It appears that Maimonides accept the Talmudic verdict that the mother rather than the father is the deciding factor in determining Jewishness.[62]

---

[55]Deut. 7:4. The pronoun he in this clause must, according to Talmudic exposition, refer to the antecedent son in verse 3, "thy daughter thou shalt not give unto his son, and not to "son" in the clause, "nor his daughter shalt thou take unto thy son." Had the reference been to the latter the verse 4 would have been read, for she (i.e., the heathen woman) "will turn away" they son. "He" must, therefore, refer to the heathen husband of the Israelitish woman who would turn away the son of his Israelitish wife, the (grand) son of her father. The son of his son born from a heathen, however, is obviously not called his (grand) son since, "for he will turn . . ." does not apply to him. See *Yebamoth*, 23a.

[56]Thy son or grandson.

[57]I.e., he is a heathen like his mother.

[58]See *Kiddushin*, p. 345, n. 5-6.

[59]This is a question in dispute, in *Yebamoth*, 45a and in a parallel passage in *Kiddushin*, 68b where the reading is, the child is a "memzer," a reading to which *Tosaf* gives preference.

[60]Literally, "called."

[61]*Yebamoth*, 23a and *Kiddushin*, 68b.

[62]See Maimonides, *Mishnah Torah*, *Nashim* (dealing with laws of sexual intercourse), Chap. 15, law 4; see also Chap. 14, law 8; Chap. 12, law 7.

Who Is a Jew: Rabbi Kagan's View

Rabbi Israel Meir Kagan followed the views of the Talmud and Maimonides that the mother determines the Jewishness of a child. A Jew can travel to distant lands but he
will retain his Jewish identity. However, Rabbi Kagan felt
that an ideal Jew must not only be born of a Jewish mother
but must also have faith in God and practice his precepts.
It is not enough to claim one's Jewishness because one's
mother is Jewish; one must study Torah and keep the commands of God to be considered an authentic member of
the Jewish fold.[63] He held that Jewish nationality cannot be
separated from its religious foundation.[64]

Who Is a Jew? Modern Era

At the dawn of the modern era the question of Jewishness
was not a significant issue anywhere in the world. The trickle
of Marranos coming out of the Iberian Peninsula ceased almost completely by 1800. In the European arena a Jew was
someone defined by Jewish law, that is one who was born
of a Jewish mother or who converted to Judaism.

With the era of emancipation the issue of Jewish identity
appeared in new forms. "The structure of law which en-
shrined a precise definition of who was a Jew came to an
end wherever any version of the modern secular state was
created."[65] Before the law religion became a matter of in-
difference and the choice to uphold one's religion became
purely voluntary. The law protected the right to private
opinion and free association for worship, provided the specific practices of a religion were not flagrantly in conflict with
public order as conceived by the state.

> This formulation had Christianity in mind, for it
> defined religion as containing dogma about God and
> the world to come and as acting in specific forms

---

[63]Kagan, *Nidhei Israel*, pp. 13ff.
[64]Kagan, *Michtevei Hafets Hayyim*, p. 468.
[65]See Arthur Hertzberg's article on "Jewish Identity," in *Encyclopaedia Judaica*, 10:50.

of worship. These premises were accepted by the founders of Reform Judaism both in Germany and in the United States, who constructed a modern definition of Jewish identity as that of individuals who belonged to the Jewish religious faith, now conceived as containing primarily ethical content and personal edification.[66]

This non-national definition of Judaism and Jewry was shared in many senses by the founder of Neo-Orthodoxy, Rabbi Samson Raphael Hirsh. He accepted the general culture and made patriotic identification with the state. What was different was that Hirsch's Neo-Orthodoxy identified the content of Jewish religion with every aspect of the inherited law, "meticulously observed as divine commandment, but whatever was national in Judaism was relegated to far-off, apocalyptic days and thus made largely irrelevant. . . ."[67] The Reform and Neo-Orthodox versions of Jewish identity were addressing themselves to the biological descendants of Jews, and held that, regardless of their self-definitions, they were part and parcel with all sorts of Jews, both in their countries and all over the world.

As anti-Semitism became ever more virulent in the last third of the nineteenth century new definitions—from Diaspora nationalism to Zionism—won many adherents. Dubnow's Diaspora Nationalism held that the unity of the Jews did not depend upon a national territory, or upon an independent state. Their unity was kept alive by communal organizations, within whose framework Jewish culture and religion had continued their growth for two thousand years after their dispersion.[68] On the other hand, Zionism, from the first days of its establishment, called for the founding of a Jewish state in Palestine, based on the historical right of the people of the Bible to the land of the Bible. But, the Jewish state of the future was conceived very clearly as a Western-type

[66]*Ibid.*, p. 59.
[67]*Ibid.*
[68]Dubnow, *Nationalism and History: Essays on Old and New Judaism.*

secular democracy, shorn of any specific traditional religious character.

Who Is a Jew? Contemporary Israel

In contemporary Israel, the issue of who is a Jew involves an interpretation based on the older, religious and *halakhic* definitions and the more contemporary but also far older communal-national emphases. Very few Israelis consider themselves Jewish Canaanites. However, many are in sympathy with the idea that the strictist of religious tests cannot be applied to those non-Jews by birth who have decided to identify with the Jewish people. On the other hand, in circles far wider than those of the Orthodox, one can sense a return to tradition which is beyond the purely secular.

> Indeed, one of the recurring problems studied by Israel sociologists is whether its population of Jews regard themselves as primarily Israelis or Jews. By all of the usually established criteria, from religious observance to involvement in the destiny of world Jewry, the Orthodox and most of the non-Sabras of all persuasions rank as "Jews." The non-Orthodox Sabras consider themselves "Israelis" on all counts except that they feel strongly about their connection to the Jews of all the world and their involvement in this international destiny.[69]

In recent years the question of Jewishness has been a matter of considerable political and social concern for Israel. The Law of Return, passed by the Kneset in 1950, states that "every Jew has the right to come to this country as an *oleh* (immigrant)." The only exceptions are persons deemed by the Minister of Immigration and later the Minister of Interior to be "engaged in an activity directed against the Jewish people," or "likely to endanger public health or the security of the state," or "with a criminal past, and likely to endanger public welfare." Under other legislation, a Jewish immigrant is entitled to receive automatic Israeli citizenship

---

[69]Arthur Herzberg, "Jewish Identity," pp. 62ff.

(unless he formally decides to waive it) from the moment
he arrives in Israel.

If one analyzes carefully the Law of Return, it does not
contain any definition of the term "Jew." The purpose of
the law is to implement the basic goal of political Zionism,
as stated in the Declaration of Independence, "to solve the
problem of Jewish homelessness and dependence by the re-
newal of the Jewish State in the Land of Israel, which would
open wide the gates of the homeland to every Jew . . ."

The issue of Jewishness under the Law of Return assumed
practical significance in Israel when large-scale immigration
brought Jewish communities that had been isolated from
traditional Judaism—such as the Falashas of Ethiopia, the
B'nei Israel of India whose lineage some Orthodox rabbinical
authorities in Israel questioned, and Jews from Eastern
Europe who had married non-Jewish wives. In the latter case,
the key question was how the children of such marriages
should be registered. The matter came to a head in 1958 after
the arrival of large numbers of Polish-Jews, who had become
assimilated and intermarried. The then Minister of Interior,
a member of the secularist, socialist Ahdut ha-Avodah party,
declared that "a person can be listed as Jewish on his identity
card simply on the strength of a personal declaration to that
effect."[70] This directive aroused the opposition of Orthodox
religious circles in Israel and the Diaspora, who warned that
"the unity of the Jewish people would be undermined and
destroyed" if Israel departed from the definition of a Jew
under Rabbinic law.[71]

The secular Israel political parties contended that an af-
firmation of national identification with the Jewish people
should suffice for such registration, whereas the religious
parties demanded that the *halakhic* guidelines should be retained. The National Religious party left the Cabinet in protest after the new regulations were approved in June 1958.

---

[70]George E. Gruen, "Again Who is a Jew?" in the *American Jewish
Committee Institute of Human Relations*, February, 1970, p. 3; see also
Raphael Posner, "Halakhic Definition of a Jew," in *Encyclopaedia Judaica*,
10:23.

[71]Gruen, "Again Who is a Jew?", p. 3.

In an attempt to resolve the controversy, David Ben Gurion, then Prime Minister, elicited answers to the question from rabbinical leaders and Jewish scholars in Israel and throughout the Diaspora; the overwhelming majority of the respondents (37 of 45) indicated that the State of Israel should follow the Orthodox identity. The final directives issued to the registering officers required that there be a bona fide conversion before the applicant could be registered as Jewish.[72] This directive enabled the National Religious party the post of the Minister of Interior.

Brother Daniel Case

One may ask the question, "Can a Christian be a Jew?" A milestone in the question of Jewishness under the Law of Return was the decision of the Israel Supreme Court in December 1962 in the case of Brother Daniel. The petitioner, Oswald Rufeisen, was a Carmelite monk, who had been born of Jewish parents and educated as a Jew. During the Second World War, Brother Daniel saved many Jews in Poland at great personal risk. After he found refuge in a convent, he decided to convert to Catholicism. However, Oswald Rufeisen continued to consider himself "ethnically Jewish and out of his strong attachment decided to settle in Israel." Upon arrival, he applied to the Minister of Interior for automatic citizenship under the Law of Return and also petitioned "that in his identity card the space provided for le'om (ethnic affiliation or peoplehood) be marked 'Jewish'."[73]

A five panel Supreme Court decided, by four to one, that although Brother Daniel was still a Jew under the strict interpretation of rabbinic law, which does not recognize conversion out of Judaism and provides that "even if a Jew has sinned he remains a Jew," the term "Jew" as used in the Law of Return was intended to be interpreted in "a secular

---

[72]Gruen, "Again Who is a Jew?", p. 4; Posner, "Halakhic Definition of a Jew"; Hertzberg, "Jewish Identity," p. 63; see also Joseph Elias, "The Search for National Identity," in the *Jewish Observer*, March, 1970, p. 5. to rejoin the government and one of its members to receive
[73]*Ibid.*

sense," that is, "as it usually is understood by the man in the street . . . by the ordinary, plain and simple Jew." The Supreme Court therefore ruled that "a Jew who has become a Christian is not called a Jew."[74] The Court instructed the Ministry of Interior to leave blank or enter "none" in his identity card next to *le'om*. The Minister of Interior offered to facilitate Brother Daniel's application for Israeli citizenship under the naturalization procedure available to non-Jews by waiving the usual three year waiting period.[75]

The importance of Brother Daniel's court decision was that for the first time an attempt was made by an Israeli court to resolve the question of Jewishness outside the realm of *halakhah*.

Who is a Jew? The Shalit Case

Benjamin Shalit, a Jew born in Haifa, married a non-Jewish Scots woman in Edinburgh. He returned with his wife to Haifa, where two children were born to them, a son in 1964 and a daughter in 1967. Since the children were born in Israel they automatically acquired Israel citizenship, as do other persons born in the country—Jews, Arabs, and Christians. Under the Law of Return, they had the right to citizenship. The question at issue was how the children should be listed in their birth certificates and in the records kept by the Ministry of the Interior under the Population Registration Law. Benjamin and Anne Shalit professed to be atheists and therefore were satisfied that their children's papers read "religion—none." But, Shalit, an officer in the Israel navy, petitioned the Haifa registration office to list his children as Jewish under the category *le'om*, the ethnic affiliation. The local registration officer, following the Ministry of the Interior's 1960 directives, wrote instead "no registration" next to the entry for *le'om*.[76] Shalit appealed this action, and the appeal finally reached the Supreme Court.

At an earlier stage in the proceedings, the Supreme Court

---

[74]*Ibid.*
[75]Gruen, "Again Who is a Jew?", p. 4.
[76]*Ibid.*, p. 5.

had recommended that the problem could best be solved by elimination of the category *le'om* altogether. The Court noted that "the concept of *le'om* was vague and was in a sense superfluous because the population registration forms of the Ministry of the Interior already had separate categories for citizenship and for religion, in addition to *le'om*."[77] Golda Meir and her government did not heed the Court's suggestion, reportedly, "because the category *le'om* on the identity cards carried by all adults provided a handy means of differentiating between Arabs and Jews for purposes of eligibility for the draft and other questions related to security."[78]

The Court ruled by a narrow five to four decision that since the Kneset "had never spelled out a definition of *le'om* and in keeping with the principle established in the Brother Daniel case that for secular laws, such as the population registry law, the Court was not required to apply strict *halakha,* therefore, Shalit had the right to have his children registered as Jewish by *le'om*."[79] In other words, a majority of the court ruled that since neither Shalit nor his children had formally converted to another religion, he had a valid right to consider himself and his children Jewish by ethnic affiliation or peoplehood even though their mother was not Jewish and neither of the parents was religious. The majority of the justice "pointed out that there were many Jews in Israel who were either agnostic or even atheists but who were still regarded as Jewish in the popular mind in view of their decision to live in Israel, to speak Hebrew, and to send their children to state schools where Jewish history and culture formed an integral part of the curriculum."[80] The minority, of course, held that one could not divorce Jewish ethnic identity from at least nominal Jewish religious affiliation.

One of the minority, Justice Silberg, wrote:

> There is not in existence . . . a Jewish-Israeli nationality; and if there were, it would not neces-

---

[77]Gruen, "Again Who is a Jew?", p. 5.
[78]*Ibid.*
[79]*Ibid.*, see also Elias, "The Search for National Identity," pp. 3ff, and Posner, "Halakhic Definition of a Jew," p. 4.
[80]Gruen, "Again Who is a Jew?", pp. 5ff.

sarily be a secular nationality. . . . It is slanderous
to say that our youth has freed itself from all al-
legiance to the heritage of our ancestors. On the
contrary, what it seeks is primarily religious values
and symbols.

This heritage of our ancestors to which we all,
or almost all, feel bound, is one of the foundations
of our rights to Eretz Yizroel. . . . Whoever sep-
arates Jewish nationality from its religious foundations touches the heart of our political claim to
Eretz Yizroel—a veritable act of treason.

The search for a new criterion of Jewish identity means in effect the denial of the continued existence of the Jewish people . . . a desire to establish a new country, without history and tradition.
The sole criterion for determining the national
identity of the Jew is the *Halakic* criterion which
views the Jewish mother or conversion as exclusive
means of identification, and not the criterion which
views a person's inclination to the Jewish-Israeli culture and values as the means of identification of a
national Jew.[81]

The decision caused an outcry among religious circles
in Israel and abroad. Many feared that the formal recognition by the Court of a category of Jews separated from
Halakha would split the Jewish people and eventually erode
the authority of the rabbinate even in religious matters. Some
of the non-Orthodox, notably Prime Minister Golda Meir,
shared the concern that the decision of the Supreme Court
would be divisive at a time when Israel needed both unity
at home and solidarity with the Jews of the Diaspora. She
stressed that she considered the Jewish people and its unity
more important than the State of Israel or Zionism, and
"there is no other explanation for our existence through the
ages, despite all suffering, than the loyalty to the faith."[82] It

---

[81]From the opinion of Supreme Court Justice Silberg, quoted in Elias,
"The Search for National Identity," pp. 3ff.

[82]*Ibid.*, p. 4.

is remarkable that the large majority of political leaders in the Kneset—secularists of all stripes—expressed feelings in the debate similar to Golda Meir's, ruling out a division between nation and religion.

In the wake of the Shalit decision the government submitted legislation to the Kneset designed to achieve a workable compromise. The legislation amends the Law of Return and the Population Registration Law to define "Jew" as "a person born to a Jewish mother or who has been converted, and who is not a member of another religion." This definition is made applicable to all registrations and documents issued under the Population Registration Law. "The effect is to apply the *Halakhic* religious definition of a Jew also to the category of *le'om* in the future. The amendment specifies that it does not have retroactive effect and does not invalidate existing registrations."[83] Thus the registration of the Shalit children as Jewish by *le'om* is left standing, but the Court's decision has been superseded with regard to all future cases.

In light of this analysis of Jewishness, one can see that Rabbi Kagan's opinion is very close to that which has since evolved in Israel. He was convinced, like Supreme Court Justice Silberg, that one cannot separate Jewish nationality from its religious foundations, and he directed his book, *Nidhei Israel*, to the non-believer and the non-practicing Jew—who, to him, would not cease being a Jew wherever he might go. He wrote: "Despite all the hardships in exile, the Jewish people exist; but the land of Israel without Torah is a land without a soul; and goodness is the result of the amalgamation of Torah and the land of Israel."[84]

Method of Educating the Dispersed of Israel

Rabbi Kagan's creativity is again in evidence in his selection of laws to be woven into a code for the dispersed of Israel. The laws themselves, such as prayer, dietary laws, Sabbath, etc., are not original in content since they are based on the *Shulhan Arukh* of Karo. But each law was clearly ex-

---

[83]Gruen, "Again Who is a Jew?", p. 6.
[84]Kagan, *Michtevei Hafets Hayyim*, p. 468.

plained in the light of Biblical, Talmudical, and rabbinical sources. Each law in the code appears to be so important that there can be no compromise with it, even in the distant lands of emigration under the most difficult circumstances. Since the Rabbi dealt with real problems, each law is presented in such a way that it has life, importance and relevance to the dispersed of Israel. His code is well organized and the language is easily understood.

Prayer

A person leaving for a distant country must become accustomed to the recital of the *Sh'ma* (Belief in one God), the Eighteen Blessings, and the putting on of fringes and phylacteries. He must take it upon himself to fulfill the regular recurring practices, even in time of suffering. The Torah is the nourishment of man's soul and the precepts are like the nourishment of the body. The Rabbi urged the immigrant to settle in a place which had a synagogue and to attend service on weekdays and on the Holy Sabbath.[85]

It is said in the Bible: ". . . and to serve Him with all your heart."[86] The rabbis taught, "Which is the service of the heart? Necessarily, prayer."[87] Rabbi Kagan's views on the greatness of prayer is based on the Talmud: "Said Rabbi Elazar; 'Prayer is greater than good works, because no one was greater in good deeds than Moses, our teacher, nevertheless, he was answered through prayer.' "[88] Thus, Rabbi Kagan held that a new immigrant must pray three times a day, and if by chance he travels, it is permissible to pray under the open sky.[89] A person who dwells in a small settlement should do his best to assemble a *minyan* (quorum).

The Study of Torah

According to Rabbi Kagan, failure to study Torah was a major cause of laxity in religious observance among immigrants. He reminds his reader that the Talmudic Sages had

[85]Kagan, *Nidhei Israel*, pp. 20ff.
[86]Deut. 6:5.
[87]Tractate *Brachoth*, p. 32.
[88]*Ibid.*
[89]Kagan, *Nidhei Israel*, p. 20.

often stated that sanctity for the Jewish people emanates from the study of Talmud. On the other hand, a lack of Torah study causes loss of sanctity. A Jew without the study of Torah is like a fish separated from the water, and though he is still alive, ultimately he will die.[90] When Jews cease studying Torah and observing its precepts, they still obey some of the commandments as long as they possess the moisture of the Torah. In due time, however, the moisture begins to dry up and finally all the Torah and precepts are abandoned. Rabbi Kagan concludes: "Who can predict the outcome of a complete separation from the study and commands of the Torah?"[91] Again, Rabbi Kagan advised immigrants to make use of the lessons of the Sages in adjusting to changing times and new conditions. He emphasized that one can and must always fit study and observance of Torah into any new environment.

The Rabbi criticized large Jewish communities in America and other countries whose leaders did not emphasize the importance of a Hebrew education. Those communities that set up a small Torah study group along with secular education stressed the secular studies more. As a result of this emphasis, Hebrew studies were swallowed up and Jewish children did not know the Bible or the practices of Jewish religion. No one seemed willing to observe the commandment to imbue their children with love for God and Torah. Rabbi Kagan blamed the leaders of the communities for neglecting this.[92] It is the view of the author that Jewish federations in the United States can benefit immensely from Rabbi Kagan's views on the importance of Torah education since for years the bulk of money from the federations has gone to hospitals and social and recreational programs rather than to Jewish education.

The Rabbi

Every Jewish community is obligated to hire a rabbi. His function is to teach the laws of the Torah and to set an ex-

---

[90]Tractate *Brachoth*, p. 61.
[91]Kagan, *Nidhei Israel*, p. 34.
[92]*Ibid.*, pp. 50-51.

ample in observing the commandments for his congregants to emulate. Rabbi Kagan scolds the towns in distant lands that lack a rabbi. It is a great sin to disregard the responsibility of hiring a rabbi. The founding of schools and the appointing of a rabbi are the pillars of Judaism. Fortunate are those Jews who dedicate themselves to these matters, and, in particular, happy are those who work to establish schools and to hire a rabbi.[93]

Shaving the Beard

Everything relating to the new immigrant and his problems as a result of the new environment interested Rabbi Kagan. For example, a new immigrant found it necessary to shave his beard. The Rabbi informed such a man that it was forbidden to shave with a razor but one might use scissors for the purpose under certain regulation.[94]

---

[93]*Ibid.,* p. 122.

[94]A controversy emerged concerning permission given by Rabbi Kagan to use a pair of scissors in rounding the corners of the head and beard. It was the custom in the distant lands to use the razor and to shave off the beards. Many immigrants began to shave off their beards and use the razor —a practice which is prohibited by the Torah. Many Jews in the old country, especially those in the Bund and revolutionary movements, were also shaving off their beards with the use of a razor. Rabbi Kagan permitted the use of scissors with the hope of checking the use of a razor. He presented proof from rabbinic law that it was permissible to use scissors. On the other hand, he admonished the users to be heedful even with scissors.

Jews from Hasidic sects began to object to the Rabbi's permission to use scissors in rounding the hair at the corners of the head and beard because in those days it was not yet the custom to round the head and beard, therefore, it was objectionable in their eyes to give sanction in public and in a book to the use of scissors. The Lubavitch Hasidim, under the leadership of their Rebbe Baal Zemach Zedek, were the most argumentative. Rebbe Baal Zemach Zedek did not permit the use of scissors, basing his interpretation on the rabbinic interpretation of the thirteenth-century rabbi, Rabbi Moses of Coucy, France, who held that the Torah prohibits the use of scissors.

The controversy over the scissors motivated Rabbi Kagan to write the *Booklet of the Glory of Man* which depicts in detail the laws of rounding the corners of the head and beard. Although he gathers ample legal rabbinic evidence to back the permission to use the scissors, the Hasidim continued to prohibit their use. When more Jews began to shave off their beards in the old country also, the booklet came to be accepted by the Hasidim. Apparently they felt it was more legal to use scissors than to shave off the complete beard. The booklet tried to strengthen the prohibition against shaving off the beard with a razor.

Dietary Laws

Since some immigrants ate forbidden foods, Rabbi Kagan impressed upon his readers the importance of following the laws of *Kashruth*. A person must show great will power in avoiding forbidden foods. Suppose a Jew is confined to a non-Jewish hospital and is told by his doctor that he must eat a piece of meat every day or, at least, a dish prepared of meat. If he does not eat he endangers his health. If he is limited to the cooking of the hospital, let him at any rate try to minimize the prohibition; i.e., let him not eat the prohibited food itself, only the soup of the cooked preparation.[95]

Just as a Jew himself is not permitted to eat anything forbidden, so he is not allowed to give the prohibited food to a friend or to aid his comrade in obtaining forbidden food. Minors are not permitted to violate the forbidden food laws.[96] By abstaining from forbidden food a Jew is sanctified by God, as it is stated: "and you shall not make your souls detestable . . . and you shall be holy unto Me; for I the Lord am Holy . . ."[97] Each time that a Jew refrains from eating a prohibited article of food, Heaven credits him with the actual carrying out of a positive precept of the Torah.[98] The rabbis stated: "If a man sat and did not commit a transgression, he is rewarded as if he had carried out a precept."[99] Also, for checking his temptation to eat prohibited food for the sake of God, he is called "mighty."

The Sabbath

The immigrant in the New World was confronted with the problem of working on the Sabbath, which was a working day in their new home. Even Jews in Europe had seen fellow Jews joining the Bund and other revolutionary movements which disregarded the observance of the Sabbath. The

---

[95]Kagan, *Nidhei Israel*, p. 161.
[96]*Ibid.*
[97]Lev. 20:25, 26.
[98]*Ibid.* p. 166.
[99]*Ibid.*

Holy Sabbath was becoming a symbol of the past to many immigrants as well as to some who remained in Europe.

Rabbi Kagan was well informed about the desecration of the Sabbath in the New and Old Worlds. In *Nidhei Israel* he devotes four chapters to a presentation of the laws dealing with keeping the Sabbath holy. His aim was to inform the violators of the Sabbath in the distant lands and at home that the Sabbath was, is, and will be, a pillar of Jewish faith.

He wrote that:

> the holy Sabbath is the immense sign and covenant that God gave to Israel so that they might be informed that in six days God created everything in heaven and earth and rested on the seventh day.[100]

It is a cardinal principle of faith to know that the universe was created *ex nihilo*; and since God created everything, He is the Lord over everything, and the Jews are his servants and are obliged to serve him with all their bodies, souls, and monies, for everything belongs to God.[101]

Twelve times the Torah states its warning to observe the Sabbath. The rabbis said: "A person who keeps the Sabbath holy, it is like he kept the whole Torah; and the one who desecrates the Sabbath, it is like he denied the whole Torah." Rabbi Kagan noted that many violated the Sabbath. In the earlier generations non-conformists were looked upon as apostates and were shunned by all Israel. But in some places, matters had become so confused that some people considered that they were also part of God's chosen inheritance but that they were exempt from the one command to observe the Sabbath. They set a bad example for others.[102]

In the *Mishnah Berurah*, Rabbi Kagan clarified more rules concerning the Sabbath. He extended the prescription for rest on the Sabbath to animals, stating that if a person rests his domestic animals on the Sabbath—even though arrangements could be made making their work permissible

---

[100]*Ibid.*, p. 181.
[101]*Ibid.*
[102]*Ibid.*

from a *halakhic* point of view— such a person would be rewarded by God.[103] In another instance, he permitted the reading of historical works such as *Josippon, Sefer Yehusin* and *Chronicles of Joseph ha-Cohen* on the Sabbath because they provide moral instruction.[104] But he prohibited newspaper reading because the Sabbath is to be a rest from all business matters.[105]

Rabbi Kagan also offered his objections to the growing practices of men and women dancing together, embracing one another, and kissing.- His objections were based on the reasoning that such acts may lead to immoral acts which may threaten the unity of the family—a key to Jewish survival.[106]

Nidhei Israel also contained details on the laws of preparation for the Sabbath, the laws for *Kiddush* (sanctification of wine, study of the Torah on the Sabbath, and general violations of the Sabbath.

Rabbi Kagan concluded *Nidhei Israel* with this thought:

> Behold my brothers after all that has been written in the book that I prepared to strengthen the dwellers in distant lands so that they will not be weakened in keeping the precepts of the Torah, nevertheless, the true way, and the most ideal, for him who wishes the grace of God, is to try arduously not to emigrate to distant lands.[107]

He goes on to say that if a person settles in a distant land for economic reasons, he should return after achieving financial success. Kagan reminds his readers that emigration to a land where open transgressions of the Torah take place will cause overwhelming fear—as if one were to see cruel people cutting off someone's limbs. The man who is conscious of God's presence will either try to stay in the "old country" or will return as quickly as possible in order to

---

[103]Kagan, *Mishnah Berurah*, III, 20.
[104]*Ibid*. III, 206.
[105]*Ibid*.
[106]*Ibid*., III, 372.
[107]Kagan, *Nidhei Israel*, p. 288.

train his children in the precepts of the Torah and love of God.[108]

Conclusion

Nidhei Israel was the response of the Rabbi to his son's suggestion that, like Jeremiah of centuries ago,[109] he should deal with the situation as it was and help those who had emigrated rather than commiserating over them. His book displays a great understanding of the religious, social, cultural, and economic problems facing Jews in other lands. His psychological and sociological insights into the pressures leading to laxity in observance of the Torah in a new environment led many to believe, wrongly, that he had lived in distant lands himself for many years.[110]

Some of the problems that Rabbi Kagan deals with in his book, *Nidhei Israel*, were not new. They had been dealt with before in the classical work of Moses Maimonides, *Guide to the Perplexed* and Judah Halevi's *Kuzari*. However, even these problems appeared in a new light under new circumstances, as Rabbi Kagan himself pointed out:

> Although the writings of the ancients, Maimonides, the *Kuzari*, and many other books have dealt in more detail with the reinvigorating of the roots of the Torah, however I did not desire to deal in detail because it is superfluous for most people and everything I have written would appear to them like one tried to prove the existence of the sun apparent to the eyes of all, likewise, there are the precepts of the Torah and its foundations and all it has set for the future and all the Prophets have set for all the Jews.[111]

Rabbi Kagan understood the religious, economic, social, political, and cultural problems of the Jews of his time. He endured, along with them, the persecutions and economic

---

108*Ibid.*
109Kagan, *Michtevei Hafets Hayyim*, p. 55.
101*Ibid.*, pp. 111-128.
111*Ibid.*, pp. 123ff.

hardships. He felt deeply the pain of the struggling immigrant Jew in the distant lands and the poverty at home. Rabbi Mendel Zaks told the author that Rabbi Kagan used "to lament and weep over the misery of the conditions of the Jews.[112]

Maimonides, Halevi, and others had been confronted with similar problems of their day, but their writings were not relevant to the problems faced by the Jews in the nineteenth and twentieth centuries. For a layman to read a book of the middle ages such as the *Guide to the Perplexed* by Maimonides was a very different experience that reading *Nidhei Israel* by Rabbi Kagan, a participant in the contemporary historical problems of the Jews. Furthermore, Maimonides and Halevi addressed themselves to the educated elite rather than to the man on the street. Rabbi Kagan was more concerned with the poor emigrant going to America than with proving the validity of Aristotle's philosophy. Therefore, in his writing of the *Nidhei Israel* the layman took priority. Not only did his book deal with very real problems faced by the immigrant Jews, but also it was written in simple language that the average Jew could understand. Rabbi Kagan's simplicity in writing brought him into close friendship with the layman and his vast knowledge of Biblical and rabbinic literature through the generations won him renown as one of the great rabbis of all time.

In more specific terms, one might point out some unique aspects of the ideas contained within Nidhei Israel. Firstly, Rabbi Kagan analyzed the causes for laxity in observance of the commands of the Torah in distant lands, and provided a program to counter them. He deals constructively with such perplexing problems as the presence of God, His testing of men, and who is a Jew.

Secondly, his selection of relevant laws from diverse sources was creative and led to a coherent code for the immigrant to follow.

Thirdly, he outlined specific programs for the functions

---

[112]Interview by the author with Rabbi Mendel Zaks, New York City, 1967.

of the Rabbi in distant lands, for communal leaders' role in establishing synagogues and schools, and for the layman's everyday religious and moral life. One can conclude that his response to the immigrant's religious and moral problems was generally programmatic.

THE ZIONIST QUESTION

In this section, the author will discuss various Zionist movements and Rabbi Kagan's response to Jewish settlement in Palestine, part of which was his work, *Likutei Halakhoth*. This section will discuss the significance of *Likutei Halakhoth* and the controversy it engendered. A conclusion will be offered at the end of the section.

The Times

The political, social, economic, and cultural discrimination under Tsar Alexander III, and the resulting pogroms against the Jews, precipitated Jewish emigration to America, Africa, England, Palestine, and other countries, as we have seen. In order to understand Rabbi Kagan's response to Jewish settlement in Palestine and to Zionism, we must trace some historical aspects of the *Hoveve Zion* (Lovers of Zion) and Zionist movements. These movements had a direct bearing on Kagan's reactions to the Jewish settlements in Palestine after 1890.

Throughout the nineteenth century Palestine had remained in a state of neglect. Vegetation and soil conservation were disregarded by the inhabitants, the roads were dangerous and impassable; and there was a scarcity of water. Epidemics, crops failures, and earthquakes brought about disease, starvation, and dangerous living conditions. In 1841 the European powers began to take an interest in Palestine and lines were drawn making the area part of the Ottoman Empire. "After church missions went into the area, consulates were set up for their protection. This protection worked to the advantage of Jews also, who flocked into the country and put themselves under the sovereignty of the various European powers."[1]

On his first visit to Jerusalem, in 1827, Moses Montefiore found fewer than a thousand souls in the city. On his seventh visit, in 1875, the estimate of the Jewish population was in excess of 12,000. By 1885, the Jewish population in Jerusalem had increased to 35,000.[2] In the early nineteenth century, Sephardic Jews[3] from the Levantine countries settled in Palestine and constituted a majority of the Jewish population. However, the pogroms and discriminations of Tsar Alexander III caused Ashkenazic Jews[4] to emigrate to Palestine in the second half of the nineteenth century and to become the majority. The hardships which they faced were similar to those confronted by the Sephardic Jews. The Ashkenazic Jews experienced tremendous difficulties in adjusting themselves to the new environment:

> The pioneer colonists in the ancient fatherland met with enormous obstacles in their path; the opposition of the Turkish government which hindered in every possible way the purchase of land and acquisition of property; the neglected condition of the soil, the uncivilized state of the neighboring Arabs, the lack of financial means and of agricultural experience.[5]

In spite of these problems, in 1882, the first year of the *Hoveve Zion* movement, the settlement of Rishon le-Zion, near Jaffa, became a reality.[6] Subsequently, a few more settlements developed: Ekron and Ghederah, Yesod Hama'alah,

---

[1]Elbogen, *A Century of Jewish Life*, p. 245; see also Sokolow, *History of Zionism*; Citron, *Toldot Hibbat Zion*; and Dinaburg, *Hibbat Zion*.
[2]*Ibid.*
[3]Jews of Spanish and Portuguese origin, whose customs, rituals, synagogue services, and Hebrew pronounciation differ from those of Ashkenazim.
[4]The name Ashkenazim applied to the Jews of Germany and North France from the tenth century on. In the middle of the sixteenth century, the term Ashkanazim came to include the Jews of Eastern Europe.
[5]Dubnow, *History of the Jews in Russia and Poland*, II, 375.
[6]*Ibid.*

Rosh-Pinah, and Zikron Yakov, in the Galilee. The last two settlements were founded by Rumanian Jews.

Rabbi Ariah Leib Kagan wrote:

> I remember that in 1890 and 1891, when they began to expel our brothers from Moscow, there emerged a big movement to our Holy Land. Hundreds and thousands of the evicted Jews hastened to take refuge in the land of our fathers. They bought land; they planted vineyards; they established colonies; inside the colony they congregated at meetings; they set up societies; they sent representatives to purchase land. Property-owners sold their homes and possessions; and with the money they settled with joy in Palestine. They were looking hopefully to find happiness and prosperity there.[7]

The *Hoveve Zion* in Russia was able to attract the support of the prominent Rabbi Samuel Mohilever (1824-1898) of Bialystok.[8] His affiliation with the *Hoveve Zion* was largely instrumental in weakening the opposition of the Orthodox masses, which were inclined to look upon this political movement as a rival to the traditional Messianic ideas of Judaism.[9]

At the same time, Moses Lilienblum and Dr. Leo Pinsker (1821-1891) organized *Hoveve Zion* societies in Odessa and other Russian cities. Towards the end of 1884 the delegates of these societies came together at a conference in the Prussian border town of Kattowitz.[10] On that occasion a fund was established under the name of "Mazkeret Moshe" (A Memorial to Moses), in honor of Sir Moses Montefiore, whose hundredth birthday was celebrated that year. *Hoveve Zion* centers in Odessa and Warsaw collected and sent money for the settlements in Palestine.

---

[7]Kagan, *Michtevei Hafets Hayyim*, p. 43.
[8]Sokolow, *History of Zionism*, II, 289ff
[9]Dubnow, *History of the Jews in Russia and Poland*, p. 377.
[10]The conference was held in Kattowitz because such a conference was impossible in Russia due to the danger of police interference.

Rabbi Kagan's Position and Response to Jewish Settlement in Palestine.

The settlement of Jews in Palestine made such a tremendous impact upon Rabbi Kagan that he was moved to contemplate settlement in Palestine. His thoughts are related by his son, Ariah Leib Kagan:

> At this time I received a letter from my father. . . .
> In it he informed me about the immense movement among our people in every corner of the country to settle in Palestine; and he calculated that the days are days of the coming of the Messiah; and since God remembered his people, perhaps it is the beginning of the gathering of the dispersed Jews that takes place before the coming of the Messiah; and if we had the means we would buy land and settle in Palestine. Since we do not have the means to settle in Palestine, let us do what is within our reach. Behold, if God shall return his exiled people to our land, are we not obligated to build the Temple and the altar, and to bring sacrifices.[11]

Rabbi Kagan and his sons were of priestly origin, and Kagan felt that they must know the laws of sacrifices if they were ever to go to Palestine. The order of the Talmud dealing with sacrificial and Temple ritual is called *Seder Kodashim*. Rabbi Israel Meir Kagan wrote the following:

> The order of the Talmud dealing with sacrifices and the Temple is very deep and profound . . . ; and we lack the expertise in sacrificial and Temple laws, as the Rambam in his time was concerned over the matter. Therefore, my son, I have decided in honor of God to study contemplatively the *Seder Kodashim,* beginning with the tractate of the Talmud dealing with the slaughtering of the sacrifices which is the most important in the *Seder Kodashim* . . . it will include the study of Rashi, Tosafoth, and

---

[11]Kagan, *Michtevei Hafets Hayyim,* pp. 43ff.

Rambam; and afterwards to derive conclusions from
the subject of study by using the method of the
general rules of the Talmud, as the Rif, and the
Rosh have already demonstrated the method. . . .
Rambam's work will be of great help to overcome
obstacles; and after each subject each law will be explained . . . ; and if we shall merit the help of God,
the book will be published; therefore the number of
people engrossing in the study of sacrificial and Temple laws will be on the increase.[12]

"This was the content of my father's letter, may he rest
in peace," wrote Rabbi Ariah Leib Kagan. "I answered that
I agreed with his proposal; and in a few days I would begin
the study of the tractate of 'slaughtering sacrifices' in order
to become acquainted with it."[13] Subsequently, Rabbi Kagan
planned to incorporate this study in a book on sacrificial and
Temple laws.

Rabbi Ariah Kagan and his tubercular younger brother
helped in the writing of the difficult book. Rabbi Ariah wrote
that he was slow in getting started because by nature he was
slow in getting things done. The most difficult subjects dealing with sacrificial and Temple laws consumed much of his
time. After two years of investigations, the Kagans showed
how the slaughtering of sacrifices could be reinstated. The
manuscript was shown to eminent rabbis who praised it. One
of the prominent rabbis said that "this manuscript is a sign
of the spark of redemption."[14] Ariah advised his father to
name the book *Halakhoth Kodashim*. Rabbi Kagan, reluc-
tant to use this title because Isaac Al-Fasi entitled his work
Halakhoth (Laws) and because he was too humble to have
his book compared to Al-Fasi's, called it *Likutei Halakhoth
(Collection of Laws)*.[15]

Before publishing the book, Rabbi Kagan sent copies for
official approval to outstanding rabbis. His son was surprised

---

[12]*Ibid.*, p. 44.
[13]*Ibid.*
[14]*Ibid.*, p. 45.
[15]*Ibid.*

that so many rabbinical approvals were solicited. But Rabbi Kagan included these because he wished to arm himself against possible critics. Rabbi Hayim Soloveichik of Brisk, Russia, who was one of the greatest Talmudical scholars of that time, wrote the following in his approval:

> Rabbi Israel Meir Kagan, a Talmudical scholar and a righteous man, has shown me parts of his manuscript *Likutei Halakhoth* on the Order *Kodashim*. I consider it a great contribution to Talmudic learning since it is a good source to the understanding of the Order *Kodashim*, for which we lack rabbinical commentaries and laws. While we have rabbinical commentaries and laws for the rest of the orders of the Talmud, this order is completely devoid of commentaries. The Rabbi, the profound scholar, has delved deeply and widely into the order dealing with sacrificial and Temple law.[16]

Rabbi Soloveichik concluded that the book would "open the door to those who try to understand the laws of sacrifices and Temple. Talmudical scholars will rejoice with the book, and they will derive usefulness from it."[17]

Controversy Over Likutei Halakhoth

Yet, when *Likutei Halakhoth* was published, controversy immediately followed. Some rabbis wrote complaining that people would think that it was not necessary to study the sources of the Talmud dealing with sacrificial and Temple laws, but instead would think it sufficient to study the *Likutei Halakhoth*.[18] They pointed out that an Hasidic rabbi had created a similar controversy by writing a Talmudical text based on the *Mishnahoth Taharoth (Studies of Purities)* which could have convinced people that the Amoraim[19]

[16]*Likutei Halakhoth*, p. 3.
[17]*Ibid.*
[18]Kagan, *Michtevei Hafets Hayyim*, p. 59.
[19]*Amoraim* means speakers or interpreters. The title was given to all teachers of Jewish law, who explained the Mishnah, discussed its rulings, and reinterpreted its decisions. Their work was eventually incorporated into what is today known as Gemara, which together with the Mishnah forms the Palestinian and Babylonian Talmud.

wrote it. They challenged Rabbi Kagan's attempt to provide practical laws dealing with the study of sacrifices and Temple ritual on the grounds that a confusion might arise concerning sources.[20]

Rabbi Kagan replied that

> other authors in past generations who compiled "Laws" like Al-Fasi and Rosh also shortened the Talmud by deriving the conclusive law. True, they did not claim to derive the conclusive law in the case of sacrificial and Temple Talmudical study, because sacrificial and Temple laws do not apply in exile; however, we, who are approaching Messianic times, are obligated to derive practical law dealing with sacrifices and the Temple.[21]

From Warsaw, Rabbi Itzhak Grodzenski informed Rabbi Kagan that one of the Hasidic rabbis strongly opposed the book, and would not be satisfied until

> he teaches the rabbi from Lithuania a lesson because he composed a new tractate of the Talmud; and because Rabbi Israel Meir Kagan was not willing to receive any advice concerning his dreams and vanities.[22]

Significance of the Work Likutei Halakhoth

The *Likutei Halakhoth* has two introductions. In the first, Rabbi Kagan wrote:

> Behold, I am surprised that people are not more engrossed in the study of the order of the Talmud dealing with sacrifices and Temple. First of all it is a religious precept to study about sacrifices just as it

---

[20]Kagan, *Michtevei Hafets Hayyim*, p. 59.

[21]*Ibid.*

[22]*Ibid.* Rabbi Kagan took the objections of the Hasidic rabbi seriously. He told Rabbi Itzhak Grodzenski to inform the Hasidic rabbi that he would publish the *Likutei Halakoth* side by side with the text of the Talmudic tractate dealing with sacrificial slaughtering. This plan met with the approval of the Warsaw rabbi and of all other critical rabbis. The Hasidic rabbi and Rabbi Kagan met later and became friendly.

is a commandment to study the other orders of the Talmud. Secondly studying about sacrifices is tantamount to offering sacrifices. Instead the opposite is happening, namely few people study the Order of Kodashim.[23]

Many of the Talmudical students do not know the basics of sacrifices, Rabbi Kagan argued. If the Jews were told that the Temple would be rebuilt, even a small boy would be glad to participate in the sacrifices. Surely, consideration should be given to the study of sacrifices. Studying does not require walking to the Temple and spending large sums of money,[24] indeed, it is very near us. Everyone in his house or synagogue can study about sacrifices.[25]

The study of Seder Kodashim is more important than the study of any other order of the Talmud because more references to sacrifices are found in the Torah than for the other orders of the Talmud.[26] The greatest part of the book of Leviticus deals with sacrifices.[27]

In the second introduction to the book Rabbi Kagan wrote:

Let no man suspect that my purpose for writing the book was God forbid to put on the garment of the Rabbis of the Mishnah and the Talmud . . . for how will a poor ragged man who exists on pieces of bread gathered by begging at the homes of the rich feel if he went and associated in the company of nobility; and to think that by associating with them, people would consider him also as a nobleman; however, in the end his ragged clothes and his begging bag will betray his humble status . . . and so I, the humble and poorly-informed in the study of Torah . . .

23Kagan, *Likutei Halakhoth*, p. 2.
24In ancient Israel Jews were required to visit Jerusalem and the Temple three times a year; on Tabernacles, on Passover, and on Pentecost. Sacrifices, first fruit, tithes to the Priests, Levites and the poor were required of the visitors.
25Kagan, *Likutei Halakhoth*, p. 2.
26*Ibid.*, p. 3.
27*Ibid.*

how can I feel that my work is like the work of the cedars of Lebanon that God has planted in the first generations, who enlightened the whole world with their learning of the Torah?[28]

Rabbi Kagan wrote that his work was meant only as a compilation of laws of the great sages of the previous generations concerning the sacrifices and the Temple.[29] Indeed, Rabbi Kagan was a man of great humility. His son, Rabbi Ariah Leib Kagan, wrote:

> I will not know to this day what strange spirit affected some of the rabbis to demean and to question the works of my father, for who can compare with him in faithfulness to God and His Torah, in instituting love for God to all Israel and in spreading Torah among all his people; perhaps if I do not commit a sin with my mouth, the cause, God forbid, was jealousy because the critics themselves did not think of writing such a book.[30]

Rabbi Kagan believed deeply that the Messianic days are approaching and that God would gather the dispersed Jews from the four corners of the earth and lead them to Palestine. Upon arriving in the Holy Land, Jews would be obligated to observe the precepts dealing with Israel, to construct the Temple, and to offer sacrifices, and the *Likutei Halakhoth* would guide them in the latter two matters.[31]

A rich man in Warsaw, Isaac Broda, contributed 24,000 rubles to provide scholarships to outstanding students engrossed in the study of sacrificial and Temple Law. Rabbi

---

[28]*Ibid.*, pp. 5ff.

[29]*Ibid.*

[30]*Ibid.*, p. 60. Once the brother-in-law of Ariah Kagan, Rabbi Zvi Levenson, told the story that one of the great rabbis of Lithuania accidentally came forth with the following words: "I should have thought to publish such a book, but Rabbi Israel Meir Kagan surpassed me in thought."

[31]Interview with Rabbi Mendel Zaks, June 28, 1967. According to Rabbi Zaks, the sudden exodus to Palestine influenced Rabbi Kagan to write *Likutei Halakhoth*. Rabbi Kagan was also convinced that the Messianic days would alleviate the persecution of the Jews.

Kagan selected ten such young men and provided them with five rubles a week to devote four hours a day to the study of Seder Kodashim. The philanthropist Hirsh Sienberg of Germany contributed money so that another five students could engage in similar study. Among the many students who devoted their time to this special course in *Seder Kodashim* were three brilliant young men—Moshe Smorgonski, his brother Isaiah Smorgonski, and David Silmanovski of Ilia, Poland—all of whom were killed in 1932 by the Nazis.[32] Rabbi Mordecai Savitsky, now of Boston, also studied *Seder Kodashim*. Rabbi Mendel Zaks, now of New York City, was in charge of this program in the *yeshiva* at Radun. One of the students spoke of Kagan's attempt to revive the study of *Kodashim*.

> But the ultimate achievement of his efforts to revive *Kodashim* was his massive *Likutei Halakhoth*. It is not his most popular work, but it is his most scholarly. . . . Rabbi Isaac ben Jacob Al-Fasi (1013-1103) had condensed the *Halakhic* parts of the Talmud. Styled "The Little Talmud," his work had omitted all those laws not applicable to the Diaspora, notably *Kodashim*. Rabbi Israel Meir Kagan, convinced by his deep faith of the nearness of Israel's restoration to the Holy Land, supplied what Al-Fasi had left out.[33]

Rabbi Kagan's Reaction to Hoveve Zion and Zionist Movement's Secularism

Rabbi Kagan firmly believed the Messianic age was at hand, but he also believed Jewry had a responsibility to help realize it. He was disturbed that the leadership of the movement to return to Palestine was vested in the hands of the *Maskilim*-inspired *Hoveve Zion* movement. He and other religious persons remembered that in the past reform Jews had mocked or, at best, ignored Palestine. They recalled that

---

[32]Letter from Mr. Leib Eckman, July 5, 1967, Chelsea, Mass. to the author.

[33]Yosher, "Israel Meir Ha-Kohen—Hafets Hayyim," pp. 468ff.

former teachers of the leaders of the *Hoveve Zion* had "erased from the Prayer Book all the blessings that make mention of the land."[34] But suddenly the *Maskilim* were gathering money for the colonies in Palestine, and establishing *Hoveve Zion* associations in Russia. Rabbi Kagan and other religious Jews were upset with some members of the *Hoveve Zion* movement in Odessa when they published virulent articles against the Mishnah and the Talmud and led the young generation astray from traditional Judaism.[35] The rabbi did not have confidence in the followers of the *Haskalah*. He said:

> Can from such people thrust forth an iota of goodness? Can such people merit the Divine Presence to guide their deeds? And if God will not construct the Temple, the work of the *Maskilim* will be in vain. If they examine the nature of the members of the *Hoveve Zion* center in Odessa, Russia, the spiritual values of the majority's members are contrary to the religion of Israel.[36]

The leader of Odessa's center of *Hoveve Zion* was perhaps the least learned of the group:

> He did not even know the holy tongue (even though his father was one of the greatest enlighteners in the generation before ours, and published books in our tongue, despite this he did not find it necessary to teach his son as part of the other studies our holy tongue and our Prayer Book) .[37]

Another leader of the *Hoveve Zion* was Moses Lilienblum, who saw the ways of the Talmud as nothing but superstition and his Orthodox education as a sin against youth. Another man who angered the rabbis was Peretz Smolenskin (1842-1885) , who battled the rabbis and Orthodoxy from the pages

---

[34]Kagan, *Michtevei Hafets Hayyim*, p. 69.

[35]*Ibid.*, p. 70.

[36]*Ibid.*

[37]Ibid., Dr. Leo Pinsker fits this description. He did not know Hebrew; he was the son of Simhah Pinsker (1801-1864), a Hebrew grammarian and the author of several books; and he was one of the most important leaders of the *Hoveve Zion* movement in Odessa.

of the literary periodical *Ha-Shahar (The Dawn)*. Both of these men became strong supporters of Jewish nationalism.

Rabbi Kagan received many letters from rabbis complaining that the Jews in Palestine, assisted financially and morally by the *Hoveve Zion* of Russia, were lax in observing the Torah and its precepts. The *Hoveve Zion* leaders were not only "guilty of leading astray the Jews in the Diaspora, but also of wanting to promulgate their ideas and abominations in the only remaining place of refuge, that is a holy place for all the Jews."[38] Letters were sent from Palestine relating that Jews in the colonies were transgressing the Sabbath and were eating forbidden food.[39]

In 1888 Rabbi Kagan met Rabbi Elijahu Kratinger of Vilna, the President of the *Halukah*.[40] Rabbi Kratinger informed him that 2,000 families in Palestine were starving. He suggested that speakers should go from city to city in Eastern Europe (as the *Hoveve Zion* leaders did) and speak about the poverty of the Jewish families to raise funds for their aid. During the discussion Rabbi Jacob Lipschitz of Kovna told the President of the *Halukah*, "It is not appropriate for the *Halukah*, which has relied for hundreds of years upon the urgent call of great Sages to raise the money now depending upon speakers." Rabbi Ariah Leib Kagan asked Rabbi Kratinger why the young people of the families didn't go to work. The answer was that they couldn't find work. Rabbi Kagan and the others were also told by Rabbi Kratinger that the settlers in the colonies did not study Torah and did not pray.[41]

Many religious Jews did not object to the establishment of a Jewish state in Palestine; but they protested the secularism of the leadership. Devout Jews were deeply hurt by the *Maskilim* belief that God would not have a hand in the establishment of the Holy Land. The *Maskilim* dis-

---

[38]*Ibid.*

[39]*Ibid.*

[40]A system for the support of Jews in Palestine with funds raised abroad. The tradition of subsidizing Palestinian Jews goes back to Talmudic times, when higher schools of learning received such support.

[41]Kagan, *Michtevei Hafets Hayyim*, p. 71.

regarded the Sages and they did not permit rabbis to interfere with their plans for Israel. These enlightened Jews referred to rabbis as "rebels of the Enlightenment who grow wise by exploiting the poor."[42]

By nature Rabbi Kagan avoided quarrels; and in the Zionist movement dispute he tried to stay clear of taking sides, even though he was heart-broken at the news that the Torah was being excluded by Zionists from the Palestinian setlements and from their life in Europe.

He spoke of his disappointment only in private to his friends and to friends of the *yeshivoth*.[43] But he received many complaints about his silence and his failure to protest the Zionist movement's mockery of religious observance. Soon his stand on the secularism of the Zionist movement became widely known among the religious elements of Jewry. The Zionist leaders, who were seeking his support, quarreled with him, claiming he had accepted false information on secular teaching and on the laxity in observance of Torah in the colonies in Palestine.

In further response to the secularism of the Zionists, Rabbi Kagan forbade his students to join the Zionist movement. His objections increased after Asher Ginzberg (1856-1927), an enlightened Zionist reputed for always telling the truth, testified upon visiting all the schools in Palestine that the critical method was applied in the study of the Holy Books in the schools.[44]

One of the many articles by Zionists was reported to have claimed:

> A nation is composed of the language and the land, and without them it is not called a nation. Therefore, they urged the people to build the land and simplify the language.[45]

Ariah Kagan wrote that when one of the *Maskilim* wrote, in

---

[42]*Ibid.*, p. 73.

[43]*Ibid.*

[44]*Ibid.*; Ginzberg became a vocal opponent of political Zionism as a solution to the Jewish problem.

[45]Kagan, *Michtevei Hafets Hayyim*, p. 74.

Ha-Meliz, that it was possible to be called a Jew without keeping the Torah, "then my father could not keep silent any longer."[46]

Rabbi Kagan's response was swift and to the point:

> Our nation exists only because of the keeping of the Torah and the precepts, and not because of the land and the language. If we do not heed the precepts of God, the land and the language will not save us. Our fathers were already there, and because they sinned they were exiled from the Holy Land.[47]

Rabbi Kagan's objections were shared by religious and non-religious Jews. Both groups knew that Rabbi Kagan was not one of the extremist Orthodox Jews opposing Zionism; he did not demand that the pioneers engross themselves in the study of Torah and prayer but only that they comport themselves according to the precepts of the Torah, as all observant Jews in exile should.[48]

Rabbi Kagan himself longed to settle in Palestine. In 1925 he wrote,

> My brothers, children of Israel, when I merit the mercy of God . . . to settle in the Holy Land . . . I said to myself that I shall separate myself from my brothers . . . with a blessing . . . I beseech God, the Keeper of Israel, He shall help his people in time of trouble, captivity . . . and he shall hasten the Messiah to them in order to bring good and comforting tidings.[49]

And in 1927 he reiterated:

> All the Jews believe in the coming of the Messiah, and Elijah will come and bring good tidings to us before the coming of the Messiah; and in every

---

[46]*Ibid.*

[47]*Ibid.*

[48]*Ibid.*, p. 76.

[49]Letter from Rabbi Israel Meir Kagan, Vilna, Rosh Chodesh Elul, 1925, in Kagan, *Michtevei Hafets Hayyim,* p. 156.

prayer we recite to God that He shall dispatch to us
our righteous Messiah, and He shall construct the
Temple as soon as possible in our days . . . therefore we are obligated to prepare ourselves in the
study of Temple and sacrificial ritual in order to
merit the Messiah.[50]

In the *Mishnah Berurah* he also claimed that revisions of
the calendar were unnecessary because the Messianic age was
at hand.[51]

In 1928 he actually completed his preparations for departure to Palestine. But when his plans became known, a
representation of leading rabbis and deans of Polish *yeshivoth*
urged him to postpone his journey because they needed his
guidance during a critical time. As a result, Rabbi Kagan
died without fulfilling his dream of seeing the Holy Land.

The Rabbi's view on Palestine can be summarized by the
statement:

The soul of Israel is the sacred Torah; and the body
of Israel is the land of Israel. Surely the soul cannot exist without the body; and all the precepts of
the Torah, depending on the land for their fulfillment, cannot be carried out without the land of
Israel.[52]

According to Rabbi Kagan, there was no future for the Jews
in exile. In one place Jews were not allowed at all; in another they were persecuted; in a third place they were forbidden to trade or own property. Despite all the hardships
of exile, the Jewish people exist; but the land of Israel without the Torah is a body without a soul; and goodness is the
result of the amalgamation of Torah and the land of Israel.[53]

---

[50]Letter from Rabbi Israel Meir Kagan, Radun, Poland, Adar bet, 1927,
in Kagan, *Michtevei Hafets Hayyim*, pp. 21-23.
[51]Kagan, *Mishnah Berurah*, IV, 575.
[52]Rabbi Israel Meir Kagan, *Hafets Hayyim al Ha-Torah*, (*Hafets Hayyim's Commentary on the Torah*), edited by Rabbi Samuel Greiniman
(Tel-Aviv: Safriti, 1943), p. 99.
[53]*Ibid.*

One of the Rabbi's students wrote:

. . . in the radiance of his faith there was no shadow of doubt. He looked confidently to the fulfillment of divine promise. . . . He prayed for Israel's total rehabilitation, not a homeland in reduced territory or mere political independence. It was not worthwhile, he said, to become another Albania or even another Belgium after nineteen centuries of suffering. A state must be re-established on Torah foundations. It must be a reign of justice and godliness, with holy Temple restored and sacrificial offerings reinstated.[54]

Conclusion

Initially, Rabbi Kagan was inspired by the settlement of Jews in Palestine to feel that the Messianic age was approaching and that he must settle in Israel. He seems to have seen the contemporary times as the beginning of Jewish redemption and return to Eretz Israel. Convinced by his deep faith of the nearness of Israel's restoration to the Holy Land, he wrote *Likutei Halakhoth* to revive the study of Temple and sacrificial ritual in preparation.

Despite his firm belief that the coming of the Messiah was near, he also believed that the Jewish people must help realize the Messianic age. He was deeply disturbed that the leadership of the *Hoveve Zion* and later of the Zionist movements was in the hands of Jewish secularists. He did not encourage mass emigration of religious Jews to Israel because of the secular orientation of the leadership and because of the laxity of observance of the Sabbath, dietary laws, and other commands of the Torah in the colonies.[55] Thus, in the later part of the nineteenth century and the first two decades of the twentieth century, Rabbi Kagan did not help organize immigration of religious Jews to Israel—a program which might have led to a more religiously oriented society there.

The Zionist leaders, who were seeking Rabbi Kagan's sup-

[54]Yosher, *Ha-Hafets Hayyim*, p. 468.
[55]Kagan, *Michtevei Hafets Hayyim*, pp. 75-76.

port, questioned his judgement in accepting information about secularism and non-observance of the Torah in Palestine. But his judgement was confirmed when Asher Ginzberg, himself an enlightened Zionist known for his honesty, testified after visiting all the schools in Palestine that the critical method was applied to the study of the Bible. It was only then that Rabbi Kagan acted upon his judgment by forbidding his students to join the Zionist movement.

When the followers of secular Zionism defined Jewish nationalism as "a nation composed of the language and the land," Rabbi Kagan disagreed. He held that the essence of Judaism is observance of the Torah and not sharing a common land or language. Jewish nationalism should consist of both religion and the land as one cannot exist without the other. The lessons of history seem to indicate that Rabbi Kagan's analytical view was correct in its claim that the precepts of the Torah rather than the Hebrew language or the dream of returning someday to Israel kept the Jews from assimilation. Moreover, in contemporary Israel, as in the Shalit case, the Israeli government has passed legislation which is based on the principle that nationalism cannot be separated from religion.[56]

---

[56]See pp. 96-100.

CHAPTER THREE

JEWS IN RUSSIA AND POLAND

JEWS UNDER COMMUNISM

T HIS section deals with Rabbi Kagan's emigration to Russia, the Russian Civil War, the Bolshevik stand on the Jews, Rabbi Kagan's departure from Russia, the Bolshevik stand on Zionism, and the Bolshevik stand on Jewish institutions. It depicts Rabbi Kagan's efforts on behalf of Soviet Jewry, and ends with a conclusion.

Rabbi Kagan's Emigration to Russia

In August, 1914, at the outbreak of the First World War, Russian Jewry found itself directly involved in the fighting. Moreover, Jews were now made to serve in the Russian armed forces to the full extent of their able-bodied manpower. It has been estimated that six hundred thousand Jews wore Russian uniforms between 1914 and 1917, and this number exceeded their ratio in the Empire's population.[1] Jewish willingness to fight for Russia was the more remarkable as the

----

[1]Baron, *The Russian Jews*, p. 187.

Russian government continued to pursue its old discriminatory policies. There were cases of Jewish soldiers who

> had distinguished themselves in the Russo-Japanese
> War. These men had thereby earned residence per-
> mits in the interior of Russia. When the former sol-
> diers were again drafted for active service, their fam-
> ilies were ordered to leave the interior of Russia,
> since the fathers had departed.[2]

When Jewish soldiers were wounded on the battlefield, they
were usually treated in hospitals in the interior, but upon
their discharge they were ordered to return to the Jewish pale
of settlement.

As the German army advanced into Polish territory, many
Jews were confronted with the problem of being taken cap-
tive by the German army or retreating to Russia proper.
Rabbi Israel Meir Kagan and his students were among those
who migrated to Russia. The Rabbi wandered as a refugee
from 1915 to 1921, from Smilovitz, to Semyatch, and to
Snovsk before returning to his hometown of Radun.

In Russia Rabbi Kagan was an eyewitness to the Bolshevik Revolution. The Russia of Nicholas II was attacked
from within by revolutionaries and from without by the
strong armies of the Germans. Many Jewish Bolsheviks recognized Rabbi Kagan and showed him respect and admira-
tion during his residence in Russia. This respect grew out of
a regard for the Rabbi's simplicity in dress, his humility, and
his stress on morality.[3]

While in Russia, in 1916, Rabbi Kagan was asked by the
Jewish leaders of the city of Smilovitz to make an appeal on
behalf of the Relief Fund for Passover. From the pulpit he
said:

> Brethren, I want your advice, I am growing old, as
> you see, and before long, expect to be summoned

---

[2]*Ibid.*, p. 188.

[3]Letter from Rabbi Mendel Zaks, to the author, June 28, 1967, Brooklyn,
New York; see also Yosher, "Israel Meir Ha-Kohen—Hafets Hayyim,"
p. 470.

before the heavenly tribunal of justice. Suppose I should be asked, 'Israel Meir, you were in Smilovitz. Tell us something about your brethren there.' What should I reply? To say that you are charitable would not be the truth; and all my life I have never lied. To tell the truth, that you are not charitable, would, on the other hand, involve evil speech, which as you know, I also guard myself against. What should I do?[4]

The Jews of Smilovitz, Russia, responded to his call by making contributions to the Relief Fund.

Also in 1916, while residing in Smilovitz, Rabbi Kagan published an article entitled, "Pursuing Charity and Loving Kindness." In it he wrote that people were starving in hundreds of cities, and he urged every Jew to help the war victims as much as possible.

As the war progressed, Jewish sufferings kept growing; they affected even the mortality figures. True, the cholera epidemic, raging in western Russia earlier in 1915, was successfully stamped out by the German forces, for their own sake, by November of that year. But because of malnutrition and overcrowded quarters in Warsaw (which at one time accommodated 80,000 Jewish refugees), Vilna and other major cities, Jews were decimated by recurrent attacks of typhoid.[5]

The policy of mass evacuation of Russian territory at the

---

[4]Yosher, "Israel Meir Ha-Kohen—Hafets Hayyim," pp. 469ff.

[5]The result was that, for instance, in Vilna, where before 1914 the annual Jewish death rate had ranged from 20.4 to 22:6 per 1,000 inhabitants, it increased to 34.4 in March, 1916, 41.4 in December, 1916, and 68.2 in 1917. In March, 1917 it reached the staggering total of 97.5 per 1,000. At the same time the number of births dwindled from 1,502 in 1913 to 489 in 1917. Similar conditions prevailed also in other occupied territories. On the Russian side of the front, too, the Jewish birth-rate declined sharply while mortality went up and up. In Elizavetgrad, symptoms of biological retardation had become noticeable before the war, the Jewish increase in population, as a result of excess natality was reduced from 201 in 1913 to 164 in 1914 and 77 in 1915. This surplus turned into a deficit of 87-88 souls in the subsequent two years. (Baron, *The Russian Jews*, p. 194).

approach of German and Austrian troops had uprooted 600,000 Jews.[6] A subsequent survey showed that only 5 percent of the evacuees were able to take their movable possessions with them; twenty-two percent were removed with such speed that they had to leave everything behind; the rest managed to take some of their possessions.[7]

> In all, these refugees, voluntary as well as forced, sustained losses estimated at 350 to 400 million dollars—a huge amount, indeed, in view of the dollar's still high purchasing power.[8]

Because of the scarcity of food and other necessities, life was very difficult for Rabbi Kagan and his students in Smilovitz, and the Rabbi tried to raise money to provide food for his students.

The Civil War

In 1918 the Rabbi and his students were forced to leave the city of Semyatch because the Civil War in Soviet Russia broke out between the Reds and the Whites.[9] With the Civil War the pogroms against the Jews were renewed. The Ukraine became the main center for anti-Semitism and pogroms during this period.[10]

---

[6]*Ibid.,* p. 191.

[7]*Ibid.*

[8]*Ibid.*

[9]The Reds were also known as the Bolsheviks, or Communists, and were led by Lenin; the Whites were opponents of the Bolshevik regime who were led by Alexander V. Kolchak in the Civil Army. See Anton I. Denikin, *Ocherki Russkoi Smutz* (Paris, 1921-1926), 5 vols. for details on the Civil War; see also *The Memoirs of General Wrangel, the Last Commander in Chief of the Russian National Army* (New York: Duffield, 1930).

[10]"The upshot was that, according to fairly reliable statistical accounts prepared in the 1920's some 30 pogroms and 50 lesser riots ravaged the Ukrainian communities in the course of 1918. Thereafter, in a constant crescendo, the monthly toll of 24 pogroms—50 lesser riots in January, 1919, increased to 120 pogroms and 20 lesser riots in May, and reached the record of 127 pogroms and 32 lesser riots in August, 1919. In all, the year 1919 witnessed 685 major and 249 minor attacks on Jews. The number began diminishing in the course of 1920, whose total of 132 major and 36 minor assaults did not greatly exceed the attacks of August 1919 alone. In the first few months of 1921 the storm blew out completely. The direct loss of Jewish lives was enormous, easily exceeding 30,000 slain. Together with those who later died prematurely from wounds, contagious and other ill-

The Bolshevik Stand on the Jews

The Red army appeared to be more humane than the White in the treatment of Jews because the Bolsheviks, led by Lenin, were not anti-Semitic. Lenin's stand against anti-Semitism stemmed from his beliefs that discrimination against the Jews itself prevented assimilation and that anti-Semitism was contrary to the basic socialist ideology of equality. Lenin and his associates sensed a danger to the Bolshevik revolution in anti-Semitism,

> especially since the early disproportionate share of Jewish leadership in the Communist Party was being used to excellent advantage by the anti-Soviet propogandists in and outside the country.[11]

On July 27, 1918 the Council of People's Commissars decreed harsh measures against any form of anti-Semitic propaganda:

> The Council of People's Commissars declares that the anti-Semitic movement and pogroms against the Jews are fatal to the interests of the workers' and peasants' revolution and calls upon the toiling people of Socialist Russia to fight this evil with all the means at their disposal.
>
> National hostility weakens the ranks of our revolutionaries, disrupts the united front of the toilers without distinctions of nationality and helps only our enemies.
>
> The Council of People's Commissars instructs all Soviet deputies to take uncompromising measures to

---

nesses contracted during these disturbances, the number may well have reached 150,000, or some 10 percent of the whole population. The massacres thus left in their wake some 100,000 new widows and 200,000 orphans over and above the multitude of war widows and orphans. In addition there was raping in Jewish women and a wholesale destruction of Jewish property, communal as well as private. No less than 28 percent of all Ukrainian Jewish houses were said to have been burned, and 10 percent abandoned by their owners." (Baron, *The Russian Jews*, pp. 222ff.; see also Elias Heifetz, *The Slaughter of the Jews in the Ukraine in 1919* (New York: T. Seltzer, 1921) and A. D. Rosenthal, *Megillat Ha-Tebah* 3 vols. (Jerusalem, 1929-31).)

[11]Baron, *The Russian Jews*, p. 214.

tear the anti-Semitic movement out by the roots. Pogromists and pogrom-agitators are to be placed outside the law.[12]

Although the last part was rather vague:

it was the only item which put teeth into the declaration. Ironically, we have later testimony that while Sverdlov, the Jew, prepared the main text of the declaration, Lenin personally added the final paragraph in red ink.[13]

Lenin took the danger of anti-Semitism so seriously that on March 31, 1919 he broadcast an appeal to the Russian people concerning the anti-Semitic menace.[14]

Rabbi Kagan's Departure from Russia

Rabbi Kagan was well informed regarding his future in the Soviet Union. Although he was well treated by the Communists he decided to leave Russia for two reasons. He knew that religion was contrary to the Communist ideology; in 1905 Lenin had written that "our propaganda includes the propaganda of atheism."[15] The pogroms, the looting, and the anti-Semitism of the Whites convinced the Rabbi that Jews would likewise have no future under the White generals Kolchak, Denikin, Petliura, and other. Therefore, he and his family decided to return to Radun, Poland.[16]

General Wladyslaw Sikorski[17] helped Rabbi Kagan return

---

[12]*Ibid.*, p. 215; see also *Izvestia*, July 27, 1918.

[13]Baron, *The Russian Jews*, p. 215.

[14]Vladimir Lenin, *Sochinoniia*, 2nd ed. XXIV (1932), 203; see also Anatolii V. Lunacharskii, *Ob Antisemitizme* (Moscow, 1929); and Solomon M. Schwarz, *The Jews in the Soviet Union* (Syracuse: Syracuse University Press, 1951), pp. 264ff., 289, n. 14.

[15]Vladimir Lenin, "Socialism and Religion," *Selected Works* (New York, n.d.), XI, 658. Lenin reiterated the Marxist view of religion. Religion is the opium of the masses and a spiritual intoxication which is used to ensure an orderly human existence by the slaves of capital. Religion teaches patience in this world for the people who work with the sweat of their brow all their lives. It teaches charity to those who exploit the working class, thus justifying their exploiting feats and providing them with tickets to paradise for a reasonable price.

[16]Letter from Rabbi Mendel Zaks to the author, June 28, 1967.

[17]During the Second World War, General Sikorski became Premier of the Pro-Western Polish Government-in-exile.

to Radun. In 1921 Rabbi Kagan wrote a letter of thanks to him. The letter, written in Polish, was published in 1930 in the Polish newspaper *Dobry Wieczor*.[18] He wrote another letter to Sikorski in Hebrew[19] wishing him long life and good fortune for his help in the departure from the Soviet Union.

Even though Kagan himself left Russia, he felt that Russia Jewry must not be forsaken and *yeshivoth* must continue to function there. Rabbi Abraham Joffin of the Navaradock *yeshivoth* consulted him regarding the future status of the *yeshivoth* in the midst of widespread religious persecution. Kagan's advice was to stay in Russia so that they could continue to spread the teachings of the Torah. Later, when students and other religious Jews were forced to work on the Sabbath, Rabbi Kagan urged Rabbi Joffin and his students to leave Russia for Poland.[20] Since the Communists had great respect for Rabbi Kagan, he was able to communicate freely with rabbis and fellow Jews. He was very disturbed by the Communist stand on religion and in this matter he had no influence over them. The fact that Kagan and his students needed Sikorski's help in leaving Russia in 1921 indicates that the Communists made it difficult for them to go.

The great author, Maxim Gorky, also intervened on behalf of the Hebrew poet, Haim Bialik, and other writers and Jews to secure their departure from Russia in 1924. Their help was well appreciated by men who wanted to be free and to practice their religion as they pleased.

The Bolshevik Stand on Zionism

The Jewish Communists were instrumental in persuading the government to outlaw all existing Jewish parties, especially the Zionist organizations. During the regime of Tsar Nicholas II, the Zionist movement "had become the most

---

[18]Letter from Rabbi Israel Meir Kagan to General Wladyslaw Sikorski, Radun, Poland, in *Dobry Wieczor*, 14 Lutego, 1930. The letter is reproduced in Yosher, *Ha-Hafets Hayyim*, I, 436.

[19]Letter from Rabbi Israel Meir Kagan to General Wladyslaw Sikorski, Radun, Poland, 1921, reproduced in Yosher, *Ha-Hafets Hayyim*, I, 436.

[20]Letter from Rabbi Mendel Zaks to the author, June 28, 1967; see also Rabbi Abraham Joffin, *Matragat Ha-Adam* (Jerusalem, 1964), I, 4.

potent force in Jewish public life despite the necessity of long operating underground."[21] By 1918, when the Zionist movement operated in the open, it had 1,200 local Zionist groups with some 300,000 members[22] But in June, 1919, the Second Conference of the Jewish Communist Sections in Moscow adopted the following resolution:

> The Zionist party plays a counterrevolutionary role. It is responsible for strengthening, among the backward Jewish masses, the influence of clericalism and nationalist attitudes. In this way the class self-determination of the Jewish toiling masses is undermined and the penetration of Communist ideas in their midst seriously hindered. Owing to its Palestine policy, the Zionist Party serves as an instrument of united imperialism which combats the proletarian revolution. In consideration of all these circumstances, the Conference requests the Central Bureau to propose to the pertinent authorities the promulgation of a decree suspending all activities of the Zionist Party in the economic, political, and cultural spheres. The communal organs, which are the mainstay of all reactionary forces within the Jewish people, must be suppressed.[23]

The Soviet government outlawed the Zionist movement and arrested some three thousand Zionist leaders, many of whom were deported to Siberia's political labor camps.[24] The government also outlawed the smaller groups of Labor Zionists, young Zionists, the People's Party (Folkisten), and the Bund. In a totalitarian government, there was no room for dissenting political organizations.

The Bolshevik Stand on Jewish Institutions

Because the Jewish Commissariat was responsible for

---

[21]Baron, *The Russian Jews*, p. 208.
[22]*Ibid.*
[23]*Ibid.*
[24]See L. Zenziper, *Eser Shnot Redifot* (Tel-Aviv, 1930) for the story of the persecutions of the Zionist movement in the Soviet Union.

abolishing Jewish political parties, it was difficult to find appointees to serve on the Commissariat. Two outstanding leaders of the Jewish Commissariat were Samuel Agurskii and Simeon Dimanshtain (appointed by the Soviet government in 1918). On October 20, 1918 the Commissariat passed a resolution calling for a prohibition on all the operating institutions in the Jewish quarter. The leaders argued that Jewish establishments no longer had a place in Jewish life, and they were detrimental to the interest of the Jewish masses. The Soviet government adopted the resolution and immediately began to liquidate all existing Jewish institutions.[25] In June, 1919 the Jewish establishments were outlawed by the governmental decree signed by both Agurskii and Stalin.[26]

The anti-Judaistic policies of both the government and the Jewish Commissariat were intended to close down the synagogues and expropriate all their possessions. Instruction in religion was forbidden to children below the age of eighteen outside their homes.[27] Religious officials were

> treated as declassed members of society, which involved sharp discrimination in securing housing, always extremely limited, in food rations and jobs, as well as in the admission of their children to schools.[28]

Efforts of Rabbis Kagan and Grodzenski on Behalf of Soviet Jewry

In 1930 Rabbi Israel Meir Kagan and Rabbi Hayyim Ozer Grodzenski of Vilna wrote:

> According to the report that came from Russia, the heart faints and the hands tremble. Approximately three million Jews are in captivity under distress and oppression. Several ten thousands of Jews, with

---

[25]Baron, *The Russian Jews*, pp. 209ff.; and S. Agurskii, *Di Yidishe Komisariatn un di Yidishe Kommunistishe Sektsies* (Minsk, 1928), pp. 19ff., 59ff.

[26]Baron, *The Russian Jews*, pp. 209ff.

[27]*Lenin, Sochineniia*, XI, 658, 661.

[28]Baron, *The Russian Jews*, p. 211.

their children and infants, were banished from their homes in the middle of the winter. They are scattered in the streets and are starving. In addition to the physical destruction that left the majority of the Jews without economic security, our brothers also experience religious persecution.[29]

The two Rabbis related that religious schools and rabbinical seminaries were closed down; and synagogues and houses of study were being converted to political and social clubs. Religious teachers and deans of rabbinical seminaries were exiled to Siberia. The majority of the rabbis were thrown out of their homes and were forced to pay a tax. The rabbis were arrested if they were found guilty of teaching religion or of avoiding payment of the tax. Charitable people were afraid to donate money to religious institutions. In many communities the slaughtering of animals in accordance with the laws of the Torah was prohibited. Those Jews who were employed by the Soviet government were fearful of circumcising their new-born male infants.[30] The tragedy was even greater in some communities where hundreds of the Holy Scrolls and all the religious books were burned in public. "Such desecration was never witnessed by the Jews."[31]

According to the law, we are obligated to fast because of evil decrees. But, since we cannot decree now a fast for all the Jews in the world, we have decided in the name of several outstading rabbis to set four days of fast including the Fast of Esther and to recite many prayers of mercy and forgiveness to God to help us from our persecutors, our enemies, and demolishers from within and without . . . and after the prayers to recite chapters of the Psalms, especially chapters 79, 80, 83. . . . Rabbis, speakers, and preachers shall say afterwards words calling for repentance, for the education of the young, for the

---

[29]Letter from Rabbis Israel Meir Kagan and Hayyim Grodzenski, Ader, 1930, in Kagan, *Michtevei Hafets Hayyim*, p. 56.
[30]*Ibid.*
[31]*Ibid.*

keeping of the Sabbath. . . . May the Lord appear
to us to obliterate the dreadful decrees, so that a portion of our brothers will not assimilate.[32]

In a second letter of 1930, Rabbis Kagan and Grodzenski
wrote that Holy Scrolls, books of the Talmud, phylacteries,
and the scrolls at the door posts had been burned in the
streets. Ritual baths were closed down and the keeping of the
family purity laws was being abandoned. The Communists
forced Jews to desecrate the Sabbath. Many rabbis and Torah
scholars were being sentenced to prison and many others were
banished to Siberia.[33]

The rabbis and Torah scholars were burdened by heavy
taxes which forced them to give up their homes. Jews who
remained faithful to God and Judaism suffered hunger and
hardship because they were denied the right to buy the necessities of life or to rent a house. Religious Jews, their children, and infants were starving in the freezing temperatures
of the street.

It was impossible, according to Rabbis Kagan and Grodzenski, to portray "the most vicious treatment of the Jews
in Jewish history."[34] They urged the Jews to repent and to
pray to the Almighty for help.

In a third letter of 1930, Rabbis Kagan and Grodzenski
exorted the Jews to send packages of food and clothing to
their co-religionists in Russia. Rabbis throughout the world
should awaken the Jews to the urgent need for saving lives
and for helping those Jews who had official permission to
leave the Soviet Union.[35]

---

[32]*Ibid.*

[33]Second letter from Rabbis Israel Meir Kagan and Hayyim Grodzenski, Adar, 1930, Kagan, *Michtevei Hafets Hayyim*, p. 57.

[34]*Ibid.*, p. 58. In the author's view, one might question this characteriza-
tion by the rabbis as "the most vicious treatment." However, one must realize that before the Bolshevik Revolution Russian Jewry gave rise to the
Hasidic, *Haskalah, Hoveve Zion* and Bund movements and they established numerous educational and philanthropic institutions. Since all these
developments and institutions were systematically eradicated, one might
have to agree with the rabbis' statement.

[35]Third letter from Rabbis Kagan and Grodzenski, Sivan, 1930, Kagan,
Michtevei Hafets Hayyim, p. 61.

In 1931, in a letter to prominent rabbis and to communal letters, they wrote:

> Behold the miserable conditions of our unfortunate and oppressed brothers in the Soviet Union are known; their economic root has been uprooted completely from them; and many hundreds and thousands of Jews are lacking food and are suffering from starvation. General aid is prohibited, but it is possible to dispatch food packages to individuals . . . and already outstanding rabbis have been informed to stress the necessity of sending packages which truthfully saves lives.[36]

People were urged to send packages throughout the year and especially before holidays. Every Jew who knew the address of a relative or friend was asked to send the package himself to the Soviet Union. Those Jews who did not have addresses of relatives or friends in Russia could forward money to the Bureau in Vilna or to Rabbis Israel Meir Kagan and Hayyim Ozer Grodzenski.

These two men were the two most respected rabbis in Poland in the 1930's. They used their international reputation and influence to secure economic help—within the limitations set by the Soviet government—for these unfortunate Jews in the Soviet Union.

In 1931 Rabbi Kagan and other great rabbis decreed that a special prayer should be recited in the synagogues throughout the world on the High Holidays on behalf of the persecuted Jews in the Soviet Union.[37] The following is the prayer, composed by Rabbi Kagan.

> May it be Thy will, O Lord my God and God of my fathers, the Mighty of Jacob, the Holy of Israel to be merciful upon the Jewish people, in partic-

---

[36]Letter from Rabbis Israel Meir Kagan and Ozer Grodzenski, Elul, 1931, *ibid.*, p. 197.

[37]Letter from Rabbi Israel Meir Kagan, on the eve of the New Year, 1931, Kagan, *Michtevei Hafets Hayyim*, p. 67.

ular, the oppressed Soviet Jewry because of our recitation of psalms. Protect them from their enemies who rise up to suppress their practice of Judaism, save them from evil, hunger, captivity, and plunder. Humble the heretic and the arrogant. We beseech three merciful and gracious King to redeem the children of Jacob from destruction and to plead the cause of the helpless for You are the Holy and the Savior of Israel. Remember Your poor and destitute children who long for Your immediate relief. The Eternal, make us miracles and wonders for the sake of our holy Torah in behalf of Your people Israel, in particular for our brothers in Russia so that they will be inspired and helped by Your holy name . . . for your God is a merciful God. He will not weaken you, and He will not destroy you. He will not forget the covenant of your fathers which He made with them. You shall redeem us hastingly for the sake of Your Name in our day, Amen.[38]

Conclusion

Rabbi Kagan was a man of great faith in God, but in time of Jewish distress, he would cry like a child.[39] His faith in God that relief would come to the suffering Jews in the Soviet Union gave him the strength—at the age of ninety-three—to work on behalf of Soviet Jewry, whose misery he understood so well. The more he understood from his own experiences in the Soviet Union, the more he lamented. He was also enough of a realist to know that one could not expect religious life and Torah learning to flourish under the atheistic Bolsheviks. In this respect, his analysis of the situation was thorough, and he saw then what people in the free world see now, that Judaism has no future in Communist Russia.

When Rabbi Kagan emigrated from Russia to Poland

---

[38]*Ibid.*
[39]Interview with Rabbi Mendel Zaks with the author, June 28, 1967.

in 1921, he left behind religious as well as communal institutions to be burned and destroyed by the Communists and by the Jewish Communists in particular. As the persecution of the religious and cultural institutions of the Soviet Jews gained momentum, Rabbi Kagan developed a guilty conscience for having left his fellow Jews behind the iron-curtain.

> I should have stayed. A Jew must be ready to die for Judaism . . . just as in the days of the Mishnah, Jews endured terrible persecution, but the future generations were blessed with the edition of the Talmud. Jews suffered similar persecutions in the medieval times, subsequently producing such illuminaries as Al-Fasi, Rashi, Maimonides, and the Baalei Ha-Tosafoth. . . . Even though the pogroms of the Cossacks during the years of 1648-1649 savaged tens of thousands of Jews who died for the sanctification of God's name and His Torah, the next generation was doubly rewarded with the appearance of Gaon of Vilna, Akiba Eger, Moses Sofer . . . and many others.[40]

In the opinion of the author, Rabbi Kagan not only manifested his guilty conscience in the above quotation, but also enlightens us with his analytical theory of the suffering of Jews in Jewish history. Jews must be willing to die if necessary for God and the Torah, but the next or future generations will doubly reap the reward by the emergence of great scholars who will be spiritual and moral guides.

Rabbi Kagan told Rabbi Elhanan Wasserman:

> The Jews erred at the time when the Jewish Communists began their persecution, they should have confronted them with war and self-sacrifice. Even though many Jews would have died, they might have weakened the power of the Satan. Because none of us volunteered to fight and die if necessary the Jew-

---

[40]Quoted in Yosher, *Ha-Hafets Hayyim*, II, 529.

ish Communists have strengthened themselves in destroying the religious and cultural life of the Jews.[41]

Rabbi Kagan blamed himself and the Jews for passivity, and for bringing upon themselves the plague of Communist pillage and destruction. It is interesting to note that Rabbi Kagan believed in the use of force for Jewish survival, although he never made use of it himself.

His regret at leaving Russia himself led him to advise Rabbi Joffin and his thousands of students to remain in Russia and to continue to maintain his chain of *yeshivoth* despite the horrible persecution of the Communists. One could perhaps criticize his judgement in advising others to make a sacrifice he himself had not made. However, he soon changed his mind and urged Rabbi Joffin and his students to emigrate from Russia to Poland.

To say that Rabbis Israel Meir Kagan and Hayyim Ozer Grodzenski succeeded in designing a program to solve the religious and cultural problems confronting Soviet Jewry would be contrary to historical facts. In fact, the religious and cultural life of Soviet Jews, instead of improving, rapidly deteriorated. The two rabbis did everything within their power to awaken Jews and men of good will throughout the world to intervene on behalf of the religious and cultural life of the Jews. Rabbi Kagan searched for all possible roads to help Soviet Jews. He even decided to write the Pope a letter requesting that he use his immense influence in relieving the religious and cultural persecution of Soviet Jewry:

> . . . it is mandatory for men of good will who follow the teachings of God to teach to those who went astray so that they might repent. If a servant sees his master experiencing disgrace at the hands of others, will not the servant come to his master's tribulation? Surely, men of God who witness the disgrace of God and religious institutions at the hands of the Soviet Communists must unite to protest since keeping silent is a criminal sin. . . . We Jews cannot resist

---

[41]*Ibid.*, II, 530.

them because we are few and because we lack the power of a government, but you who represent the religion of the majority of people in many countries must try to resist Communist oppression. . . .[42]

Rabbi Kagan never sent the letter to the Pope because he decided that it would do more harm than good to Soviet Jewry. One can conclude that he was analytical in his decision to write to the Pope and later in cancelling it.

It is interesting to note that perhaps the letters and protests of Rabbis Kagan and Grodzenski did have a positive effect in the economic realm and the economic life of the Russian Jews improved. Jews as workers could contribute to Soviet economy and technology and would not harm the Soviet Union by receiving economic equality. On the contrary, this was a means of assimilating the Jew into the Soviet way of life. By permitting economic equality but denying religious and cultural rights, the Soviet government controlled the Jew's body and deprived his soul of spiritual values. Economic privileges would not maintain the unity of the Jews in Russia, but religious and cultural values would strengthen the unity of the Jews in Russia, abroad, and in Israel.

We can see that Rabbi Kagan's fears of a half century ago have been confirmed today and can still believe that only a miracle, for which the Rabbi cried and prayed, will open the doors of the Soviet Union for Soviet Jews to leave or to receive religious and cultural rights.

POLAND BETWEEN THE WARS

In this section the author deals with Rabbi Kagan's response to the Polish government's discriminatory legislation, his leadership in the Polish Torah community's religious and communal problems, his dedication to establishing and maintaining *yeshivoth,* his method of teaching, and his influence

---

[42]Quoted in Yosher, *Ha-Hafets Hayyim,* II, 531ff.

on students and other rabbis. It includes a discussion of his opinions on the existence of the Torah, on the Jewish people, and on dark forces in the world.

Historical Background

Rabbi Kagan's role in combating the Polish government's discriminatory legislation can best be understood in the light of Polish and Jewish history. The causes of the First World War were not engendered by Poland, but that country—which was simultaneously under the role of Tsarist Russia, Austria, and Germany at the outbreak of the war—became a battlefield. President Wilson's stand on an independent Poland, and the pronouncement of the leaders of the Russian revolution supporting a free Poland, motivated the Poles to take a pro-ally stand. On June 3, 1918 President Wilson declared:

> An independent Polish state should be erected which should include the territories inhabited indisputably by Polish populations, which should be assured a free and secure access to the sea, and whose political and economic independence and territorial integrity should be guaranteed by international covenant.[43]

Britain, France and Italy stated that "the creation of a united Poland with a free access to the sea constituted a condition of a just peace."[44]

While Poland was engaged in a diplomatic struggle at the Paris Peace Conference, Pilsudski pursued the military struggle on the battlefield against the Russians. In 1918 he was able to drive the Bolsheviks out of Vilna, his birthplace. He expressed the desire to federate Lithuania, White Russia, and the Ukraine with Poland. The Allies urged Poland to take a strong position against the Bolsheviks in the light of the danger of Communism. Pilsudski captured Kiev in the Soviet Ukraine. However, the eminent Soviet General Tuchachevsky

---

[43]Raymond Leslie Buell, *Poland: Key to Europe* (New York and London, 1939), p. 68.
[44]*Ibid.*

began to push Pilsudski back to Polish territory and re-captured the city of Vilna. In the battle of Warsaw on August 16, 1920, Pilsudski's forces were once more able to drive the Russians back. In 1921 Lenin and Pilsudski signed the Riga Treaty stating that the Vilna question was a matter between Poland and Lithuania. Poland received a large White Russian and Ukrainian population, both parties agreed not to meddle in each other's internal affairs, and a collection of trophies and other property were restored to Poland.

As a result, the Jewish population of the new Poland became the largest Jewish community in Europe. When Rabbi Kagan returned to Poland in 1921, he found that Warsaw had more than 300,000 Jews, Lodz 194,000, Lemberg approximately 100,000, Vilna 55,000, and Lublin 44,000.[45]

Relations between the Jews and the Poles deteriorated during and after the First World War. During the war, Dmowski, the leader of the National Democratic Party, accused the Jews of supporting Germany. The pogroms in Kiev and the Ukraine as a whole set an example for the Poles. In 1919 the Jews of Eastern Galicia declared themselves neutral in the struggle over the province between the Poles and the Ukrainians. In 1919 other Poles accused the Jews of cooperating with the Bolsheviks. The Polish government held the Jews

> responsible for the minorities treaty it was induced to accept at the Paris Peace Conference; in addition to providing general minority guarantees, this treaty contained special provisions protecting the Jews in Poland; according to Article 10, Education Committees appointed locally by the Jewish communities were subject to the general control of the State, provided for the distribution of the proportional share of public funds allocated to Jewish schools and for the organization and management of these schools.[46]

---

[45]Elbogen, *A Century of Jewish Life*, p. 532. However, the Jewish community as a whole was in a precarious position.

[46]Buell, *Poland: Key to Europe*, p. 295.

The Language Laws of 1924, which gave minorities the prerogative to use their native language in courts and public institutions, did not pertain to the Jewish people because it was deemed impossible for so many functionaries to learn Yiddish.

In 1926 Pilsudski's regime came to power and to some extent changed the discriminatory conditions of the Jews. Marshall Pilsudski himself had no use for anti-Semitic slogans. His government had members of the Jewish faith as well as of other minorities in the *Sejm*. To be sure, certain anti-Jewish laws prevailed from the past and a segment of the Jewish population protested against government interference in internal Jewish affairs and curtailment of the traditional autonomy of Jewish communities.

The Jewish community law of October 14, 1927 recognized

> the existence of the Polish Jews as a religious federation composed of individual communities, and with local councils for each community. Nevertheless, the legislation limited the rights of these communities, largely in religious and charitable matters, and gave the government large powers of supervision.[47]

The government had the right to veto the selection of officers of the Jewish communities and even to remove them under special circumstances. The deposed Jewish leaders could be replaced by commissioners of the government. The government had the right to control the budget of the community for the support of synagogues, supply of kosher meat, Jewish charitable institutions, and religious education of children.

There were many Jews who felt that the government's control over the Jewish communal affairs was in violation of Article 10 of the minorities treaty between Poland and the Principal Allied and Associated Powers. The Allies recog-

---

[47]*Ibid.*, p. 297.

nized the right of existence of Jewish communities. Jews also protested that only "the repulsive features of the law were enforced." The more progressive Jews also

> criticized the right given to the communal election board to deprive all those not practicing their religion of the right to vote. They regarded such provisions as a reward paid to the Orthodox Jews for their support of the Pilsudski regime.[48]

Rabbi Kagan's Response to the Polish Government's Discriminatory Legislation

Rabbi Kagan lived in independent Poland from 1921 to 1933 and his relationship to the Polish government, on behalf of the Jews can be traced through articles and letters. In 1928, in response to dissension caused by an election of the Polish Chamber of Deputies, he wrote an article entitled "Tochahah L'Hasarat Sinah V'riv ("Rebuke for the Removal of Hatred and Quarreling") . In it he claimed that there

> developed among certain Jews a hatred and antagonism against God-fearing Jews who guarded the Jewish religion or because of the election of *Sejm*. All sort of schemes were used to disgrace the religious Jews and thereby caused the curtailing of the number of Jews in the *Sejm*. In addition, they brought about the decline of the Jewish Deputies' influence in the *Sejm*.[49]

"Great is the sin of those who embarrass the God-fearing and the learned." Rabbi Kagan continued to appeal to

> the God-fearing Jews who dedicate themselves to keep the religious teachings of the holy Torah not to lose the spirit; and not to be discouraged because their Redeemer is strong; His name is God and He can help us in many ways.[50]

---

[48]*Ibid.*, p. 298.
[49]Rabbi Israel Meir Kagan, "Tochahah L'hasarat Sinah V'riv" ("Rebuke for the Removal of Hatred and Quarrels"), in Kagan, *Michtevei Hafets Hayyim*, p. 40.
[50]*Ibid.*

He ended the article with the hope that God would make peace between the fighting Jews in order to merit the redemption and the coming of the righteous Messiah, so that the honor of God would be exalted in this world.

From this article one can conclude that Rabbi Kagan approved of Jews serving and cooperating with the Polish government and the Chamber of Deputies. He was concerned that the religious qualifications of the candidates be strong so they would help to strengthen the Torah and religion. The Rabbi possessed an ability to bring about harmony among the diverse elements of Jews. People of every walk of life respected him for his honesty and disregard for politics. He was convinced that a religious Jew possessed the ability to serve the religious interests and the political, economic and social interests of all Jews. Rabbi Mendel Zaks told the author that politics was foreign to Rabbi Kagan and the welfare of the Jewish people was his primary reason for taking a stand on political issues.

Rabbi Kagan felt that unity among the Jews could bring them positive results in the *Sejm,* therefore the hatred and quarrels must cease. As a moral person, the Rabbi also felt that hatred and bickering were abominable in the eyes of God and God-fearing men. He was also concerned lest the Polish government take advantage of the divisions among Jews and increase discrimination against them. In 1931 he wrote an "Open Letter":

> As we stand now close to the elections of the *Sejm* and the Senate, and as the past experience has taught us of the necessity of selecting religious representatives, surely it is a great obligation upon everyone who is God-fearing, not to be evasive and not to be indecisive in this matter which touches things that stand upon the apex of the world for strengthening the Torah and our holy religion; and with all our arduous effort we must try to elect there people, energetic and dedicated to God, His Torah with all their soul in order to defend our holy reli-

gion against those who stand in every corner to destroy and obliterate it.[51]

He urged that Jews vote for the representatives under Number 18 on the ballot because they were representatives approved by the greatest rabbis to defend the Jewish faith and the Jewish general welfare. He requested that they not support those candidates whose goal was to destroy the teachings of the Torah, and who fought without justification against the holy Torah, and against the keepers of the precepts.

In this letter Rabbi Kagan again approved of Jews serving in the Polish *Sjem* and the Senate but only of candidates who were committed to the Jewish cause in general and to preserving the Torah in particular. He took a stand against candidates who tried to break the control of the rabbis over the masses. In Poland the progressive elements among the Jews, such as the Bundists, Communists, and non-religious Zionists, were antagonistic towards religion. Since the rabbis controlled the masses, the progressive elements lacked support from them. There were many schemes to mock religion in order to weaken the position of the rabbis and of orthodoxy. Rabbi Kagan opposed the candidates from these progressive elements.

Rabbi Kagan and President Moscicki of Poland

In 1929 the President of Poland, Ignacy Moscicki, visited the city of Radun, the home of Rabbi Kagan. The Rabbi met him personally and bestowed on him the following blessing:

Honorable President!
   Blessed be the guest!
   Thank God that I merited at time of my old age
to greet with a blessing the President of the Polish
government, Ignacy Moscicki. I am fortunate in witnessing the Polish nation that was established after
a long time of having been ruled by foreign powers;

---

[51]Letter from Rabbi Israel Meir Kagan, Mar Hesvan, 1931, Kagan, *Michtevei Hafets Hayyim*, p. 67.

and now it rises and blossoms into a mighty nation. I am happy for the opportunity to bestow my warm blessing upon you, President of the nation, on your visit to this city, which is the center of Torah because of the sixty year old *Yeshiva*. May I bless you with longevity for the honor and happiness of the whole nation in which shadow we take refuge and for its welfare we always pray.[52]

Rabbi Kagan thanked the Polish government on behalf of all the Jews for the Palestinian Polish Council's work in helping the Jews in Palestine in a time of Arab attack, looting, and murder.[53] He also requested the President of Poland to withdraw the orders requiring religious teachers to have a secular education; to abandon the idea of establishing a Central Religious Council; and to change plans for the council's role in determining qualifications for the appointment of rabbis—which was contrary to the consensus of the rabbis of Poland and against Jewish tradition.[54] He expressed the hope that Polish ideals and tolerance would allow the Jews self-autonomy in religious matters. Polish Jewry for hundreds of years had provided the greatest Torah scholars, and even in his time Poland was the main Torah artery for the

---

[52]Rabbi Israel Meir Kagan, "Ha-brachah L'fnei ha- President B'eit Bikuro B'Radun" ("The Blessing Before the President at the time of his Visit in Radun"), Kagan, *Michtevei Hafets Hayyim*, p. 215.

[53]*Ibid.* The cause of the trouble was the Wailing Wall. In 1928 the Jewish worshippers wanted to erect a curtain to separate the men from the women. On Rosh Hashanah there was no commotion, but before Yom Kippur the Arabs pressed the British police to prohibit the erection of a curtain. The British police came in during the Yom Kippur service on September 24, 1928 and removed the curtain by force. Jews all over the world were disturbed by the tactless act of the police. The Mufti of Jerusalem saw in the erection of the curtain an opportunity to arouse the religious passions of the Moslems to wage a Holy War. The passions and the propaganda motivated by the Mufti were so fierce that murder, looting, and attacks against the Jews were the order of the day. In Hebron sixty innocent and defenseless persons were murdered. The results were that the Arabs killed 133 Jews and wounded 339, while they themselves lost 144 dead and 232 wounded through the interference of the British troops. In this troubled strife between the Arabs and the Jews, the Polish Council had tried to help restore order and end the bloodshed.

[54]Letter from Rabbi Israel Meir Kagan to President Ignacy Moscicki, Radun, Poland, Elul, 1929, Kagan, *Michtevei Hafets Hayyim*, p. 215.

whole Jewish Diaspora. He hoped the President would be able to spare time to read the letter.

Rabbi Kagan waited in vain for an answer to his letter. He finally wrote the President a second letter reminding him of the first and stating:

> The most important matter that I want to discuss is the legislation for the establishment of a Central Religious Council . . . whose purpose will be to answer and to decide on all questions dealing with the religious life of the communities; it will have the power to deal with the appointment of rabbis for Jews; it will have the authority to establish new institutions, which will have the general characteristic of serving all Jews in Poland; there is already grave concern among the religious circles of Jews over the establishment of a Central Religious Council which is dangerous to the religious life of the Jewish people.[55]

The Rabbi also mentioned that the President of the Board of Rabbis in Poland had already explained in detail to the Minister of Culture the negative side of the work of the Central Religious Council. He explained that in the past, election representatives from the leftist parties such as the Bundists and the Zionists were elected and that their negative attitude towards religion was a factor causing dissension among the Jews in different communities. A Central Religious Council could not be entrusted, Kagan felt, to representatives of communities who try to secularize those communities. At that time each community had the right to determine its religious life, and each community—through its religious leaders—maintained the religious life of the people. The Central Religious Council might deny each community the right to follow the ways of the Torah because many non-religious representatives would be running the council. As an example of the degradation of religious life during the

[55]Letter of Reminder from Rabbi Israel Meir Kagan to President Ignacy Moscicki, Radun, Poland, 1929, Kagan, *Michtevei Hafets Hayyim*, p. 217.

seventeenth and eighteenth centuries, Rabbi Kagan cited the Council of Four Lands of Poland. He wrote:

> The religious life of Jews stressed in its religious education two goals which are important and fundamental and which cannot be compromised with: 1. To teach the students the knowledge of Torah of Israel and the fundamentals of Judaism through the teaching of Bible, Prophets, and the rudiments of the Talmud through the primary sources. To implant in them the true faith in God and His Torah, until the new generation not only will acquire the knowledge of the Torah, but also will observe the statutes of God and will keep the precepts that we were commanded.[56]

The Rabbi again urged the President not to require secular education for religious teachers. The primary purpose of the religious teachers, he argued, was to instill knowledge of the Torah and complete faith in God and His Torah. Only religious and delicated teachers could perform these two important goals of religious education.

Rabbi Kagan explained to President Moscicki that he had seventy years of experience in guiding the religious life of the Jewish people and he believed the religious education of children should be left in the hands of the religious leaders without instituting new laws, such as secular training of religious teachers. The Rabbi felt that his experience qualified him to warn the President of Poland of the danger in changing the status quo in Jewish education: It was rare for him to come out with a statement praising himself, but he felt that he must do everything possible to forestall the possibility of required secular education for religious teachers.

Rabbi Kagan also objected to the Polish government's proposal for community election of rabbis followed by governmental confirmation. He advised the President and the Polish government to consult the Board of Rabbis before

---

[56]*Ibid.*, p. 219.

passing any legislation contrary to the consent of the Board. He ended his letter with the following:

> I hope fervently that the President of our country with his great kindness will be concerned with matters stated in the letter, and will listen to the words of a man whom God guided to old age and to be chief spokesman of religious Jewry.[57]

Rabbi Israel Meir Kagan was ninety years old in 1929. As the oldest and most respected rabbi in the world, he used his prestige to press for Jews to maintain their traditional ways of selecting a rabbi. His attempts at resisting secular influences were at least partially successful.[58]

Rabbi Kagan's Lobbying Against a Proposal Concerning the Slaughtering of Animals

In 1930, the Polish government proposed that the slaughtering of animals according to Torah law should be under the supervision of the entire Jewish community, rather than being left to the rabbis. Rabbi Kagan anticipated that the position of rabbis would be weakened by this move and felt that the secular leaders of the community would be lax in observing the regulations for slaughtering. Community control of slaughtering animals would not only challenge the authority of the rabbis but would also deny them one of their independent sources of income.[59]

On August 12, 1930 Rabbi Kagan wrote to Rabbi Israel Kirshbraun, a Deputy of the Polish *Sejm*, urging him to lobby to kill the bill for communal supervision of slaughtering.[60] He pointed out that the rabbi would lose a source of

---

[57]*Ibid.*

[58]The author was told by Mr. Leib Eckman, a contemporary of Rabbi Kagan, that the latter was successful in lobbying against legislation affecting the religious life of the Jews.

[59]The author recalls from his experience in Poland that the supervision of slaughtering animals and kosher butcher shops was an important source of income for the rabbi of the community.

[60]Letter from Rabbi Israel Meir Kagan to the Deputy of the Polish *Sejm*, Rabbi Israel Kirshbraun, Radun, Poland, AB 12, 1930, Kagan, *Michtevei Hafets Hayyim,* p. 230.

income and his authority would be undermined, and asked him to persuade other Deputies to leave the supervision of animal slaughter in the hands of rabbis. A similar letter was written on the same day to a member of the Senate, Asher Mendelsohn. Rabbi Kagan wrote that the proposal for community supervision of slaughtering was a "dangerous and frightening decree to an understanding person and to one who sees the future."[61] Since the rabbi will not be able to earn a living by the new proposal, there is a danger—particularly in a small community—that he will be forced to leave and the smaller groups of Jews would be left without a rabbi. Rabbi Kagan urged Mendelsohn to try hard to defeat the proposal, which was, in fact, never passed.[62]

It is remarkable that Rabbi Kagan, at the age of ninety-one, was able to carry on correspondence with the Deputy of the *Sejm* and a member of th Senate in order to preserve the slaughtering of animals according to prescribed Torah law in the hands of rabbis. In addition to being concerned with the livelihood of the rabbis, he felt that, according to the highest law of the Jews, the Torah, a hands-off policy by the progressive elements of Jews was the right policy. In his old age Rabbi Kagan had the courage to challenge the Polish government's proposal for the supervision of this important tradition in the Jewish community.

Rabbi Kagan's Lobbying Against a New Universal Calendar

In 1918 the League of Nations in Geneva was discussing the possibility of a new universal calendar, which could upset the scheduling of the Jewish Sabbath and Jewish holidays. Rabbi Kagan objected to this recommendation and he urged the Polish government not to consent to a universal calendar.

On May 9, 1931, he wrote a letter to the Deputy of the *Sejm* Wislitski, urging the Polish government and the Dep-

---

[61]Letter from Rabbi Israel Meir Kagan to the Senator Asher Mendelsohn, Radun, Poland, AB 12, 1930, Kagan, *Michtevei Hafets Hayyim*, p. 231.

[62]According to Leib Eckman and Rabbi Joseph Epstein, contemporaries of Rabbi Kagan, the proposal was defeated as a result of the latter's efforts.

uties to reject the proposal because it endangered the Jewish Sabbath.[63] He pointed out that some countries had already refused to accept a universal calendar under pressure from their Jewish citizens. Poland, with the largest Jewish population in Europe, should do no less. He exhorted Deputy Wislitzki to do everything within his power to persuade the government to reject the proposal.

Rabbi Kagan wrote a similar letter to Senator Asher Mendelsohn asking him to speak to all the officials who had a voice in the calendar issue and urge them to abandon it.[64] Through lobbying and arduous effort, he hoped to persuade the government to vote against the calendar.

Rabbi Kagan's Lobbying Aaginst Legislation Affecting the Ordination of Rabbis

The Polish government, under the influence of secular elements of Jewry, was pressed to pass legislation requiring the rabbis to receive ordination from an elected Rabbinical Council instead of being ordained by outstanding rabbis and to demand that rabbis acquire a secular education.

On May 15, 1931 Rabbi Kagan wrote a letter to the Minister of Religions and Culture, Dr. Stefan Tservinski:

> As I am the oldest Rabbi of Poland and I was fortunate to educate several generations of rabbis among the Jews, I have the authority to request from the splendid and honorable Minister the following petition:
>
> The past year I and the outstanding rabbis and Hasidic rabbis of Poland gathered to express to the splendid and honorable Minister our feeling and the feeling of the God-fearing community concerning the matters of the order of the elections of the rabbis and rabbinical judges in Poland. The paramount

---

[63]Letter from Rabbi Israel Meir Kagan to Deputy of the *Sejm* Wislitski, Radun, Poland, Iyar 9, 1931, Kagan, *Michtevei Hafets Hayyim*, p. 241.

[64]Letter from Rabbi Israel Meir Kagan to Senator Asher Mendelsohn, Radun, Poland, Gyer 9, 1931, Kagan, *Michtevei Hafets Hayyim*, pp. 239ff.

issue that confronted us consisted of the following two principles: 1. The ordination of rabbis should remain as in the past, namely the rabbi shall receive his ordination from a well versed in Torah and God-fearing rabbi, and no more. 2. Rabbis' consensus was not to require from a rabbi a secular education and the present day custom shall prevail.[65]

He urged the government to pass legislation in accordance with these two principles. He pointed out that ordination of rabbis by an elected Rabbinical Council would present the possibility of unqualified rabbis being elected to the Rabbinical Council and the inevitable lowering of ordination standards, with a subsequent weakening of the fundamental pillar of Judaism—the Rabbinate. The secular leaders would try to destroy the authority of the rabbis by their attempt to control the elected Rabbinical Council. They wanted rabbis to be required to have a secular education because they knew that Torah-educated and God-fearing rabbis would never go to universities to obtain this. They hoped to obtain puppet rabbis who would obtain a secular education and whom they could control.

Rabbi Kagan's Involvement in Religious Conferences

In 1924 Rabbi Kagan participated in the Rabbinical Assembly in Vilna, which met to devise ways of strengthening observance of the Torah. At the conference he said:

According to the custom of the world, when a certain partnership's transaction is about to fail, the partners of the transaction gather to look and to search for the causes of the failure and they seek ways to ameliorate conditions of the business.

We all received the Torah in partnership, we all said, 'We will do and we will heed.' And now, when

---

[65]Letter from Rabbi Meir Kagan to Minister of Religion and Culture, Dr. Stefan Tservinski, Radun. 15/V, 1931, Kagan, *Michtevei Hafets Hayyim*, pp. 238f.

> we realize that the Torah has become lax among us,
> we gathered together to search for answers in order
> to improve our condition.[66]

He also said that without the Torah it is impossible to be
a Jew. A person who removes himself from the responsibilities of the Torah excludes himself from the Jewish way of
life. The soul of a person is similar to the body. Just as the
body cannot exist without food, so the soul cannot survive
without Torah. However, as long as the pulse beats there is
hope. He told the rabbis that:

> Recently we see that the Torah is transgressed more
> and more among us; we forget the principle, namely
> that learning Torah is not only a command but also
> an obligation upon each and every person, as the
> law stated that even the poverty stricken person who
> goes around begging is obligated to set free time for
> the study of Torah. The Torah annoints man with
> a holy spirit. And without Torah we are like the
> rest of the nations.
>
> But what shall those do who are always busy with
> their concerns over livelihood, and how can they ob-
> tain a portion in the Torah? On this the sages pro-
> vided us with sound advice—to support those who
> study Torah, to finance the rabbinical schools, by
> which they can buy a portion in the Torah, as if
> they studied themselves.[67]

In the days of the Temple, Jews had to give contributions and tithes to the priests and the Levites, but with its
destruction priests and Levites lost the privileges of receiving these gifts. Rabbi Kagan held that the students in *yeshivoth* had taken the place of the priests and Levites and every
Jew was, therefore, obligated to support them because they
carry the flag of the Torah.[68] Because of the laxity with which

---

[66]Rabbi Israel Meir Kagan, "Portions of His Speech in the Rabbinical
Assembly of Vilna," Kagan, *Michtevei Hafets Hayyim*, p. 143.
[67]*Ibid.*
[68]*Ibid.*, p. 144.

Jews were observing the teachings of the Torah, Rabbi Kagan urged its strengthening through financial support for the students in rabbinical schools. Also, in the *Mishnah Berurah* Rabbi Kagan ruled that the people engaged in Torah study are permitted to rely on others for financial support.[69]

In the same year, 1924, a rabbinical convention was held in Grodno, at which Rabbi Kagan was the main speaker. No decisions were made without his approval. He told the assembly that in those cities where no study of Torah took place and which lacked a *yeshiva*, Judaism was non-existent. Judaism, according to the Rabbi, could not survive without financial support for *yeshivoth*. In the same conference Rabbi Kagan pointed out that since troubles in the world were growing, Jews must occupy themselves with the Torah and loving-kindness to help them to survive suffering. He spoke of a person who asked the Gaon of Vilna, Rabbi Elijahu (1720-1797), about the topic of a sermon. The Gaon answered that the topic would be the strengthening of the Torah because it applied to everyone.[70]

> It is necessary to try that every Jew shall have a portion in strengthening the Torah. On account of the Torah the whole creation exists. . . . Because of the Torah, we shall merit the true redemption, as it is said, 'remember the Torah of Moses, my servant' and afterwards, "behold, I am sending to you Elijah, the Prophet' and the Sages added, "the Jews will not be redeemed, but for the merit of the Torah.' And whenever the Torah is forgotten by us, we are not forgotten by it, as it is said upon finishing a tractate of the Talmud, "Do not leave us and we will not leave you." It is a holy responsibility upon us to do whatever is possible on behalf of Torah. Rabbis shall travel to neighboring cities to arouse the people regarding the circumstance of the Torah. They do not have to travel the whole year,

---

[69]Kagan, *Mishnah Berurah*, II, 289.
[70]Rabbi Israel Meir Kagan, "Portions of His Speech in the Rabbinical Conference of Grodno," Kagan, *Michtevei Hafets Hayyim*, p. 145.

as Samuel the Prophet did, but a week or two during the year they must travel to stimulate the people to give money according to their means for the
support of the rabbinical schools.[71]

In 1925, Rabbi Kagan participated in the Rovna Conference. For many generations the district of Volhynia had
not had *yeshivoth*. Before the First World War attempts were
made to establish an important *yeshiva* there, but every attempt was abortive because there was no dedicated leader to
arouse the Jews into making the necessary contributions to
obtain land. After the First World War, however, *yeshivoth*
had been founded in the cities of Zvihil, Kuritz, and Lutzk,
Volhynia.

The assembly at Rovna revealed feelings of pride among
the *yeshivoth*. They had come to feel that they should be
given independence from the supervision of the *yeshivoth* in
Vilna. At the assembly, Rabbi Joel Sarin, the dean of Zvihil,
and later of Kunitz, urged such independence. He recommended that Volhynia participate as an equal partner in
the administration of the collection of money, but that the
division of the money and the governing of internal affairs
of the *yeshivoth* be dependent upon the executive committee
of Volhynia.

Rabbi Kagan reminded the convention of his lifelong
concern with the problems created by evil tongues, talebearing, and in particular, quarrels. He urged all factions to
unite and stop quarreling, and because of the esteem in which
he was held he succeeded in uniting the conflicting parties.
He became the motivating force in preventing the secession
of the Volhynia *yeshivoth*.

Rabbi Kagan also spoke at the Rovna assembly concerning the atheistic books used in modern Jewish schools:

As yet I have not seen a history text which is taught
at the present time to our children. I thought it was
a general history of Africa or of America, I opened
it and behold, it contained heresy and atheism.

---

[71]*Ibid.*, pp. 146ff.

Let me cite an example. Concerning the sacrifice of Isaac the Torah tells us that an angel of God called upon our father Abraham from heaven and did not permit Abraham to sacrifice Isaac, his son . . . and they, the new heretics, write that his heart did not allow him to do this. There is no mention of an angel who did not permit it. . . . They came to uproot from a child all roots and fundamentals of the faith . . . and in a similar manner they treat the rest of the material in the Torah.[72]

The books did not mention the miracles of the splitting of the Red Sea and the drownings of the Egyptians. Denying such miracles robs a child of a source of wonder and faith in God. The subject of circumcision, which is the basis of the Covenant between God and the Jewish people, was not even mentioned in the history book. The story of the ten plagues was also omitted.

It is tragic if parents do not take any interest in the education of their children. And it is possible that the father is a very religious and believing Jew, and the son is being educated without Torah, and without faith. The principle of the thing is that without faith, he is hopeless.[73]

Rabbi Kagan went on to remind his listeners that the Holy Torah is not in heaven; it is accesible to all and a father must send his child to a teacher who believes in the Torah. If a father permits his child to study atheistic history books, the father and the son will both suffer forever. A father must provide his son with an education in the Bible, the Prophets, the Talmud, and the Code of Law to which the fathers of the past were accustomed, rather than an education emphasizing dancing, singing and skipping.[74]

When a great rabbi comes to a city, many people ask

---

[72]Rabbi Israel Meir Kagan, "Portions of his Speech in the Rovan Conference," Kagan, *Michtevei Hafets Hayyim*, p. 148.

[73]*Ibid.*, p. 149.

[74]*Ibid.*

his blessing. But they forget that the most important blessing one can obtain is for the strengthening of Torah. If a person tries to fortify the Torah, he has everything and without the Torah he has nothing.

There are many troubles that befall the Jews in this world, but some Jews do not even stop to think of the causes of their suffering. Has God created a world of troubles and malicious sicknesses? God is good and, therefore, He is good to man. The various diseases and troubles are a result of the laxity of Torah among us.[75] Every man with intelligence must understand that without Torah the faith will be weakened, and only *yeshivoth* can strengthen faith.

In 1925 Rabbi Israel Meir Kagan addressed the convention of rabbis and deans in the city of Bialystok, Poland. The purpose of the assembly was to find ways to save the *yeshivoth*, which were not only confronted with competition from the modern Jewish schools but also with financial difficulties. Rabbi Kagan was aware of their financial hardship and urged every Jew to contribute according to his means. He said in part:

> The Torah is our existence, "It is your existence," it is also the existence of our children, as it is written "to us and to our children forever." On the words "to our children" are placed dots—what do these dots indicate? It is like one writing to another a letter and underlining some words, to show that they are the essence of the letter; so the dots remind us to better raise our children in the path of Torah and to preserve the Torah forever.[76]

Rabbi Kagan told the delegates that enemies of the Jews wanted to take the Torah away from them because they knew that without the Torah Jews lost their strength. Therefore, Jews must be careful not to give up their strongest weapon—the Torah.[77]

---

[75]*Ibid.*, p. 151.
[76]Rabbi Israel Meir Kagan, "Portions of His Speech in the Conference of Bialystok," Kagan, *Michtevei Hafets Hayyim,* pp. 126ff.
[77]*Ibid.*

In 1929, because of poor health and old age, Rabbi Kagan was unable to attend a conference in Vienna. But he wrote to the convention saying that because of the modern secular schools the young generation was being brought up without religion or truth. The secular schools were spreading everywhere, but the religious schools and *yeshivoth* were faced with financial and administrative problems. He suggested that every new religious school should establish adult education classes and groups for workers in order to increase the number of people learning and living the Torah. He realized the importance of educating not only children, but also their parents who could help the children transfer the learning of the Torah into the living of the Torah and its laws.[78]

In the letter Rabbi Kagan also expressed his great concern over the transgression of the Sabbath because it had become a week-day in many cities. He was grateful for the establishment of Sabbath-observant organizations throughout the world whose purpose was to strengthen the observance of the Sabbath among Jews.[79] The Rabbi noted that many Jews transgressed the law because they were led astray by sinners, and it is a worthwhile deed to show understanding towards those so led astray. Teaching the way of the Torah to Jews who sin unintentionally is of paramount importance. Rabbi Kagan felt that a person should receive a second chance to abandon his sinning ways and he urged the rabbis at the Vienna Assembly to correct the ways of those led astray.[80]

At the age of ninety, Rabbi Kagan called for a rabbinical assembly at Vilna, writing in 1930 to Rabbi Ezekiel Lipschitz of Kalish (among others) :

> I cannot portray in a letter my distressed heart
> concerning the troubles and the frightening decrees
> that are about to come forth, which set afire our
> holy religion; why do we keep still? Surely, we will

---

[78]Letter from Rabbi Israel Meir Kagan, Radun, Poland, Elul, 1929, Kagan, *Michtevei Hafets Hayyim*, p. 211.

[79]*Ibid.*, pp. 211ff.

[80]*Ibid.*

be responsible for this because the fault of the generation falls upon the leaders, as it is known from the sages and for such matters we are obligated to sacrifice our lives. . . . Therefore, we have to do everything within our power. First matter on the agenda is to gather the leaders of Jews to find a solution to the problems. Even though it is very difficult for me to travel at this old age, I will disregard my condition and, God willing, I will be present among those assembled. But we selected Vilna which is situated near our city in order to lighten my burden of travel and also there will be no concern for us over troublemakers. I shall do the inviting for the assembly . . . and we must do everything within our power to honor God and His Torah.[81]

The assembly was held in Vilna in 1930 and rabbis and deans came together to search for solutions to the pressing problems of the day. The paramount problems to solve were the financial difficulties of the religious schools, laxity in observance of the Sabbath, and the decrees of the Polish government requiring secular education for rabbis and ordination by a central Rabbinical Council.

In his speech to the conference Rabbi Kagan told the guests that one could find only old people praying and learning in synagogues. There were hardly any young people in the house of God. Without youth, it would be difficult to wage war against laxity in learning and observance. As time passed, he claimed, Judaism would become weaker and weaker. The fundamentals of Judaism, such as putting on phylacteries, were being ignored. He continued:

If one shall recall the religious life of his city twenty years ago, he will be shocked. In such a short period of time the learning of Torah has declined. Let us take, for example, the city of Vilna which was for a long time a city full of learned Jews and

---

[81]Letter from Rabbi Israel Meir Kagan, Radun, Poland, Tevet, 1930, Kagan *Michtevei Hafets Hayyim*, p. 226.

writers. And today? Today there is a handful of students of the Torah. The situation is similar everywhere. We see what has happened to Judaism in Germany which in the past had so much Torah learning and today—nothing.

We have to remember that the Rabbinical Schools in our districts are the last iota of Torah that we have; and we must cherish and keep it, because without Torah we are nothing. Each rabbi in his city and town must strengthen the learning of Torah and the exercise of loving-kindness.[82]

In concluding his speech, Rabbi Kagan described the plight of Soviet Jewry:

We find ourselves now in a very oppressing circumstance, nevertheless, we must remember our brethren in Soviet Russia whose plight is even worse than ours. They are prohibited from engaging in business and also from leaving the country. What shall they do? Three million Jews experience such a dreadful circumstance. We have to help them with whatever we can. The least we can do is to send food packages to still the hungry. Every Jew, even the poor, must send the minimum of two food packages during a half year to our destitute brethren in Soviet Russia—this is a holy matter.[83]

Rabbi Kagan's Involvement in Communal Problems

We have seen despite his prolific scholarship Rabbi Kagan found time to participate in conferences dealing with matters directly affecting the rabbinate and the religious life of his people. He was, however, deeply concerned with communal problems as well and made himself available to help solve them. Although he was a modest man and did not try to stand in the place of great rabbis, he did not hesitate to take a stand on serious communal problems.

---

[82]Rabbi Israel Meir Kagan, "Speech at Vilna Assembly of Rabbis," Kagan, *Michtevei Hafets Hayyim*, p. 139.
[83]*Ibid.*

At the outbreak of the First World War, Rabbi Kagan was distraught over the consequences of war for the Jews and for the whole world. He urged Jews to pray to God for peace. He called upon the rabbis in each community to set aside a fast day and to recite prayers of forgiveness.

> In this critical time, it is an obligation, upon every man, to strengthen the characteristic of loving-kindness toward his friend. In particular, as of today, the families looking for loving-kindness have increased; and it is obligatory to take them into consideration, and not to deny loving-kindness. One who shows compassion for people, God has mercy upon him.[84]

During the years 1925 and 1926 the Rabbi denounced the tendency among the Jews to prefer secularly-oriented education to Torah study. Some Jews had begun to compare the Hebrew University in Jerusalem to the "Third Temple." Also in 1925, he helped found *Horeb*, a Central Religious Committee. Its function was to augment the religious schools in every city, and he requested that rabbis not on the Committee cooperate with *Horeb* to preserve religious education.[85]

In 1926 the first Religious Educational Conference met in Vilna to seek ways to increase study of the Torah among the young and to prevent them from studying in atheistic schools. Rabbi Kagan, in a letter to the conference, blessed the rabbis and leaders of the conference for gathering to consider such a worthwhile cause and expressed his hope that God would guide them in their deliberations.[86] Also in 1926 he wrote a letter urging the rabbis to explain to parents the danger of sending their children to the Tarbut and Yiddish schools, which were sponsored by the Zionist and Bundist or-

---

[84]Rabbi Israel Meir Kagan, "May God Rest Among Our Jewish Brethern," Kagan, *Michtevei Hafets Hayyim*, p. 170.

[85]Letter from Rabbi Israel Meir Kagan, Radun, Poland, Tebet, 1926, Kagan, *Michtevei Hafets Hayyim*, pp. 77-81.

[86]Letter from Rabbi Israel Meir Kagan, Radun, Poland, Tamuz, 1926, Kagan, *Michtevei Hafets Hayyim*, p. 86.

ganizations respectively. He recommended that in every city the rabbis set up a committee composed of God-fearing Jews for the purpose of preventing parents from educating their children in secular schools.

In 1927 the secular elements among the Jews called for a general conference in Vilna to discuss communal problems such as granting the right to vote to women, loosening the control of the rabbinate over the community, and modernizing religious life. In a letter of 1927, Rabbi Kagan urged the rabbis and the lay community leaders not to attend this general gathering. He notified the public that in the near future rabbis and religious communal leaders would attend a general assembly to discuss these communal problems.

In 1928 the Jews were preparing to vote to select communal leaders. Rabbi Kagan wrote an article entitled "Unity Among the Religious Jews and Their Responsibilities in the Communities," in which he told the Jews to unite to participate in the communal elections and to help select religious leaders who wuld dedicate themselves to strengthening the teachings of the Torah and to saving Jewish children from the atheistic education received in the Zionist and Bundist schools. The rabbis must set an example in unity for they carry the responsibility for educating the Jews and their children in the ways of the Torah. Rabbi Kagan wrote that rabbis should be sure that there would be a religious school and religious teachers in every city. Unity among the religious Jews meant harmony with the Hasidic Jews. Rabbi Kagan was well respected among the Hasidic rabbis and their followers united to combat the secular elements among the Jews. In communal elections also, Hasidic and other religious Jews were able to unite in electing religious leaders.

One way in which the secular element among the Jews combatted religiosity and the authority of the rabbis was by printing newspaper articles mocking the rabbis and the traditional religious mode of life. The mockery and the criticism of rabbis and religion were influencing many Jews to rebel against the authority of the rabbis and the teachings of the Torah. Rabbi Kagan realized the danger of the newspapers to the masses, and in 1928 he wrote an article entitled, "To Abstain From Mockery and Newspapers," in which he objected to the newspapers which, he said, were filled with mockery, evil tongue, tale-bearing, quarrels, atheism, and heresy and were read by Jews not only on weekdays but also on the Sabbath and holidays.[87] He warned the Jews not to read such newspapers which stressed factors destructive to communal unity and traditional Judaism.

Rabbi Israel Meir Kagan felt strongly that the rabbi of any community must hold a position of influence and authority. Thus, he was shocked by the majority communal decision in Vilna in 1929 to discourage the influence of rabbis in the religious life of the Jews. The article "Insult of the Torah" said:

> How shocking it is to hear now the happening in the city of Vilna concerning the question of the rabbinate . . . behold, it is known that for several hundreds of years the city of Vilna was the center of great rabbis and leaders of Jews. . . . Behold, Satan has blocked the path before us, for they decided to alienate the great rabbis and teachers of Israel from the religious community, so they will not have influence in religious matters, and to appoint a leader who is not fitted for the position.[88]

The Rabbi urged every Jew to protest the decision. In a letter to Rabbi Hayyim Ozer Grodzenski in 1929, Rabbi Kagan advocated an unyielding stand concerning the honor of the rabbinate and the Torah in Vilna. Regardless of public opinion on the decision of the Vilna communal majority, the Torah and the authority of the rabbinate must be respected. A religious Jew must stand firm in time of insult to the power of the rabbinate and the Torah; in this there could be no compromise. An adamant opposition to compromise would show to the world, to the secular elements among the Jews,

---

[87]Kagan, "To Abstain from Mockery and Newspapers," Kagan, *Michtevei Hafets Hayyim,* p. 97.
[88]Rabbi Israel Meir Kagan, "Insult of the Torah," Kagan, *Michtevei Hafets Hayyim,* p. 43.

and to the ministers of the Polish government that there was
no such thing as give and take concerning the strict observance of the laws of the Torah and the authority of the rabbinate in carrying out the teachings of the Torah.[89] As in all
matters dealing with the honor of the Torah and the authority of the rabbinate, Rabbi Kagan displayed a firm stand.

In 1931 Rabbis Israel Meir Kagan and Hayyim Ozer
Grodzenski wrote an article entitled, "Grave Warnings Concerning the Rabbinate." In it they defined the duties of a
rabbi:

> Behold, the establishment of the rabbinate is the
> educational pillar among Israel, it is venerated and
> sanctified from generation to generation. The rabbis
> are the teachers who guide the path of the Jews and
> their practice. . . . The most significant requirement
> of the rabbinate is the knowledge of the Torah and
> of every aspect of the Law. The rabbis are chosen
> to serve in their position for a lifetime, and they shall
> know that they are assured in their position, and
> their lives shall not be dependent upon compromises
> with opposition and their words shall be heeded.
> The rabbis were always the glory of Israel, and with
> their wisdom and by their righteousness they in-
> fluenced the journey of general and specific events,
> and they shall be the true bearers of the flag of the
> Torah.[90]

Rabbi Kagan also concerned himself with the daily problems of the working Jew. The tobacco factory in Grodno
employed Jews. Although the workers in the Grodno factory
had two days off each week, the non-Jews preferred not to
have two consecutive days off—such as Saturday and Sunday.
They did not work on Sunday, of course, and preferred to
stay home on another day in the middle of the week. This
meant that the Jews in the factory had to work on the Sab-

---

[89]Letter from Rabbi Israel Meir Kagan, Radun, Poland, Sivan, 1929,
Kagan, *Michtevei Hafets Hayyim*, p. 209.
[90]Kagan and Grodzenski, "Grave Warning Concerning the Rabbinate,"
Kagan, *Michtevei Hafets Hayyim*, p. 115.

bath. Rabbi Kagan wrote to Rabbi Aaron Lewin, Chief Rabbi of Reisa, Poland and a deputy to the Polish *Sejm* asking permission for the Jews in the factory to abstain from work on the Sabbath. Rabbi Lewin wrote to Rabbi Kagan in 1931 informing him that the Director of Tobacco Factories of the Polish government had been notified of the Sabbath problem in Grodno. He urged the Jewish workers to ask the management of the Grodno factory to write to the Director and to the religious Deputies of the *Sejm*. He expressed the hope that the Jewish workers would be allowed to observe the Sabbath.[91] With the help of Rabbis Kagan and Lewin, the workers were eventually allowed to do so.

In 1931 Rabbi Kagan delivered a sermon before several thousand women and men in the large synagogue in Vilna, in which he stressed the importance of keeping the family purity laws. In the big cities in particular, where women were influenced by secular education, many were not keeping the family purity laws strictly enough. Vilna, which had been known as the Jerusalem of Lithuania, began to emerge as a showplace of secular enlightenment and progressive elements among the Jews. The Rabbi reminded his listeners that Vilna had been a holy city full of Torah and God-fearing people for the last fifty years. In order to remain holy in the eyes of God, Jews must try in every generation to keep all the laws of the Torah. Men are born and they die; but the Torah remains unchanged for every new generation to study and keep. The Jews are considered holy only if they keep the Holy Torah.[92] The family purity laws had been observed faithfully by mothers in the past, and the women must continue to study the laws dealing with family purity and keep them in order to preserve the holiness of Israel.

Rabbi Kagan's Involvement in the Agudat-Israel Organization

In 1912 the Union of Liberal Rabbis in Germany, under

---

[91]Letter from Rabbi Aaron Lewin, Reisa, Poland, Iyar, 1921 to Rabbi Kagan, Kagan, *Michtevei Hafets Hayyim*, p. 242.

[92]Rabbi Israel Meir Kagan, "Portions of his Speech in the Vilna Synagogue," Kislev, 1931, Kagan, *Michtevei Hafets Hayyim*, pp. 195ff.

the supervision of Caesar Seligmann, recommended a new set of principles under the title, "Principles of a Program for Liberal Judaism" (Richtlinien Zu Einem Programm Fur Das Liberale Judentum"). Although the fundamental truths and eternal morals of the Jewish faith were retained, new forms of faith and practice were urged. Moderation was the goal of the Union. Both radical and Orthodox Jews declared war on the principles. The radicals felt that the requirements were too numerous and too positive; the Orthodox objected to the principles' destructive tendencies and claimed that religious education in the spirit of the principles was dangerous to Judaism. They felt that rabbis who followed the formulations were unfit to hold a rabbinic post.

Agudat-Israel, the world organization of orthodox Judaism, undertook to wage a war against these principles. The organization was established in Kattowitz in May, 1912 and was led by Jacob Rosenheim in Frankfurt. Its purpose was to search for solutions to the contemporary problems of Judaism in the spirit of Torah and its means were

> the combination and common action of Orthodox groups in the east and west, large scale promotion of the study of Torah and of Jewish education, measures of relief, and, finally, representation to the outer world and defense against attacks directed against the Torah and its adherents.[93]

From its inception, Rabbi Israel Meir Kagan was one of Agudat-Israel's greatest guides in dealing with contemporary common problems of Judaism in the spirit of the Torah. In 1929, in an article concerning Agudat-Israel, he wrote:

> Brethren Jews! How grave and threatening is our time, how dangerous is the present moment in which we live. The prophet says: 'Then will the God-fearing man speak to his friend.' (Malachi 3:16) With their friends they will be able to converse, but not with the people, because the people do not listen.

---

[93]Elbogen, A Century of Jewish Life, p. 422.

And if the people do not listen, then the God-fearing people converse only with their friends. Hillel the Elder had said thus: If you see a generation that has love for the Torah then be active and dedicated in spreading the learning of Torah; and if it has no love for Torah, be passive, sad, so the Torah will not be insulted. And if the people say: In vain do we worship God and there is no profit for us—then there is no sense to spread Torah among them; but only among the God-fearing Jews in every city, it is a good deed to unite and to inspire each other in the worship of God.[94]

He went on to describe the laxity of religious life among the Jews and the aims of Agudat-Israel.

Brethren and friends! We live today in a generation that has no love for the Torah. There are very many who are lax in keeping the Torah. The dislike for religion increases from day to day. There is a constant attempt to uproot the foundation and existence of the Jewish people. . . . It is a must to strengthen ourselves in behalf of the worship of God and the love of Torah by organizing ourselves into a united party. . . . Therefore, each one who feels God in his heart must more dedicate himself in the honor of God. All God-fearing people in all the cities must unite themselves and assemble in their company all those who have not as yet completely abandoned the Jewish way of life; and all shall unite under the name of "Agudat-Israel." Their main concern shall be to see that in every city shall be a Hebrew school as in the past, where the Bible with Rashi's commentaries (without skipping) also the prophets shall be taught; and the teachers shall be God-fearing men who educate the children in the path of the Torah and the faith in

---

[94]Rabbi Israel Meir Kagan, "Agudat Israel," Kagan, *Michtevei Hafets Hayyim*, p. 134.

God. For better boys, there shall be in every city elementary rabbinical academies. Also there must be guidance for keeping the Sabbath and the family purity laws. And no strength and effort must be spared, for you shall know, brethren, that Satan with his companions are fortifying all their strength to cause the forgetfulness of the Torah among the Jews and thereby prolonging the exile . . .

I ask you brothers and friends in Lithuania and in all near and distant lands to unite yourselves under the flag of "Agudat Israel" and to follow God and His Torah. Because this will merit us God's help and the quick redemption.[95]

In a letter of 1930 to the leaders of Agudat-Israel in Poland, Rabbi Kagan urged them not to unite with the secular parties in the coming elections. God, who had guided the Jews for such a long time, would be the partner of the religious Jews. With the help of God the God-fearing Jews would be successful in the election without a coalition with secular Jews.[96]

*Rabbi Kagan's Dedication to Establishing
and Maintaining Yeshivoth*

In 1869, at the age of 31, Rabbi Kagan had established a *yeshiva* in his home of Radun, Poland. The Yeshivath Hafets Hayyim of Radun eventually became one of the most important centers of Talmudic learning in Europe. The Jews in Radun and its environs loved the Torah and shared in the expense of construction and maintenance of the *yeshiva.*

In the early stages of the growth of the *yeshiva,* students from out of town ate in the homes of Radun Jews; later a kitchen was established to provide sustenance for the students. Rabbi Kagan's wife and daughters were responsible for collecting the necessary food from the Jews of Radun and for the preparation of the meals. Before the Second World

[95]*Ibid.,* pp. 135ff.
[96]Letter from Rabbi Kagan, Radun, Poland, Elul, 1930, Kagan, *Michtevei Hafets Hayyim,* p. 233.

War, students at the *yeshiva* were provided with money for food, clothing, mail, and other necessities. A married man received an additional stipend for his wife and family.

In the beginning, only students from Radun and neighboring towns came to study at the *yeshiva*, but it grew and attracted students from more distant places such as Germany and England. Rabbi Kagan gave each student his personal attention, guiding each with fatherly love and understanding.

In 1927, he wrote a letter concerning the leadership of the Radun *yeshiva*.

Behold I shall inform the public of every matter of our holy *yeshivah*, the establishment took place upon my return from the city Washilishok . . . to Radun in the year 1869. When I came to Radun, I was inspired to gather single and married students to learn Torah; and also God motivated me to arouse the people of the community concerning the importance of the proposal. And with the help of God my words concerning the establishment of a *yeshiva* were acceptable to the people . . . even though I was occupied with the publications of my books dealing with morality and legal code, yet I did not remove my eyes from *yeshiva* to strengthen it and to increase it, and to attend all its necessary matters. And thus it went on until the year 1886 in which God merited me to marry my daughter to a man, a genius in the Torah and righteous in deeds, Rabbi Zvi Levinsohn, a student of our *yeshiva*. And when he came to my home, blessed by the Lord, the *yeshiva* was more strengthened because both of us worked to strengthen it and to increase it; and my son-in-law dedicated his life to the existence of the *yeshiva* until his death in 1921. After that his sons merited to be the financial and spiritual leaders of the *yeshiva*, for they are Rabbis Joshua Leib Levinsohn and Eliezar Zev Kaplan; and they are trying arduously to strengthen the holy *yeshiva* from the day their father passed away, may his memory be blessed. And now, at the time of my old age, I was thinking to settle in our holy land Israel and to leave the *yeshiva* in its place. And I made all the necessary preparations for this; however, from heaven I was prevented because on the day of my trip, my wife took very ill and is not able to make the trip; and according to the diagnosis of the doctors she will not be able to make the trip in the future; and, therefore, I must remain here . . . God merited me to marry my second daughter to a man great in Torah learning by the name of Rabbi Mendel Joseph Zaks, the son-of-Jacob Mordecai. I gave my son-in-law the authority to be a dean of the *yeshiva* and to teach before the students . . . and the main source of his livelihood should come from the *yeshivat* treasury. And my grandchildren, Rabbis Joshua Leib and Eliezer Zev shall be the materialistic and spiritual leaders of the *yeshiva* as before and no one can intervene in their authority.[97]

Rabbi Kagan was always ready to extend his leadership and counsel to the establishment of rabbinical seminaries in other cities throughout the world. His guidance was sought everywhere, even in America, and his readiness to help *yeshivoth* won him an everlasting reputation as a true friend of the Torah and of rabbinical schools. Rabbi Mendel Zaks, his son-in-law, told the author that Rabbi Kagan was invited to come to America to strengthen Judaism and to establish *yeshivoth*. Unfortunately, he was not able to do so because he was needed in Europe. His authority and determination to spread the Torah and to establish *yeshivoth* ignited the flame in the hearts of many Jews to support his endeavors. The *yeshiva* of Radun was one of the greatest centers of Torah learning and Rabbi Israel Meir Kagan was one of the greatest *yeshiva* deans.

---

[97]Letter from Rabbi Israel Meir Kagan, Radun, Poland, Tebet, 1927, Kagan, *Michtevei Hafets Hayyim*, p. 256-258.

In 1924 Rabbis Kagan and Hayyim Ozer Grodzenski
wrote an article entitled "Voice of Torah." In it they wrote:

> And behold, we saw that the position of the rab-
> binical seminaries has declined immensely; as it is
> known before the First World War there were many
> rabbinical seminaries in several Jewish populated
> cities, and in every rabbinical seminary hundreds
> of students studied Torah. . . . And now the num-
> ber of *yeshivoth* decreased, because the rabbinical
> seminaries cannot exist due to the lack of sources of
> support; several *yeshivoth* are on the verge of clos-
> ing down because of little financial support—the
> deans cannot provide even bread to the students.[98]

The two rabbis issued the following regulations to help the
yeshivoth:

1. Every Jew must make an annual contribution for the
support of the *yeshivoth*.
2. The contribution must be a dollar every half-year.
3. If a person can afford more he must give according
to his means.
4. Rabbis and followers of the Torah must donate two
weeks during the year to collecting the contributions and to
arousing the Jews in neighboring surroundings to strengthen
the Torah.
5. Each city must establish a local committee headed by
the rabbi to carry out this decision.
6. Payment must be made for the summer during the
Ten Days of Penitence and the contribution for the winter
must be paid up by Yom Kippur.
7. Every local committee must deliver the money to the
Central Yeshivoth Committee in Vilna.[99]

This Committee was organized by Rabbis Kagan and
Grodzenski and others to alleviate the financial burdens of

---

[98]Rabbis Israel Meir Kagan and Hayyim Ozer Grodzenski, "Voice of
Torah," Kagan, *Michtevei Hafets Hayyim*, p. 154.
[99]*Ibid.*, p. 155.

the *yeshivoth*. A *yeshiva* in great financial need now had a national committee to come to its aid and to keep its door open. The Central Yeshivoth Committee was very successful in aiding faltering seminaries, according to Rabbi Joseph David Epstein, an active participant in the Central Yeshivoth Committee.[100]

In another article, "Voice Calls for Strengthening the Yeshivoth," of 1925, Rabbi Kagan wrote:

> And behold, now the summer payment for the year 1925 has been completed; and it is appropriate to say that the year brought financial success which enabled us to strengthen the economic position of disastrous yeshivoth.
>
> And behold, I thank and bless abundantly all the workers, the contributors and the leaders who dedicated themselves in the project of strengthening our holy Torah; and may God repay them meritoriously for their outstanding work.[101]

In closing the article, Rabbi Kagan urged the Jews to continue to support the *yeshivoth;* and expressed the hope that God would reward them generously for their charity on behalf of the *yeshivoth*.

In another letter of 1925, Rabbi Kagan asked various rabbis to travel to surrounding communities and collect the annual dues for the Central Yeshivoth Committee. Since the majority of Torah educated Jews were poor, the payment to the Central Yeshivoth Committee should be considered as fulfilling the obligation of charity and kindness.[102] He also wrote to Jews in America:

> . . . and behold, until now our brethren in America had a great merit in strengthening the Torah, supporting students of Torah in Palestine and in the

[100]Interview by the author with Rabbi Joseph David Epstein, Brooklyn, New York, October 28, 1967.
[101]Rabbi Israel Meir Kagan, "Voice Calls for Strengthening the Yeshivoth," Kagan, *Michtevei Hafets Hayyim*, p. 73.
[102]Letter from Rabbi Israel Meir Kagan, Radun, Poland, first day of Elul, 1925, Kagan, *Michtevei Hafets Hayyim*, p. 157.

dispersion through the contributions of individuals
and through the very noble foundation, the Central
Relief whose support financed successfully the holy
yeshivoth and places of learning . . . to our sorrow,
as it is already known, the Central Relief will cease
to provide financial support in the near future and
all the holy *yeshivoth* and establishments of Torah
learning will find themselves in a very grave financial crisis.[103]

The Rabbi implored American Jews to change their minds
about the dissolution of the Central Relief agency. Since it
had been able to support the *yeshivoth* in the past; there
was no reason, according to Rabbi Kagan, for American
Jewry to abandon such a worthwhile charitable institution.
Since American Jews had not experienced the destruction
of the First World War, they were in a position to help their
poor brethren in Europe. Since God had kept American Jews
from the horrors of war and provided them with economic
stability, it was their obligation to help their poverty-stricken
brethren in Europe through maintaining the Central Relief
agency. Rabbi Kagan later came to realize that Americans
were at that time in the midst of an economic depression
and did not have the funds to keep the agency going.

Russian Jews were under the rule of Communism and
were forbidden to support religious schools of learning. The
Polish masses managed to support countless schools and
charitable institutions despite their poverty, but they needed
financial support from American Jews to continue the upkeep of the *yeshivoth*. Rabbi Kagan noted that many outstanding students were denied entrance to the *yeshivoth* because of financial difficulties. The schools were on the verge
of economic disaster and unless God showed his mercy upon
them they would close up. He concluded by calling for a
day of fast and prayer by the deans and students of the *yeshivoth* in order that God would relieve them from economic

---

[103]Letter from Rabbi Israel Meir Kagan, Radun, Poland, Hesvan, 1932,
Kagan, *Michtevei Hafets Hayyim*, pp. 175ff.

disaster.[104] In 1929 Rabbi Kagan selected the prominent Rabbis Simon Skop, dean of the Grodno seminary, Reuben Katz, Rabbi and Dean of Stavisk seminary and later chief rabbi of Petach-Tikva, and others to raise funds in America for *yeshivoth* in Europe.[105]

Rabbi Kagan's Method of Teaching and His Influence on Students and Other Rabbis

Rabbi Kagan's method of teaching was a combination of clarity in presentation of difficult material and derivation of practical legal conclusions based upon Biblical, Talmudic, Midrashic, and other rabbinic sources. He was not interested in using the pilpulistic (casuistical subtlety) method in his teaching because he said that the time was short and precious and because the practical application of the teachings of the Torah was to him of paramount importance.[106] His method of teaching stressed deep understanding of the material and ability to transfer complicated subjects meaningfully.

In 1925 Rabbi Kagan was influential in initiating the following ordinances in his *yeshiva*:

1. The study of laws dealing with gossip and tale-bearing to take place at least three times a week.

2. The study of laws dealing with daily observance to take place every day, on the Sabbath, and on holidays.

3. The observance of the above-mentioned ordinances to be supervised by the deans of the seminary.[107]

In 1931 a conference of rabbis and deans gathered in Radun. The group decided that students in the *yeshivoth* should:

1. Strengthen the earnest study of the Torah, morality, and the fear of God;

2. Be cautious in speech and avoid speaking in vain; (The appropriate advice was to study the laws dealing with gossip

---

[104]*Ibid.*, p. 150.
[105]Katz, *Shaar Reuben*, p. 7.
[106]Interview by the author with Rabbi Mendel Zaks, June 28, 1967.
[107]Rabbi Israel Meir Kagan, "Ordinances in Yeshiva," Kagan, *Michtevei Hafets Hayyim*, p. 174.

and tale-bearing which can be found in the book *Sefer Hafets Hayyim*.)

3. Not commit any deed which profanes God's name;

4. Organize groups with a leader to evaluate the diligence in studying Torah of each member;

5. Not study secular subjects, but devote themselves to the study of the holy Torah and the fear of God;

6. Not read atheistic and blasphemous books or newspapers which write abominable articles; and

7. Be expelled for reading unacceptable books.[108]

In the same assembly the following ordinances were instituted concerning the enhancement of the spiritual life of the *yeshivoth*:

1. Every year, before Passover or at the time of the meeting of the Central Yeshivoth Committee for the materialistic welfare of the *yeshivoth*, it is necessary to congregate to evaluate the spiritual matters of the schools.

2. Twice a week in every *yeshiva* students in the first two years of study must attend lectures in addition to their independent work.

3. Every student must be examined twice per term or at least once per term.

4. Students shall not be accepted from Rabbinical Academies to Rabbinical Seminaries unless they pass the examination based on the material studied the last year in attendance at the Academy and are capable of carrying on independent study.

5. Students are permitted to go to summer camps only for a month and the weak students shall have priority.[109]

In the *yeshiva* at Radun, outstanding single and married students were selected to study the tractate of the Talmud dealing with sacrificial law. In 1931 Rabbi Kagan wrote the

---

[108]Rabbi Israel Meir Kagan, "Ordinances that were made and accepted in the Assembly of rabbis and deans," Kagan, *Michtevei Hafets Hayyim*, p. 184.
[109]*Ibid.*

following ordinances to be observed by the students engrossed in the study of sacrificial law:

1. A student must abstain from gossip, tale-bearing, mockery, falsehood, flattery, deceit, fraud, putting to shame, profanity of God's name, and passion of the eyes.

2. A student must repent every day before sleep, on the eve of every new month, on the eve of every Sabbath, and on the eve of Yom Kippur.[110]

Rabbi Kagan's Teaching on the Existence of the Torah, the Jewish People, and Dark Forces in the World

According to Rabbi Mendel Zaks, Rabbi Kagan was convinced that keeping the Torah was the most important reason for the existence of the Jewish people. Only through the practice of the teachings of the Torah could the Jews hope for the coming of the Messiah and redemption. Rabbi Zaks informed the author that Rabbi Kagan was deeply grieved by the persecution of the Jews and his advice to the Jews was to endure the persecutions through faith in God and through study of the Torah. Rabbi Kagan felt that observing the holy Torah had kept the Jews from assimilation throughout the centuries and would do so in the future.

According to Rabbi Zaks, Rabbi was well informed about such forces as Communism, anti-Semitism, and the emergence of Nazism and Fascism. He lamented the calamities he knew these forces would inflict upon the world in general and upon the Jews in particular, but he was convinced that only belief in God and observance of the laws of the Torah could save the Jews from disaster. He died in 1933, and was saved from seeing one of the worst tragedies in Jewish history befall his beloved people and from being one of the victims of the holocaust.

Conclusion

After Rabbi Kagan returned from Russia to Poland, he emerged as a leader of Polish Orthodox Jewry. He also dis-

---

[110]Rabbi Israel Meir Kagan, "Ordinances of Rabbi Israel Meir Kagan," Kagan, *Michtevei Hafets Hayyim*, p. 187.

played for the first time skills for diplomacy and made practical attempts to remove legislation he thought detrimental to Jewish religious and cultural autonomy. Even though he held that a Jew must be law abiding, he also believed that if the law of the land threatened the autonomy of Jewish religious and cultural institutions, it was necessary to use lobbying, diplomacy, and even bribery to attempt to change such legislation.

As we have seen, Rabbi Kagan encouraged Jews to participate in elections to the *Sejm* and the Senate, he actively campaigned on behalf of his endorsed candidates, whom he trusted to fight discriminatory legislation, and he met with the President of Poland and other high officials to remove anti-Jewish legislation. His analysis of the political events affecting Jews often led him to design specific programs for change and to do all he could to implement them.

Rabbi Kagan was a powerful personality with whom the Zionists, Bundists, and other secularists had to reckon or even fear since he was quite often instrumental in uniting Hasidic and Orthodox Jews during elections to the *Sejm* and to positions of leadership in the Jewish community. Thus, Rabbi Kagan's influence often produced a majority of votes for the candidates whom he supported.

Rabbi Kagan rejected secular education under any circumstances and particularly when he was aware that the Polish government's requirement was intended to break the power of the old guard rabbis over the Jewish masses, who were Hasidic or pious Orthodox Jews.

Since Rabbi Kagan saw that the Polish government's discriminatory legislation of the late twenties and thirties was aimed at weakening the power of rabbis and breaking down religious and cultural autonomy among the Jews, we see again that he might have encouraged mass Jewish emigration to Israel or America, where the Orthodox might have had a better chance to flourish.

In Poland, he continued to blossom as a leader of the Torah community. He participated in many conferences dealing programmatically with the religious and communal problems of the Jews. His following was wide and diversified; he enjoyed the loyalty of Orthodox and Hasidic Jews and was held in high esteem even by non-observant Jews. Certainly, he was the decisive force in many of the conferences.

In 1933, the year that Hitler rose to power in Germany, one of the *Roshei Yeshivoth* asked Rabbi Kagan, "What will the destiny of European Jewry be, after the wicked one has made public his intention of destroying the Jewish people . . . ?" "God forbid," answered Rabbi Kagan, "for anyone to conceive the idea of annihilating the Jews." For it is written, "If Esau attacks one camp, the other one will be for a refuge." The *Rosh Yeshiva* understood that the danger was immediate, and he continued to ask: "If, God forbid, Hitler destroys European Jewry, the most populated and most prolific culturally and spiritually, where will the place of refuge for the other camp be?" Rabbi Kagan answered that even this is explained in the prophets: "On Mount Zion there will be a refuge and a place of holiness." The *Rosh Yeshiva* left Rabbi Kagan very disturbed, but at the same time convinced that at least the holy land would escape the terrible slaughter of the Nazis.

Very few men in the twentieth century had the vision to foresee the diabolical consequences of Hitler's hostility towards the Jews. Certainly Rabbi Kagan foresaw the suffering of his people, but he was unable to overcome his objections to Jewish life in America or Israel in order to encourage mass emigration. He spoke of the danger, but very few listened to design a program to encourage mass departures of Jews to escape that danger.

Chapter Four

LASHON HARA:[1] A MAJOR PIETISTIC CONCERN

Rabbi Israel Meir Kagan considered gossip and talebearing great evils and spent his life preaching against them. In this chapter we will look at the problem of gossip and slander in the Eastern European Jewish Community, the effects of the problem on life in that community, and the often tragic results wrought by informers who used it to achieve their goals. Rabbi Kagan's first and most important work, *Hafets Hayyim,* will be analyzed in the light of classical-ethical literature, and gossip and slander will be defined in the light of Talmudic and rabbinic law and in terms of their significance in *Hafets Hayyim.* We will also discuss some negative precepts, some positive commands, and some curses associated with gossip and tale-bearing. An analysis of material from Rabbi Kagan's other book on the subject, *Shemirath ha-Lashon* will be offered, and the chapter will end with a conclusion.

Gossip and Tale-bearing in the Eastern Europe
Jewish Community

As we have seen, the Eastern European Jewish community went through profound changes in the nineteenth century and there was a clamor for innovations and reforms. Rabbi Kagan was particularly grieved that in the process of making

---

[1]*Lashon Hara* are the Hebrew words for *gossip.*

changes, man degrades himself by misusing and profaning speech—an attribute which elevates him above other animals and can be the means of achieving excellence. This concern motivated him to write his compendium, *Hafets Hayyim*.[2]

To be sure, Rabbi Kagan was not the first to deal with the problem of gossip and tale-bearing; other voices bemoaned the low moral climate. Rabbi Isaac Blazer (1837-1907), a leader of the Musar movement,[3] wrote:

> Piety has declined . . . houses of worship are deserted, sins have multiplied beyond control, ugly traits mount . . . falsehood is replacing righteousness and truth is lacking. In generations study of Torah was not separated from piety, but now, the bond has been almost broken . . . and without piety, the study of Torah is meaningless.[4]

And Rabbi Israel Salanter wrote:

> . . . an individual refrains from committing many sins, even at a time when he is forced to transgress a precept. . . . There are more serious transgressions than these that a person will violate. An example is: a large portion of our brethren will not eat without washing the hands. . . . However, in the case of gossip, a grave sin, they will trespass easily. . . . Even the learned and God-fearing are guilty of gossip and are lax in keeping the ethical precepts of the Torah.[5]

The polemics exchanged on a personal level between the rabbis and the *Maskilim* fit the definition of gossip,[6] and gossip

[2]Kagan *Michtevei Hafets Hayyim*, I, 13ff.

[3]For a discussion of the life and works of Rabbi Blazer, see Katz, *Tenuath ha-Musar*, II, 220-273. See p. 2 for a description of the Musar movement.

[4]Blazer, *Or Israel*, p. 4.

[5]Israel Salanter, "Igeret ha-Musar," in *ibid.*, pp. 106ff.

[6]Abraham Mapu's novel, *Ayit Zavua (The Painted Hawk)*, depicted a certain rabbi under the name of Rabbi Gadiel as "blind fanatic, an enemy of *Haskalah* and of Hebrew literature." (p. 225). See also Glenn, *Israel Salanter*, p. 43, where Glenn identifies Rabbi Salanter, the personification of truth and morality, as Rabbi Gadiel.

and slander were the primary tools of informers who threatened the very life of the Jewish community.

Informers

The conscription horrors of Tsar Nicholas I fostered informing among the Jewish communities.[7] They produced the type of professional informer who blackmailed the *kahal* authorities by threatening to disclose irregularities in the administration of the canton system. The informers made life intolerable, and "there were occasions when people took the law into their own hands and secretly killed the most despicable among them."[8] In 1836 a case of this kind took place in the town of Novaya Ushitza, Podolia province. Two informers named Oxman and Schwartz, who had terrorized the entire province, were found dead and Russian officials blamed the local Jewish community for the crime. Twenty *kahal* elders were sentenced to exile in Siberia and a like number were sentenced to hard labor.[9]

Informers were also involved in the Mstislavl affair. In 1844, a Jewish crowd in the market place of Mstislavl, in Moghilov province, resisted a detachment of soldiers who were searching for contraband goods in a Jewish warehouse. Arye Briskin, a converted Jew, joined the local police and officials to inform the government that the Jews had organized a mutiny. A swift resolution followed: "To courtmartial the principal culprits implicated in this incident, and, in the meantime, as a punishment for the turbulent demeanor of the Jews of that city, to take from them one recruit for every ten men."[10] The decree arrived in Mstislavl on the eve of Purim, and threw the Jews into consternation. Several eminent leaders of the Jewish community were arrested and had to submit to disfigurement by having half of their beards and

---

[7]Informing during the *rekruchina* (1825-1855) was a peculiar circumstance since the *kahal* was involved. In fact, quite a class conflict resulted from it because the minors of the poor were recruited by the leaders of the *kahal* while the sons of the rich were able to buy their exemption.

[8]Dubnow, *History of the Jews in Russia and Poland*, II, 84ff.

[9]*Ibid.*, p. 85.

[10]*Ibid.*, p. 86.

their heads shaved off, and the recruits were hunted down, irrespective of age.[11]

Another example of the damage informers could cause is offered by the case of Jacob Brafman. At the end of the 1860's, the Jew Jacob Brafman appeared in Vilna to offer his services as an informer against his co-religionists. He felt bitter toward the authorities of the Jewish Community in Minsk who had tried to recruit him during the *rekruchina*. Brafman recommended curtailment of the last traces of Jewish autonomy through the closing of all religious and charitable institutions.[12] His *Book of the Kahal*,[13] filled with the usual misrepresentation of facts concerning Judaism and the *Kahal*, was dispatched to all government officials as a guide to dealing with local Jewish groups. The book indirectly caused the death in pogroms of many innocent Jews who had had nothing to do with his conscription into the army.[14] These events helped confirm Rabbi Kagan's conviction that gossip and tale-bearing can lead to informing which can inflict great harm upon society.[15]

Classical Ethical Literature

Prior to the publication of *Hafets Hayyim*, other ethical works were used as texts for the study of *Musar*. The classical books *Hoboth Halebaboth* (*Duties of the Heart*), *Sefer Hasidim* (*Book of the Pious*), *Mesilath Yesharim* (*Path of the*

---

[11]The lobbying of Isaac Zelikin, the merchant and popular champion of the interests of his people, in the Court of Nicholas I, resulted in an "imperial Act of Grace." The imprisoned Jews were set free, the conscripts were returned from service, the governor of Moghilov was severely censured, and several local officials had to face trial. *Ibid.*, pp. 86ff.

[12]*Ibid.*, pp. 187-190.

[13]The *Book of Kahal* was printed at public expense. The first edition appeared in 1869, the second in 1871.

[14]Dubnow, *History of the Jews in Russia and Poland*, II, 191-198.

[15]The problems created by tale-bearing were experienced personally by the author. In 1939 some Jews of Ilia, Lithuania, informed the Communists that the author's father, Leib Eckman, was a capitalist working for the overthrow of the Soviet government. He was also alleged to be a spy for England and America. As a result, he was arrested and detained for five years.

Righteous),[16] were used in the *yeshivoth* and other schools. These works are concerned with character building and Jewish values, and not with such details as gossip and slander. Furthermore, they were written not for the layman but for Torah scholars. Most Jews found these texts difficult to comprehend as they required special study. But not so the *Hafets Hayyim*. It was written in a language that was easily understood; it was patterned after the form of the *Shulhan Arukh* (for which a majority of Jews harboured a deep respect and reverence), and it became a kind of accompanying text to the code of law which every educated layman in Eastern Europe could understand and follow. At the same time it was suitable for study by scholars.

Definition of Slander and Gossip in the Light of Talmudic and Rabbinic Law

According to the Talmud, slander is a serious crime. It is defined as the dissemination of either false or true statements about a person in order to defame his character. The slanderer is like one who denies God. "He and I cannot live together in the world," God says of the slanderer.[17] The Talmud based this statement on a verse: "Thou shalt not

---

[16]*Hoboth Halebaboth* deals with the unity of God; examination of creation, the service of God, trust in God, wholehearted devotion, humility, repentance, spiritual accountings, abstinence, the love of God, the ten strophes, admonition, and petition. See Bahya ben Joseph iben Pakuda, *Hoboth Halebaboth*, translated by Moses Hyamson (Jerusalem: Boys Town Publishers, 1965), 2 vols.

Sefer Hasidim deals with the conduct of man in relation to God, in relation to one another, in relation to gentile neighbors and to government authority. It includes worship and prayer, sin and repentance, Sabbath observance and the study of Torah. It embraces rules concerning matters of business; the treatment of servants, and the care of animals. It includes such topics as the sacred relationships of marriage and love, with emphasis on chastity, self-restraint, education of children, writing, copying and treatment of books, and minutiae of personal conduct. See Rabbi Judah Ha-Hasid, *Sefer Hasidim* (Jerusalem: Mossad Harav Kook, 1964). See also Simon G. Kramer, *God and Man in the Sefer Hasidim* (New York: Bloch Publishing Company, 1966).

Mesilath Yesharim deals with man's duty in the world, various functions of zeal, how to acquire spiritual cleanness, different phases of abstinence; purity, saintliness, humility, fear of sin, and holiness. See M. H. Luzzatto, *Mesilath Yesharim* (New York: Shulsinger Bros., 1942).

[17]Tractate *Arakin*, p. 15b.

go up and down as a talebearer among thy people; thou shalt not stand idly by the blood of thy neighbor."[18] The Torah connects the sin of slander—which destroys a man's reputation—with the sin of imperiling a man's life. Gossip is defined as an utterance that may be true, but may expose the person to contempt or derision. According to Rabbi Kagan, a talebearing tongue convicts three: itself, the slandered one, and the one who listens to the slander. Uncharitable comment on one's fellowman is classified as *"avak lashon hara,"* a shade of slander, or more literally dust of evil speech. The Midrash describes the spreading of gossip in the following manner: "What is spoken in Rome may kill in Syria."[19]

Slander

It is important to trace the definitions of gossip and slander in the light of Talmudic and rabbinic sources so that differences between them can be ascertained and Rabbi Kagan's views concerning them can be placed in proper perspective. The Hebrew word for slander is *rekiluth*. The Talmud depicts *rekiluth* as an act of revealing a secret.[20] Maimonides defined slander as that which a person peddles from neighbor to neighbor, saying "someone said thus," "such and such I heard about a certain man." Even though the tale may be true, a person who tells it is guilty of destroying the world. Maimonides presented the example of Doag the Edomite, who was responsible for Saul's slaughter of innocent people.[21] Maimonides also held that a person who spies on his friend commits a very grave transgression and causes the murder of many innocent Jews since the verse "thou shalt not stand idly by the blood of thy neighbor" follows the verse "thou shalt not go up and down as a tale-bearer among thy people."[22]

Prohibitions against slander are also included in civil

---

[18]Leviticus 19:16.
[19]*Genesis Rabba*, 8:23.
[20]Tractate *Sanhedrin*, 31a.
[21]Maimonides, *Hilkhoth Dea'yoth* (Mt. Kisco: Yeshiva Press, 1958), p. 61.
[22]*Ibid.*

law. According to Wilfred A. Button, slander is a "defama-
tory statement which is published by the word of mouth or
by gesture."[23] Slander is a tort actionable at a suit of the
person defamed by it. A plaintiff in a slander action must,
with four exceptions, prove actual damage in order to suc-
ceed. The four exceptions are:

1. when the words impute a crime punishable with imprisonment;
2. when the words impute leprosy or venereal disease;
3. when the words are spoken of a person in the way
   of his trade, profession, or calling, and impute to him
   misconduct in or unfitness for that trade, profession
   or calling;
4. when the words impute unchastity or immorality to
   a woman or girl.[24]

In civil law one can bring a slanderer to court if evidence
can be shown. However, in Talmudic law a slanderer cannot
be taken to court.

Gossip

The Talmud depicts *lashon hara* as a devastating quality:
Rabbi Yohanan said in the name of Rabbi Yosi ben Zimra;
"one who indulges in gossip is guilty of denying the existence
of God and of His commands . . . such a man is punished
with leprosy. . . ."[25] Rabbi Ishmael said: "One who engages
in gossip is guilty of a sin equal to the three prohibitions
for which a Jew must accept death, namely, idolatry, adultry,
and murder. . . ."[26]

The Talmud expands the definition of *lashon hara* to
include *avak lashon hara* (shade of *lashon hara*) as gossip. If
one indulges in *avak lashon hara,* he is as guilty as if he engages in gossip: Rabbi Dimi said, "a person must never speak

---

[23]W. A. Button, *Libel and Slander* (London: Sweet and Maxwell, Ltd.,
1946), p. 19; see also Sir Hugh Fraser, *Principles and Practice of the Law
of Libel and Slander* (London: Butterworth and Co., 1935), pp. 1ff.
[24]Button, *Libel and Slander*, p. 19.
[25]Tractate *Arakin*, p. 15b.
[26]*Ibid.*

about his neighbor's goodness since he might also mention his weakness in the narration."[27] Rabbi Amram said in the name of Rav: "Each day a person is held accountable if he is guilty of transgressing the following three prohibitions: meditating to commit a sin, meditating that God must reward him for his prayers, and speaking a shade of gossip."[28] Rashi defines a shade of gossip in the following manner: "If someone asks of a fellowman, 'where can I find fire?' and he replies, 'fire can be found in the house of so and so where there is plenty of meat, fish and where they are always cooking something,' by adding the words, "that they are always cooking something,' he is committing a shade of gossip, implying that they are always eating there."[29]

Rabbi Kagan accepted these definitions and views from Maimonides concerning gossip and slander, and expanded on them. He included the fourteen positive and seventeen prohibitive commandments of the Torah relating to an evil tongue. Further, like Maimonides, he cited the Talmud's comparison of gossip and slander to the most grievous sins of idolatry, adultery, and murder. Gossip is a sin not only when false, but even if true; not only when spread against Jews but even against non-Jews.

Traditionally, gossip and talebearing consist of any verbal or non-verbal activity—even if based on the truth—which can cause minor harm or discomfort to the one who is its object. Certainly, the polemics of Mapu and Gordon against rabbis would be considered *lashon hara* and slander since the exchanges were harmful. It may be difficult to understand how such exchanges could be called gossip or slander, but one must remember that Rabbi Kagan considered the feelings of another person as his own and believed that no one had the right—even under the justification of truth—to hurt the feelings of another of God's creatures. Thus, if the criteria of the slightest damage is applied, gossip and slander come to include a great variety of acts and deeds.

---

[27]*Tractate Baba Bathra*, p. 164b and 165a.
[28]*Ibid.*, p. 164b.
[29]Commentary of Rashi in tractate *Arkin*, p. 15b.

Significance of Gossip and Slander in Hafets Hayyim

Rabbi Israel Meir Kagan was concerned with the evil resulting from slander and gossip, but was perhaps more concerned that people were ignorant of the basic Torah law: "Thou shalt not go up and down as a talebearer among thy people." The precepts of gossip and slander were scattered throughout the Torah and cognate rabbinic literature and as a result were not available to most Jews. So Rabbi Kagan set out to systematize and classify all aspects of Jewish law having to do with talebearing and gossip, beginning with the basic law of the Torah. In the introduction to *Hafets Hayyim* he pointed out:

> . . . laws of gossip and talebearing are scattered throughout the Talmud and early rabbinic literature . . . even Maimonides . . . did not elaborate on these laws and many specifics were omitted by them. . . . I, therefore, girded my loins with the help of God . . . and gathered all the laws of gossip and talebearing from all sources starting with Talmud, codifiers and responsa literature. . . . I codified these laws into one book consisting of two parts; laws forbidding gossip and laws forbidding slander.[30]

Rabbi Kagan's discussion of *lashon hara* and slander is a broad one that attempts to show how central this prohibition is and what relevance it has to the community. He did not see the act of speaking evil as an independent incident relating only to the culprit and the victim, but as an evil act which starts a chain reaction that ultimately spreads its poison to the entire community.[31] He also tried to show that gossip has a tendency to lead one to violate other laws.

---

[30]Rabbi Israel Meir Kagan, *Hafets Hayyim (He Who Desires Life)*, (Jerusalem: Va'ad Shemirath ha-Lashon, 1967), pp. 4ff.

[31]*Ibid.*, p. 13; see also Kagan, *Shemirath ha-Lashon (Guarding the Tongue)* (Jerusalem: Va'ad Shemirath ha-Lashon, 1967), pp. 39ff.

It is the beginning of all evil.[32] Because of gossip, Rabbi Kagan states, Jews were exiled into Egypt; because Joseph spoke evil about his brothers to his father, he was sold into Egypt.[33] Again, it was on account of gossip which the spies brought from Canaan that the children of Israel were condemned to stay in the desert for forty years.[34] It is written: "before the blind do not put a stumbling block . . ."[35] There is also in the Torah a curse upon those who cause the blind to go astray. The Rabbi considered the talebearer the "pusher" of an evil that disrupts the harmony of humanity. Consequently the evil bearer is also violating the precept "thou shalt love thy neighbor as thyself."[36] By disparaging one's neighbor, one negates the love one is to have for him.[37] The talebearer is soiling the image of God with which every human being is endowed.[38] He impairs the dignity of his neighbor and, in essence, denies both reverence and fear of God.[39] According to Rabbi Kagan, the love and goodness of God for mankind depend on their abstinence from gossip and talebearing, which are major causes for controversy and evil.[40]

Thus Rabbi Kagan was responsible for a new body of *Halakhah,* broad in scope, philosophical in nature, and universally accepted among Jews as the final word in matters dealing with gossip and talebearing. Concerning the content of the book, the remainder of this chapter will analyze some of the negative precepts, some of the positive precepts, and some of the curses that the Torah connected with the prohibition of gossip and slander, and will deal with two sections of answers to questions about gossip and talebearing.

---

[32]Kagan, *Hafets Hayyim,* p. 2; and Kagan, *Shemirath ha-Lashon,* p. 11ff.

[33]Kagan, *Hafets Hayyim,* p. 9; and Kagan, *Shemirath ha-Lashon,* pp. 158-165.

[34]Kagan, *Hafets Hayyim,* p. 9; and Kagan, *Shemirath ha-Lashon,* pp. 173-178.

[35]Leviticus 19:14.

[36]Leviticus 19:18.

[37]Kagan, *Hafets Hayyim,* pp. 26ff.; and Kagan, *Shemirath ha-Lashon,* pp. 59ff.

[38]Kagan, *Hafets Hayyim,* p. 38.

[39]*Ibid.,* pp. 31-34.

[40]*Ibid.,* p. 9; and Kagan, *Shemirath ha-Lashon,* pp. 13-15.

Some Negative Precepts

Gossip is considered an even greater sin than talebearing and is part of the negative command. What is gossip? It is words which embarrass a friend, even though they might be the truth.[41] Suppose, on the other hand, the gossip is false; the gossiper is also guilty of damaging his innocent friend's reputation.[42]

The one who tells and the one who listens to gossip are equally guilty of trespassing the negative precept of "thou shalt not utter a false report."[43] The teller as well as the listener are guilty of violating the precept "before the blind do not put a stumbling block." However, there is a difference between one who gossips and one who listens. The gossiper is guilty whether there are many or few listeners, and surely the greater the number of listeners the greater is the sin since he has caused many to stumble. However, the listener is, by virtue of his listening, only responsible for himself.

Rabbi Kagan ruled that one who gossips is also guilty of breaking the negative command: "thou shalt not hate thy neighbor in thy heart."[44] Such a person speaks peace with his friend while bearing false tales about him in his absence. Rabbi Kagan held that one who gossips also transgresses the negative command of "thou shalt not take vengeance nor bear any grudge."[45] If one man says to another, 'lend me your sickle,' and the latter says to him, 'no,' and on the morrow the second man says to the first, 'lend me your axe,' and the first man says to him, 'I will not lend it to you; just as you did not lend it to me,' this is vengeance.[46] What is bearing a grudge? If one says to another, 'lend me your axe,' and the latter says to him, 'no,' and on the morrow the latter says to the first, 'lend me your sickle,' and the first man says to him,

---

[41]Kagan, *Hafets Hayyim*, p. 9.
[42]*Ibid.*, p. 12.
[43]Exodus 23:1.
[44]Leviticus 19:17.
[45]Leviticus 19:18.
[46]Tractate *Yoma*, 23:1.

'here it is; I am not like you who did not lend it to me,' this is bearing a grudge. For such a person guards the hatred in his heart even though he does not take vengeance.[47] According to Rabbi Kagan, the principles of vengeance and bearing a grudge apply equally to material, monetary and verbal matters.[48] Gossip and talebearing result from taking vengeance or bearing a grudge when, after the episode, a person finds fault with his friend and defames him before others.[49] It appears to the author that Rabbi Kagan was original and unique in extending the precept of "thou shalt not take vengeance nor bear any grudge" to gossip and slander.

Some Positive Commands

One who gossips against his friend transgresses the positive command of "remember what the Lord thy God did unto Miriam by the way as you came forth out of Egypt."[50] Miriam who was a righteous prophetess and loved her brother Moses as herself, was not forgiven for her gossip concerning Moses' wife. The more so must the average man be careful in his speech and abstain from gossip so that he will not be punished.[51] One who engages in gossip and talebearing is also guilty of trespassing the precept of "thou shalt love thy neighbor as thyself,"[52] since this positive command teaches us that a person must value his friend's life and money as his own, and one who gossips or endangers his friend's livelihood by talebearing does not do so.[53] Just as a person will hesitate to reveal his own shortcomings, similarly he must be thoughtful not to defame his friend.[54]

The person who indulges in evil-tongue is also guilty of breaking the command of "but in righteousness shalt thou judge thy neighbor."[55] Suppose one sees his friend doing or

[47]*Ibid.*
[48]Kagan, *Hafets Hayyim,* pp. 16ff.
[49]*Ibid.,* p. 17; and Kagan, *Shemirath ha-Lashon,* pp. 60-63.
[50]Deut. 24:9.
[51]Kagan, *Hafets Hayyim,* pp. 25ff.; and Kagan, *Shemirath ha-Lashon,* pp. 75-77.
[52]Leviticus 19:18.
[53]Kagan, *Hafets Hayyim,* pp. 26ff.
[54]*Ibid.,* p. 27.
[55]Leviticus 19:15.

saying something which could be judged either favorably or unfavorably; the Torah commands us to judge the friend favorably. Suppose one judges his friend unfavorably in such a case and gossips about it, he transgresses the command "but in righteousness shalt thou judge thy neighbor."[56] Suppose, further, that through gossiping about his friend and accusing him of incompetence he causes his friend to lose his job, he is also guilty of transgressing the command of "and if thy brother be waxen poor, and his means fail with thee; then thou shalt uphold him: as a stranger and a settler shall he live with thee."[57] It is mandatory to abstain from gossip which might cause one's friend to lose his livelihood.[58]

If a person gossips to another about a third person, the listener must immediately rebuke the gossiper lest he commit a transgression of the positive command "thou shalt surely rebuke thy neighbor."[59] Suppose one decides on a rebuke later—after hearing the gossip. He will be guilty of transgressing the command, since the rebuke must take place immediately just as when a Jew eats pork the rebuke must be given at the time.[60]

There are three other positive commands which are transgressed when one indulges in gossip and tale-bearing. One must abstain from doing so in the synagogue as well as in the house of study for it is written "my sanctuary shall you reverence."[61] "Thou shalt fear the Lord thy God,"[62] and study of Torah are the two remaining positive commands. One must remember that he is born in the image of God and that the Torah enumerates the ethics which God requires of man. Wasting precious time on gossip instead of studying Torah, according to Rabbi Kagan, is one of the gravest of sins.[63]

---

[56]Kagan, *Hafets Hayyim*, p. 27.
[57]Leviticus 25:35.
[58]Kagan, *Hafets Hayyim*, p. 27.
[59]Leviticus 19:17.
[60]Kagan, *Hafets Hayyim*, p. 29.
[61]Leviticus 19:30.
[62]Deut. 6:13.
[63]Kagan, *Hafets Hayyim*, pp. 34, 38.

Some Curses

In the third section of *Hafets Hayyim* Rabbi Kagan deals briefly with the curses[64] that the Torah connected with the prohibition of gossip and talebearing and made these teachings relevant to the pressing ethical problems of his day. Someone who engages in gossip and talebearing is inviting upon himself the punishment "cursed be he that smiteth his neighbor in secret."[65] He falls also under the punishment of "cursed be he that caused the blind to go astray in the way."[66] It is interesting to note that Rabbi Kagan felt that many of the matchmakers as well as business agents of his day fell within the category of this latter curse.[67] He held that gossip, talebearing, bad advice, and selfishness are part of the broad definition of causing the blind to go astray from the way.[68] Someone who indulges in gossip is guilty, therefore should be punished by the curse: "That confirmeth not the words of this Torah."[69] Just as without the ethical teachings of the Torah there would be moral chaos, allowing people to continue their gossipping and talebearing would permit them to contribute to the moral laxity of the times.

Replies to Questions About Gossip

In the fourth section of the *Hafets Hayyim,* Rabbi Kagan deals with inquiries about gossip. We turn now to a discussion of five such inquiries.

1. Is an individual permitted to tell a story which contains even an iota of gossip about another person at the urg-

---

[64]Rabbi Kagan referred to the curses that took place on Mount Ebal before the children of Israel entered the land of Israel. In their clarity and succinctness, these solemn dooms recall the Decalogue. They relate to extreme cases of irreligion and immorality: idolatry, dishonor of parents, removal of landmarks, injustice to the helpless, incest and immorality, murder, bribery, and general disobedience of the law. The offenses selected ar such as could not readily be brought to justice before a human tribunal. See Deut. 27:15-26.

[65]Deut. 27:24.
[66]Deut. 27:18.
[67]Kagan, *Hafets Hayyim,* p. 34.
[68]*Ibid.*
[69]Deut., 27:26.

ing of his friend, father, or teacher? Rabbi Kagan wrote that it is prohibited to relate a story which contains an iota of gossip about another person even under duress or pressure from his friends. The request of his father or teacher is not to be heeded and he is not permitted to repeat the episode. This reply shows how far Rabbi Kagan extended his prohibition against gossip—to the point that one must even break the commandment to honor one's father and teacher in order not to violate the prohibition against spreading gossip.[70]

2. If a person works for a firm whose management makes use of gossip in its business transactions, is he permitted to follow the company's policy lest he lose his and his family's livelihood? The Rabbi replied that a person must be ready to lose his job and livelihood rather than indulge in gossip.[71]

3. If someone is in the social company of people who indulge in gossip, may he join in the conversation lest he appear to them to be mentally unbalanced, threatening his own honor and self-dignity? Rabbi Kagan held that it is better to be considered mentally unbalanced than to engage in gossip.[72]

4. Are listeners of a rabbi's speech given in a synagogue permitted to gossip that his speech is worthless? The Rabbi wrote that he observed that many people were in the habit of gossiping about the uselessness of a rabbi's speech. He prohibited such gossip, even if it is true, because it can cause the rabbi shame and threaten his livelihood.[73]

5. Are people permitted to gossip about an adopted child and his new parents? Rabbi Kagan prohibited gossip about an adopted child and his new parents because it could cause harm to the child should the parents decide to send him away because they were vulnerable to the gossip. On the other hand, if the truth concerning the adoption can benefit the child, then it can be told.[74]

---

[70]Kagan, *Hafets Hayyim*, p. 46.
[71]*Ibid.*, pp. 46ff.
[72]*Ibid.*, p. 47.
[73]*Ibid.*, pp. 69-71.
[74]*Ibid.*, p. 147.

Replies to Questions about Talebearing

In the last section of the *Hafets Hayyim*, Rabbi Kagan deals with inquiries concerning talebearing.

1. Is a person permitted to listen to talebearing from his wife? Rabbi Kagan prohibited even listening to the talebearing of one's wife. If a man displays an interest in his wife's talebearing, she would continue to supply stories which eventually would cause him heartache and would open the door for quarrels with her. Therefore, a man must scold his wife when she engages in talebearing.[75]

2. If someone knows that his friend plans to enter into a business partnership with another man and he is convinced that the partnership would cause hardship to the friend, is he permitted to tell his friend why he should not enter the partnership even though he might be guilty of talebearing against the other person? Rabbi Kagan permitted the truth in this instance because his friend might be hurt by the relationship. However, the Rabbi stipulated, the following conditions must surround the telling: the man must not decide immediately that the partnership is bad. He must attempt to inquire into the real circumstances. In his narration of the story he should minimize the evil aspects and he must be sure that his motivation for telling the truth is a desire to help his friend rather than hostility to the business partner.[76]

3. Is a person who knows the bad traits of a bridegroom permitted to reveal them to the bride and her family? Again, the Rabbi permitted a person to tell the family about the shortcomings of a bridegroom. However, if the shortcomings consist of unnoticeable physical disability or limited education, telling about them would be considered talebearing.[77]

4. X is engaged in talebearing against Y in the presence of Z. Afterwards, Z goes to tell Y about X's talebearing. Is Y permitted to go to X and ask him the reason for his slander in front of Z? In this case, the Rabbi held that Y is not per-

---

[75]*Ibid.*, p. 210.
[76]*Ibid.*, p. 112.
[77]*Ibid.*, pp. 112ff.

mitted to go to X and scold him for his talebearing in front of Z.[78]

5. A person naive in business matters enters a store whose owner is known for his exploitation of innocent people by charging higher prices and fixing weights. Is a third man who is well informed about the shortcomings of the store-keeper permitted to tell the innocent person about the dishonesty? Here the rabbi held that it was permitted to inform others of such a deceitful storekeeper and it is not considered talebearing.[79]

As a general rule and as an antidote to the widespread malady of gossip and talebearing, Rabbi Kagan suggested that every person should endeavor, first of all, to develop an ability to think before uttering words, to reflect before giving vent to ideas, and to refrain from discussing situations which might reflect badly on another person.

The Rabbi was disturbed that many Jews, even Torah scholars, were oblivious to the enormity of evil which Jewish law ascribes to gossip and talebearing. He could not conceive why the slightest violation of the dietary law disturbed many people, but the same persons would indulge themselves in speaking with an evil tongue—which is a greater transgression. In 1926 Rabbi Kagan wrote:

> . . . evil tongue and talebearing are as lawlessness in the eyes of many people; and they think that it is only a good and righteous custom to follow; and I came to awaken only the wise who possess the Torah-knowledge; nevertheless, it does make a difference to them between the prohibition of a soup prepared from forbidden meat and the prohibition of evil tongue. If a person is given forbidden soup to eat by his friend, he would not speak with the man that stumbled him for several years, surely the prohibition of evil tongue is more severe.[80]

[78]*Ibid.*, p. 193.
[79]*Ibid.*, p. 223.
[80]Rabbi Israel Meir Kagan, "B'enyan lashan hara' v'rechilut," in Kagan, *Michtevei Hafets Hayyim*, II, 84.

In the hope that people would form study groups dealing with the laws of gossip and talebearing, the Rabbi reduced the price of *Hafets Hayyim* for study groups.[81] Three years after the publication of *Hafets Hayyim* he wrote a complementary treatise, *Shemirath ha-Lashon (Guarding the Tongue)*. In it, he reiterated many of the ideas of *Hafets Hayyim* and added some important thoughts.

According to Rabbi Kagan, there were three main reasons why people indulge in gossip. (1) They do not know how to distinguish between gossip and conversation. (2) There is an overwhelming inner temptation to gossip. (3) People lack the moral discipline to control this temptation.[82]

He pointed out that the punishment for indulging in gossip is equal to the one for transgressing all the precepts of the Torah. The reason for such a severe penalty is the fact that speech is considered a spiritual act and does not involved material objects as do the precepts about wearing fringes, putting on phylacteries, and sitting in a Sukkah.[83] Gossip can cause a person harm in this world as well as in the world to come. Abstention from talebearing carries a reward in this world and the world to come since the individual can maintain harmony between man and man as well as between God and man. A person careful in his speech also causes God to be merciful towards him as well as towards others. Since the punishment for the sin of indulging in gossip is harsh in this world and the world to come, one must realize that a good life in this world and the world to come demands self-control in matters of gossip.[84]

A person who is careful in his speech and avoids gossip sanctifies his power of speech.[85] He is also credited with bringing peace between people for they will entrust him with their confidential matters.[86] A person must abstain from indulging in a controversy even if his own parents are involved

81*Ibid.*
82Kagan, *Shemirath ha-Lashon*, p. 5.
83*Ibid.*, p. 12b.
84*Ibid.*, p. 15.
85*Ibid.*, p. 31.
86*Ibid.*, p. 34.

in it because the chances are good that gossip will be used.[87]

Conclusion

Even though Rabbi Israel Meir Kagan was responding to the communal problems of his time, his writing of *Hafets Hayyim* and *Shemirath ha-Lashon* best reflected his own personal principles and conduct. One who presents a codification of the sins of gossip and talebearing might expect to be greeted with much scorn—private if not public. Yet, in the case of Rabbi Kagan, people sensed a singular individual, an honest man whose love for his fellow Jews was expressed in his trying to bring them closer to the Torah; a man who believed in the obligation and ability of people to pursue perfection. People were convinced that the purpose for writing *Hafets Hayyim* and *Shemirath ha-Lashon* was not for self-recognition or for library shelves, but for working people and scholars to form study groups and to learn and implement the laws which he had codified.

It was not easy to attack the sin of gossip and talebearing which the Talmud considers a universal one. However, Rabbi Kagan's exemplary ethical conduct in matters dealing with gossip and talebearing made him a unique personality, the first one in Jewish history to attempt to deal with the problem in depth.

Rabbi Kagan was a genuine folk hero. While scholars respected him, common people loved him with a rare passion. The reasons are many and no doubt complex, but the most logical explanation is simply that he considered himself one of them, sharing their common problems—one of which was gossip and talebearing. He did his best to systematize and codify all aspects of the problem and to offer a plan of action in dealing with it.

Rabbi Kagan was concerned not only with the evil resulting from gossip and slander, but also with the fact that people generally had no knowledge of what he saw as a basic law of the Torah: "Thou shalt not go up and down as a

---

[87]*Ibid.*, p. 39.

talebearer among thy people."[88] In realizing his objective in *Hafets Hayyim,* he also displays his entire outlook on *Halakhah* and its relevance to society. For example, he did not conceive the act of speaking evil as an independent incident relating only to the culprit and the man who was affected by it, but as an evil act which starts a chain reaction that ultimately spreads its poison to society. Moreover, he pointed out that gossip has a tendency to lead one to violate other laws. He considered the talebearer as the "pusher" of evil that disrupts the harmony of humanity. Consequently the evil bearer is violating the precept, "thou shalt love thy neighbor as thyself."[89] By disparaging an individual, one negates the love one is to have for one's neighbor. The talebearer is soiling the image of God with which every human being is endowed. He impairs the dignity of his neighbor and, in essence, denies both reverence and fear of God. His teachings emphasized a character building which was important in his day and could have profound relevance to our own.

Thus, Rabbi Kagan was responsible for a new body of *Halakhah*—broad in scope, philosophical in nature; and universally accepted among Jews as the final word in matters dealing with gossip and talebearing.

REVERED BY ALL

It is rare in Jewish history for one man to leave behind him a legacy of great works in rabbinic literature, significant individual contributions, noble deeds, and outstanding personal attributes. Rabbi Israel Meir Kagan was such a man, revered by all. His creations and involvement are those of a complicated individual and not simply reflections of the time and place in which he lived. Outstanding rabbi, codifier, scholar, thinker, author and humanitarian, Rabbi Kagan shared in the political, social, economic, and cultural trials and tribulations of his time, but he transcended these in continuing man's age-old examination of his purpose in

---

[88]Leviticus 19:16.

life and his relationship to God and to his fellowman. His spirit and writings made important contributions to his generation, yet they have meaning for our generation and will remain inspiring to future generations. Rabbi Kagan is a legendary personality whose accomplishments and characteristics are real and well-documented. His life and works stand as an example for other men to follow.

There was no situation, no edict, no tribulation of his time which Rabbi Kagan did not inquire into. He sought to understand what the will of God was regarding them, and to discern because of whom and because of what the evil had befallen his generation and why his generation was held responsible for it. His writings contain eternal value though they came about as a response to the conditions of his particular generation, its contemporary events, and its experiences.

His impact on the dissemination of the teachings of the Torah, on the education of children, on the establishment and maintenance of *yeshivoth,* is immeasurable. His contributions to rabbinic literature show him to be one of the most prolific and influential writers of his time, his pen enriching almost every aspect of rabbinical literature and his concerns encompassing all Jews and every aspect of their relations with one another, with the non-Jewish world, and with God.

There are two kinds of knowledge—that acquired from books and that acquired from life experience. Rabbi Israel Meir Kagan was blessed with a longevity of ninety-four years which enabled him to amass great book learning and more importantly, life experience. There is no substitute for a man who possesses both types of knowledge. Rabbi Kagan's contributions and his impact on his own generation hold inspiration for our generation—beset as it is by so many societal problems. If relevance of scholarship and deeds is the cry of our generation, certainly Rabbi Kagan is an ideal example of a man who was concerned with every aspect of life. His writings remain relevant and meaningful to our day.

89Leviticus 19:18.

BIBLIOGRAPHY

A. Works by Rabbi Israel Meir Kagan[1]

Ahavath Chesed (lit. *Loving Mercy*, but the subject of the book is more nearly described as "loving kindness"). Warsaw, 1888.[2]

Baith Yisroel (House of Israel). Petersburg, 1928.

Chomas Hadas (Fortress of Faith). Petersburg, 1905.

Geder Olam (Everlasting Fence). Warsaw, 1890.

Hafets Hayyim (He Who Desires Life). Jerusalem: Va'ad Shemirath ha-Lashon, 1967. (First published in Warsaw, 1873.

"Kosher Essen Far Yuddishe Zelner," (Kosher Food for Jewish Soldiers"). *Der Jud*, LXIV (1923).

Likutei Halakoth (Collection of Laws), Vol. I. Petersburg, 1900.

Mahaneh Israel (Camp of Israel) New York: Saphrograph Co., 1943.

Michtevei Hafets Hayyim (Letters, Articles, and Speeches of Hafets Hayyim). Edited with an introduction by Ariah Leib Kagan. New York: Saphrograph Co., 1953.

Mishnah Berurah (Lucid Learning). Vol. I. Warsaw, 1884.

Nidhei Israel (Dispersed of Israel). Warsaw, 1893.

Shem Olam (Everlasting Memorial). Warsaw, 1893.

Shemirath ha-Lashon (Guarding the Tongue). Jerusalem: Va'ad Shemirath ha-Lashon, 1967.

Toharath Yisroel (Purity of Israel). Warsaw, 1910.

Torath Habaith (Home and Family Study) (The book deals with the importance of the study of the Torah by the family at home. Thus, the title *Home and Family Study* suggests the essence of the book.) Petersburg, 1907.

B. Secondary Sources

Agurskii, S. *Di Yiddishe Komisariatn un di Yiddishe Komunitishe Seksies*. Minsk, 1928.

---

[1]All of Rabbi Kagan's works were written in Yiddish or Hebrew.

[2]When no publisher is given, the reader should assume that none appeared within the edition of the book consulted.

"Alexander III." *Evreiskaia Enciclopedia*. 1906. I, 825-839.

Babylonian Talmud. Vilna edition. Tractates *Ktuvoth, Arakin, Sanhedrin, Baba Bathra, Yoma, Sotah, Makoth, Gittin, Sukkah, Sabbath, Megillah, Hulin, Brachoth*.

Bahya, ben Joseph Ibn Pakuda. *Hoboth Halebaboth*. Translated by Moses Hyamson. 2 vols. Jerusalem: Boys Town Publishers, 1965.

Balaban, Majer. *Historja i Literatura Zydowska Ae Szezegolnym Uwzqlednieniem Histoyi Zydow w Polsce (Jewish History and Literature, with Special Emphasis on the History of the Jews in Poland)*. 3 vols. Lvov-Warsaw-Krakow, 1924.

"Balfour Declaration." *American Jewish Yearbook*. Philadelphia: Jewish Publication Society of America, 1919-1920. p. 659.

Baron, Salo W. *The Russian Jews: Under Tsars and Soviets*. New York: Macmillan Co., 1964.

—————. *A Social and Religious History of the Jews*. Vol. I. New York: Columbia University Press, 1937.

Berlin, Meir. *Fun Voloshin Biz Yerushalayim*. New York: Orion Press, Inc., 1933.

"The Bialystok Pogrom." *American Jewish Yearbook*. Philadelphia: Jewish Publication Society of Ameria, 1906-1907. Vol. 8, pp. 36-37, 79-89.

Blazar, Isaac. *Or Israel*. Vilna, 1800. New Edition by Bnei Brak, Israel-American Off-Set, 1959.

Braude, Simhah Zissel Ziv. *Hokhma Umusar*. Vol. I. New York: Aber Press, Inc., 1957.

—————. *Hokhma Umusar*. Vol. II. Jerusalem: Hat'hiyah Publishers, 1964.

Buell, Raymond Leslie. *Poland: Key to Europe*. New York and London, 1939.

Button, W. A. *Libel and Slander*. London: Sweet and Maxwell, Limited, 1946.

Citron, S. L. *Toldot Hibbat Zion*. Odessa, 1914.

Commission on Jewish Chaplaincy of the National Jewish Welfare Board, "Kashruth Observance in the Military Establishment of the United States."

Cohen, A., ed. *The Soncino Books of the Bible*. 14 vols. London: Soncino Press, 1948.

Curtiss, J. S. "The Army of Nicholas I: Its Role and Character." *American Historical Review*. LXIII (1959).

Danby, H. *The Mishnah*. Translated from the Hebrew with introduction and brief explanatory notes. London: Oxford University Press, 1933.

Denikin, I. *Ocherkii Russkoi Smutz.* 5 Vols. Paris, 1921-1926.

Dinaburg, Benzion. *Hibbat Zion.* Vol. I. Tel-Aviv: Dvir, 1932.

Dubnow, Simon M. *History of the Jews in Russia and Poland.* 3 vols. Translated from the German by I. Friedlander. Philadelphia: Jewish Publication Society of America, 1946.

——————. *Nationalism and History: Essays on Old and New Judaism.* Edited with an introduction by Koppel S. Pinson. Philadelphia: *Jewish Publication Society of America,* 1918.

——————. *Veltgeshikhte fun Yiddishn Folk (World History of the Jewish People).* 10 vols. Buenos Aires-New York, 1956.

Elbogan, Ismar. *A Century of Jewish Life.* Translated from the German by Moses Hadas. Philadelphia: Jewish Publication Society of America, 1946.

Elias, Joseph. "The Search for National Identity." *Jewish Observer.* March, 1970, p. 5.

Epstein, Isadore, ed. *The Babylonian Talmud with Introduction and Commentary.* London: Soncino Press, 1935-1952.

Finkel, Abraham S. *N'tivot Ha-Musar.* Tel-Aviv: Tziyoni Publishers, 1961.

Florinsky, Michael T. *Russia: A History and an Interpretation.* 2 vols. New York: Macmillan Co., 1964.

Fraser, Sir Hugh. *Principles and Practice of the Law of Libel and Slander.* London: Butterworth and Co., 1935.

Freedman, H. and Maurice Simon, eds. *Midrash Rabbah.* Translated with brief notes. Vol. 1-10. London: Soncino Press, 1939.

Friedman, A. A. *Sefer ha-Zichronoth.* Tel-Aviv, 1926.

Ganzfried, Solomon. *Code of Jewish Law.* Translated by Herman Golden. New York: Hebrew Publishing Co., 1927.

Ginsburg, Saul M. *Historishe Werk.* 3 vols. New York, 1937.

Glenn, M. G. *Israel Salanter: Religious Ethical Thinker.* New York: Bloch Publishing Co., 1953.

Glueck, Nelson. *Hesed in the Bible.* Cincinnati: The Hebrew Union College Press, 1967.

Gordon, Judah Leib. *Kol Shirei Gordon.* Vol. IV Tel-Aviv: Dvir, 1931.

Graetz, Heinrich. *Geschichte der Juden (History of the Jews).* 11 vols. 1853-1875.

Greenberg, Louis. *The Jews in Russia.* New Haven: Yale University Press, 1965.

Grinstein, Hyman. *The Rise of the Jewish Community of New York.* Philadelphia: Jewish Publication Society, 1945.

Gruen, George E. "Again Wo is a Jew?" *American Jewish Committee Institute of Human Relations.* February, 1970, p. 3.

Halevi, Judah. *Kuzari.* Tel-Aviv: Hadaran, 1959.

Heifetz, Elias. *The Slaughter of the Jews in the Ukraine in 1919.* New York: T. Seltzer, 1921.

Heilperin, I., ed., *Bet Yisroel B'Polin (The Jewish People in Poland).* 2 vols. Jerusalem, 1948.

Hertz, Jacob Sholem. *Doires Bundisten.* 2 vols. New York: Verlag Unzer Zeit, 1956.

Hertz, Joseph. *Authorized Daily Prayer Book.* New York: Bloch Publishing Co., 1948.

Herzen, Alexander. *Biloe i Dumy (Life and Thoughts).* 6 vols. London: Chatto and Windus, 1924-1927.

Herzl, Theodor. *Gesammelte Zionistische Werke.* 5 vols. Berlin: Judisicher Verlag, 1934.

—————. *A Jewish State.* Translated by S. D'Avigdor. 2nd Revised edition with a foreword by Israel Cohen. London, 1934.

—————. *Tagebucher.* Edited by Leon Kellner. 3 vols. Berlin: Judisicher Verlag, 1922-23.

Hurwitz, Joseph. *Madregat Ha-Adam.* Jerusalem: Israel Publication Committee, 1964.

Isserles, Moses. "Ruling on the Building of a Synagogue." *Haggahoth,* Paragraph 163.

Joffin, Rabbi Abraham. *Matragat Ha-Adam.* Jerusalem, 1964.

Josephus. *Antiquities.* 11: 8, 2 (306-312).

Judah He-Hasid. *Sefer Hasidim.* Jerusalem: Mossad Harav Kook, 1964.

Karo, Joseph. *Shulhan Arukh.*

Karpovich, Michael. *Imperial Russia, 1801-1917.* New York: H. Holt, 1932.

Katz, Dov. *Tenuath Ha-Musar (The Movement of Morality).* 5 vols. Tel-Aviv: Bitan Ha-Sefer, Abraham Tzioni Publishers, 1952-1963.

Katz, Reuben. *Shaar Reuben.* Jerusalem: Mossad Harav Kook, 1952.

"The Kishinev Pogrom." *American Jewish Yearbook.* Philadelphia: Jewish Publication Society of America, 1903-1904.

Kizevetter, A. A. *Storicheskie Ocherkii.* Moscow, 1912.

Kliuchevsky, V. O. *Kurs russkoi istorii (Lectures in the History of Russia).* 5 vols. Petrograd, 1918-1921.

Kornilov, A. A. *Kurs istorii Rossii v XLX veke (Lectures in the History of Russia in the Nineteenth Century).* 3 vols. Moscow, 1912-1914.

Kramer, Simon G. *God and Man in Sefer Hasidim.* New York: Bloch Publishing Company, 1966.

Lauterbach, J. Z. *Mekilta.* 3 vols. Philadelphia: Jewish Publication Society of America, 1941.

——————. *Midrash and Mishnah.* Philadelphia: Jewish Publication Society of America, 1941.

Lenin, Vladimir. *Selected Works.* 3 vols. Moscow: Progress Publishers, 1970.

——————. *Sochinoniia.* 2nd edition. XXIV (1932) 203.

——————. "Socialism and Religion." *Selected Works.* New York, n.d., XI, 658.

Leo XXIII. *The Great Encyclical Letters of Pope Leo XIII.* New York, 1903.

Leslie, R. F. *Reform and Insurrection in Russian Poland 1856-1865.* London: University of London, The Athlone Press, 1963.

Liashchenko, Petr I. *History of the National Economy of Russia to the Revolution.* Translated by L. M. Herman: New York, Macmillan, 1919.

Lilienblum, Moses. "Nefesh Tahath Nefesh." *Ha-Meliz,* 4 (1878), 75-80.

Lipschitz, Jacob. *Sichron Jacob (Memoirs of Rabbi Jacob Lipschitz).* 3 vols. Kaunas, 1930.

Lunacharskii, Anatolii V. *Ob Antisemitizme.* Moscow, 1929.

Luzzatto, M. H. *Mesilat Yesharim.* New York: Shulsinger Bros., 1942.

Mahler, Raphael. *Geshikhte fun Yidn in Polyn, Letste Yerhunderer (Jewish History in Poland, Last Centuries).* New York, 1957.

Maimonides. *The Code of Maimonides.* Julius Obermann, ed. New Haven: Yale University Press, 1949.

——————. *The Commandments.* Translated by Charles B. Chavel. 2 vols. London: Soncino Press, 1967.

——————. *Eight Chapters: Introductory to Tractate Avot.* Warsaw, 1924.

——————. *Guide to the Perplexed.* Jerusalem: Offset S. Monzon, 1960.

——————. *Hilkhoth Dea'yoth.* Mt. Kosko, New York, 1958.

Malia, Martin. *Alexander Herzen and the Birth of Russian Socialism.* New York: Grosset and Dunlop, 1961.

Mapu, Abraham. *Ayit Zavua.* 5 vols. Warsaw: Alexander Ganz, 1873-74.

"The Memorial to the Tsar by the Jews of England." *Sichron Jacob.* Kaunas, 1930. III, 44-48.

Miller, David. *The Secret of the Jewish Law.* New York: Hebrew Publishing Company, 1927.

"Pahlen Commission," *Evreiskaia Enciclopedia,* 1906.

Pinson, Koppel S. "Arkady Kremer: Vladimir Medem and the Ideology of the Jewish Bund." *Jewish Social Studies,* VIII (1945), 233-64.

Platanov, Sergei Fedorovich. *History of Russia.* Translated by E. Arnsberg, edited by F. A. Golder. New York: Macmillan, 1905.

Pobedonostsev, Constantine. "The Jews." *Ha-Meliz,* No. 18 (1882).

——————. *Reflections of a Russian Statesman.* London: Grant Richards, 1898.

Posner, Raphael. "Halakhic Definition of a Jew." *Encyclopedia Judaica,* 10:23.

Reddaway, W. F. *Cambridge History of Poland.* Cambridge: Cambridge University Press, 1950.

Ringelbum, Emanuel. *Capitlen Geschikhte fun Amoliken Yiddishen Leben in Polyn (Chapters of History from Early Jewish Life in Poland).* Edited by Jacob Shatzki. Buenos Aires, 1952.

Rosenthal, A. D. *Megillat Ha-Tebah.* 3 vols. Jerusalem, 1929-31.

Salanter, Israel. "Ma'orer Ha-Nirtamin." *Ha-Meliz,* No. 8 (1879), 149-154.

Schapiro, Leonard. *The Communist Party of the Soviet Union.* New York: Vintage Books, 1964.

Schwarz, Solomon M. *The Jews in the Soviet Union.* Syracuse: Syracuse University Press, 1951.

Seton-Watson, Hugh. *The Decline of Imperial Russia, 1855-1914.* New York: Praeger, 1956.

Smith, W. R. *The Prophets of Israel.* Edinburg, 1882.

Smithline, Jacob. "Scientific Aspects of Sexual Hygiene." *Torah Laws for the Modern Woman*. New York: G. N. T. Typographic Corp., for United Jewish Women for Taharas Hamispocho, Inc., 1965.

Sokolow, Nahum. *History of Zionism, 1600-1918*. With an introduction by A. J. Balfour. Vol. II. London: Longmans, 1919.

Treadgold, D. *Twentieth Century Russia*. Chicago: Rand McNally, 1959.

Venturi, Franco. *Roots of Revolution: A History of the Populist and Socialist Movements in Nineteenth Century*. Introduction by Isaiah Berlin. New York: Knopf, 1960.

Witte, Sergei. *The Memoirs of Count Witte*. Translated by Abraham Yarmolinsky. New York: Doubleday, 1921.

Yosher, Moses M. *Dos Leben Un Shafen Fun Hafets Hayyim*. New York: Shulsinger Bros. Linotyping and Publishing Co., 1946-47.

——————. *Ha-Hafets Hayyim*. Tel-Aviv: Nezach, 1958, 1959, 1961.

——————. *Israel in the Ranks*. New York: Shulsinger Bros., 1943.

——————. "Israel Meir Ha-Kohen—Hafets Hayyim." *Jewish Leaders*. Edited by Rabbi Leo Jung. Jerusalem: Boys Town Publishers, 1953.

——————. *Saint and Sage*. New York: Shulsinger Bros., 1937.

Zeitlin, Solomon. "Offspring of Intermarriage." *Jewish Quarterly Review*, LI (October, 1930).

Zelikin, Isaac. *Book of Kahal*. 1869, 1871.

Zeman, Z. A. B. *The Break-up of the Habsburg Empire, 1914-1918*. London: Oxford University Press, 1961.

Zenziper, L. *Eser Shnot Redifot*. Tel-Aviv, 1930.

INDEX